1991

Chaucerian Theatricality

Chaucerian Theatricality

John M. Ganim

PRINCETON UNIVERSITY PRESS

PRINCETON, NEW JERSEY

Library of Congress Cataloging-in-Publication Data

Ganim, John M., 1945–
Chaucerian theatricality / John M. Ganim.
p.   cm.
Includes bibliographical references.
ISBN 0-691-06779-1
1. Chaucer, Geoffrey, d. 1400. Canterbury tales.   2. Chaucer,
Geoffrey, d. 1400—Knowledge—Performing arts.   3. England—Popular
culture—History—Medieval period, 1066–1485.   4. Performing arts—
England—History.   5. Performing arts in literature.   6. Popular
culture in literature.   7. Carnival in literature.   I. Title.
PR1875.P45G36   1990
821'.1—dc20   90-8469

This book has been composed in Linotron Galliard

Princeton University Press books are printed
on acid-free paper, and meet the guidelines
for permanence and durability of the Committee
on Production Guidelines for Book Longevity
of the Council on Library Resources

Printed in the United States of America by
Princeton University Press, Princeton, New Jersey

10 9 8 7 6 5 4 3 2 1

For May Lattof Ganim
and for
Jessica and Dominick

CONTENTS

ACKNOWLEDGMENTS

PARTS OF THIS BOOK began as papers presented at various meetings, including the Modern Language Association, the Medieval Association of the Pacific, the New Chaucer Society, and the Philological Association of the Pacific Coast. I would like to thank especially the Medieval Club of Columbia University for inviting me to speak, and Traugott Lawler for arranging a paper before the Department of English at Yale University. Along with everyone else who participated in the remarkable 1988 conference on "History/Text/Theory: Reconceiving Chaucer," I owe a debt to Tom Hahn of the University of Rochester. Part of Chapter 7 appears in the proceedings of that conference published in *Exemplaria* 2 (1990), edited by R. A. Shoaf, and part of Chapter 2 appeared in *Studies in the Age of Chaucer*, proceedings vol. 2 (1986), edited by John V. Fleming and Thomas Heffernan. Part of Chapter 4 appeared as an article in *Assays* 4 (1987), edited by Peggy Knapp, and part of Chapter 5 appeared in *Chaucer Review* 22 (1987). I am grateful to the editors of these collections and journals for permissions to reprint materials here, however substantially changed. For financial support related to the writing and research of this book, I would like to thank the Research Committee of the Riverside Division of the Academic Senate of the University of California. The assistance of the library of the University of California, Riverside, especially the Interlibrary Loan Department, has been essential; in the Reference Department, Monica Fusich has been especially helpful, and in the English department library, Dr. Elizabeth Lang.

It is a pleasure once again to work with the literature editor of Princeton University Press, Robert Brown. The readers for the press, Robert Hanning and Seth Lerer, made many helpful suggestions for revision. A penultimate version was saved from errors and heresies by James Dean and Alfred and Linda David. Donald R. Howard read some early drafts of some chapters after we appeared on an MLA panel together. Everyone who knew him knows how much I, we, miss his counsel.

I would like to thank my colleagues and the office staff of the Department of English at the University of California, Riverside, most especially Steven Axelrod, Jean-Pierre Mileur, Helene Mankowski, and George Haggerty, for their support and friendship. The department is something of an extended family, so I would also like to include Philip Brett, Rise Axelrod, and ex-colleagues Laura Brown, Walter Cohen, Stan Gontarski, and Brian Finney. I also owe much to conversations with Gary and Mary Sposito, Dan Rubey, Stephanie Hammer, Georg Gugelberger, Martin

Green, R. Howard Bloch, Ben Stoltzfuss, and Serena Anderlini. For their hospitality during the writing of this book, I would like to thank Milton Wexler, Jeffrey and Michelle Adelman, Donna O'Neill, Maryline Barnard, Herb Pardes, Nancy Wexler, Laurent Charlet, Mary Jane Ganim, Cynthia Coss, Mike Ganim, and Kathy Ganim. For guidance she may not remember, I would like to thank Barbara Jones Guetti.

I doubt whether a book about Chaucer's theatricality and artistic performance would have taken the shape it did if it weren't for years of being influenced by the work of my artist and writer friends who probably wouldn't be able to find that influence here: David James's poetry and criticism, Laura Farabough and Chris Hardman's Snake Theater, David Schickele's films, Vija Celmin's work, Susan Frecon's paintings, Frank Gehry's buildings. But I would have not fully understood or enjoyed any of these if I had seen or read them alone. Everyone who knows Alice Wexler knows how much I owe her. Lately, I find that all my thoughts are either begun or completed with her.

Chaucerian Theatricality

Chapter One

INTRODUCTION: CRITICAL METAPHORS AND
CHAUCERIAN PERFORMANCE

THIS BOOK is an essay on some related problems both of Chaucer criticism and of Chaucerian poetics. The terms defining twentieth-century Chaucer criticism could not have been set forth more clearly than in Kittredge: "Structurally regarded, the *Canterbury Tales* is a kind of Human Comedy. From this point of view, the Pilgrims are the *dramatis personae*, and their stories are only speeches that are somewhat longer than common" (1911–12, 435). Kittredge was writing in the decades following the innovations of Ibsen's drama and James's novels. To claim psychologically subtle characterization and thematic unity based on social questions was, for Kittredge, to claim poetic relevance for Chaucer. Victorian medievalism and the great editorial efforts of the later nineteenth century had recovered many of the lost contexts of Chaucer's work, but at the risk of subsuming him to a very Victorian picture of his age or dispersing his intentions among discrete scholarly questions. Kittredge's critical move, something of a tour de force, was to make the links and prologues, rather than the tales, the center of attention, and as a result to proclaim a new coherence for Chaucer's work and a new agenda for criticism. The success of this agenda is attested to by the fact that even as the present century moves towards its close, extended critical studies of the *Canterbury Tales* inescapably engage Kittredge's categories, either by proposing alternate groupings to his version of thematic and structural unity, or by attacking head-on his assumptions concerning character and literary meaning. Although it is difficult to find someone today willing to espouse a wholesale dramatic reading of the *Canterbury Tales*, these categories prove surprisingly resilient against the impressive artillery arrayed against them. D. W. Robertson's (1962) powerful promulgation of an "allegorical" aesthetic for medieval literature was directed squarely against the psychological and characterological interests of the dramatic thesis. Charles Muscatine (1957) questioned the realistic assumptions of the generally Kittredgian consensus by pointing to the conventional basis of Chaucer's style. Robert M. Jordan (1967) attempted to argue for a nondramatic and nonorganic aesthetic for medieval poetry in general and for Chaucer in particular. Jordan, Muscatine, and Robertson, all very different, are just a few examples. It would have seemed as if medieval literary study in the 1950s and 1960s, by having to grapple with Kittredge's proto-New Critical literary assumptions, might have predicted the postmodern, structuralist, and poststructuralist critique of the humanist and formalist enterprises. But the Kittredgian ghost continues to haunt the house of Chaucer criticism. Recent books such as C. David Benson's *Chaucer's Drama of Style* (1986) must insist once again that the coherence of the *Canterbury Tales* does not lie in the pilgrims and their dramatic interchange. Derek Pearsall (1985) warns us of the interpretative lacunae that have resulted from the Kittredgian valorization of the settings of the tales above their narratives.

Amid the flurry of attempts to drive a stake into the heart of the "dramatic" reading of the *Canterbury Tales*, I propose a relatively minimal revision. What would happen if we revised rather than replaced the metaphors of Chaucer criticism? Instead of the metaphor of "drama," I propose that of "theatricality." My intention is to orient contemporary critical positions, largely those that grow out of the dramatic metaphor, towards some long-neglected materials such as urban and court spectacle and certain forms of late medieval performance. I also seek to preserve the most powerful contributions of the arguments for the unity of the *Canterbury Tales* while accounting for some of the obvious contradictions in those arguments. Even if the obsession with unity has created certain critical dead ends, it has paradoxically generated remarkable local explanations that are not invalidated by the failure of the larger thesis.

The attempt to revise the central critical metaphor of Chaucer studies has in fact been one of the strategies of attacks on the dramatic thesis. The chief of these is the metaphor of Gothic art and architecture, but others, less metaphoric than metonymic, would have us read the *Canterbury Tales* as we would a scriptural text. These rejections of the dramatic paradigm, however, result in a poetry fixed in its values and highly directed in its statements. We are forced to assume a virtual identity between the poetic and philosophical conceptions of reality. The danger of such a tendency is that we are inventing a Chaucer who is always, as he is sometimes, an orthodox voice. In contrast, my argument here points towards a much less stable avenue to meaning, suggesting even that meaning is generated in the act of reading and is more akin to theme than to statement. The Chaucer that results is one more conditional, more provisional, appropriating the improvisational and performative qualities of medieval theatricality.

Chaucer places the stories of the *Canterbury Tales* within the structural setting of the pilgrimage and frequently introduces or comments on those stories by means of interactions among the pilgrims. The *Canterbury Tales* is therefore usually described as a framed fiction, along with other collections of tales, chiefly Boccaccio's *Decameron*, with its elaborate "cornice," Gower's *Confessio Amantis*, and also the *Thousand and One Nights*. Such a description is obviously important and helpful, and I do not suggest we discard the term entirely. Nevertheless, the interaction of Chaucer's stories and the pilgrimage setting is obviously much more dynamic than in these and other similar collections. The *Canterbury Tales* are not merely framed, they are reframed, reset, changed by the very process of their presentation. If, as I argue, our critical reference points can be helped by importing the notion of "theatricality," we must also rethink the notion of a stable, independent or dominant "frame."

I am suggesting that we consider the formal presentation of the *Canterbury Tales* as akin to a linguistic rather than an architectural gesture. Given the fiction of the *Canterbury Tales* as talk, as recorded speech, I would stress the illusion of multivocality in Chaucer, not only in the fluctuating relations between teller and tale, but between tale and tale, and between Chaucer and his sources. I seek to underline the presentation, and self-presentation, of the *Canterbury Tales* and its narrators, as social performances, subject to response and correction. But the notion of theatricality also accounts for the duality of the work, as artifact and as performance, as talk and as text. The concept acknowledges the destabilizing force of Chaucerian recourse to authorities and sources, including his own earlier works, as they are transformed by their new context. By focusing on the nature of Chaucerian theatricality, we can read as significant apparently troublesome moments in the frame or within the pilgrims' stories, which seem to transgress narrative or dramatic decorum.

. . .

By the term *theatricality*, I mean not to suggest so much a study of the drama of the *Canterbury Tales* narrowly conceived, or even an affiliation between Chaucer's poetry and the forms of medieval theater, though the latter is part of my project. Rather, I mean to locate a governing sense of performance, an interplay among the author's voice, his fictional characters, and his immediate audience. Theatricality, in the sense I use it here, is a paradigm for the Chaucerian poetic, and what I seek to define is Chaucer's own manipulations of the forms of popular culture and the varying discourses of inherited high literary forms.

This definition has certain critical consequences. Instead of towards concern with how Chaucer's style or narrative movement is unified, the concept of theatricality points us towards ways in which the consistent surface of the work is almost programmatically violated. Instead of a concern with the dramatic consistency of the Chaucerian narrator, the "pilgrim" or the "poet," the concept of theatricality attunes us to the ease with which the *Canterbury Tales* (and other fourteenth-century works) move among different levels of fictional address.

My definition of theatricality is then primarily stylistic rather than sociological; but that style is immersed in social and political contexts ranging from popular theatrics to court ceremony. Taken as a form of integral cultural expression, as it is in Huizinga's *Waning of the Middle Ages* (1954), medieval theatricality shares with the theatricality of other periods the dramatization of both interior states and of shared social values. Whereas Huizinga read medieval theatricality's obsessive dramatization of both private experience and public events as a vaguely overripe efflorescence, studies in slightly later periods have alerted us to the socially adaptive and politically calculated quality of Renaissance or eighteenth-century theatricality. In *The Illusion of Power* (1975), for instance, Stephen Orgel describes the essentially political ritual of Renaissance court theater and masques. Though medieval courts may have had impressive spectacles with specific meanings, those meanings had by their nature to communicate something other than the monarchical ideology Orgel locates. In their very form, medieval spectacles and processions suggest a much less clearly centralized and symptomatically much less loosely structured and formalized aesthetics or politics. However careful their preparations, medieval court ceremonies and royal processions took place in settings that, however stage-like to modern eyes, were by no means the planned theater-like spaces of Renaissance courts. For that matter, permanent public theaters are themselves a product of the Renaissance. In contrast, medieval popular and court theatrics shared a temporary, provisional, and occasional quality. Robert Weimann in *Shakespeare and the Popular Tradition* (1978), for instance, implies that the Renaissance public theater owes its participatory and improvisatory quality to medieval popular traditions.

The more general use of theatricality to locate a certain conception of social existence, even self-creation, also grows out of Renaissance rather than medieval studies. In his *Renaissance Self-Fashioning* (1980), Stephen Greenblatt describes the means by which Renaissance literary and historical figures theatrically create their "selves." Here again Chaucerian characters both resemble and do not resemble the Renaissance dynamic. Chaucer's most apparently self-fashioning characters emerge in his longer prologues, such as those of the Wife of Bath and the Pardoner. Here, long, only briefly interrupted monologues create in their own words the most fully realized characters in literature before Shakespeare. But this apparent self-creation owes much to highly conventionalized and even ritualized forms such as the equally long self-descriptions of allegorical characters and the self-examination of the confessional mode that developed in the wake of the institutionalization of regular confession in the high Middle Ages. The theatricalization of character in Chaucer exists as much to admit as to evade social constrictions upon the invention of the self. Moreover, the most elusive Chaucerian character, the figure of Chaucer himself, is theatrically represented, both in the early poems and in the *Canterbury Tales*, so much so that it has become one of the tropes of modern Chaucer criticism to address his degree of fictionality, precisely that which theatricality simultaneously invites and frustrates.

From an empirical point of view, it is Chaucer's early poetry that is most obviously theatrical. Court poetry often has a ceremonial, presentational, and official dimension quite apart from its manifest content or meaning. It is part of court life, part of a system of signs and gestures, decorations, clothing, manners, all of which proclaim the unique character of the court's world. Indeed, it has become commonplace to speak of the social significance of continental court and courtly literature (Salter 1973, Hauser 1951). The initiatory experience of the protagonists of the *Romance of the Rose* or Chretien's romances may have reflected the social refashioning of a military caste into a chivalric elite. But it is just as likely that constant self-definition is a marked quality of courtly literature. Stevens's *Music and Poetry in the Early Tudor Court* (1961) shows how the courtly-love tradition had a "sociological" function in establishing the role of the courtier; Caspari's *Humanism and the Social Order in Tudor England* (1954) shows how many aspects of humanist education and early Tudor court culture involved retooling the feudal aristocracy for increasingly complex administrative and diplomatic tasks.[1] Although I agree with Mathew (1968) that the courts of Richard and Edward introduced a new phase of royal court culture in England, there is very little evidence that their courts promulgated the relatively coherent adaptive and educative programs of the Tudor courts. We need to look elsewhere for the kind of experience codified in courtesy books, court ceremony, and early humanist education. One place to look is poetry. The ritual and almost experimental quality of Chaucer's early poems, despite their traditional trappings, must have filled some need in the life of the court.

The court of Edward III represented a highly self-conscious attempt to appropriate knightly chivalry to royal protocol, in ways that were publicly accessible rather than hermetic. This cultural move is reflected in the early poems, which include within themselves, sometimes with a touch of parody or irony, the quality of court theater. A poem like the *Parliament of Foules* at times predicts the elements of a masque. However skeptical one may be about such explanations, the description of Fame in her temple in the *House of Fame* more than slightly resembles the apocalyptic image of Alice Perrers disguised as the Lady of the Sun as she rides to and is seated at the jousts at Smithfield in 1374 (Wickham 1959, 20). Even the wicker construction of the House of Rumor suggests a material that might well have been widely used in the elaborate sets of indoor court entertainments.

But the theatrical quality, the bizarre mechanics, and the strange contrivances of poems such as the *House of Fame* and even the *Squire's Tale* have more than a single parallel. In 1377, for instance, the year in which Richard was crowned, for one entry an imitation castle was equipped with a mechanical angel that somehow bowed down and offered Richard a crown (Wickham 1959, 55). In 1392, in a pageant meant to soothe rumpled feathers between Richard and the citizenry, two children disguised as angels appeared to float down and offer the King a crown (Wickham 1959, 71). Even more elaborate pageants and mimes are recorded in the French royal court during the century, one of which may be alluded to in the description of magic in the *Franklin's Tale* (L. Loomis 1958, Braswell 1985). I do not mean to suggest either direct references to these events in Chaucer's text, nor am I suggesting Manly-like identifications. Instead, I want only to point to the ways such theatricality is included in Chaucer's poetry and suggests the uneasy but crucial relation, celebratory and subversive at once, of his poetry to court life. One can read the *Book of the Duchess* and the *Parliament of Foules* as part of court theatricality, even if wittily ironic about it while the *House of Fame* seems in many ways explicitly satiric and critical. In the *Canterbury Tales*, the references to ceremonial theatricality are part of complex thematic statements about power and control, usually, but not always, political.

It may not have been so much that Chaucer combined aristocratic and bourgeois perspectives as that in certain social sectors, and particularly in a relatively centralized political situation like that of London, these perspectives may have been broadly shared.[2] Even the evidence of Edwardian, if not of Ricardian, court ritual is striking. The most elaborate processions and entries of Edward's reigns were not exclusively "courtly" in an elitist sense. More often than not, they were meant to celebrate the sometimes shaky political unity of the city, the nation, and the court. The distinction between civic and aristocratic theatricality was sometimes blurry. Chaucer might not have remembered, for instance, a tournament in which Edward and his nobles appeared in the lists disguised as the Mayor and aldermen of London, a disguise probably meant to be complimentary, but he no doubt took part in similar events in which citizens, not always as closely connected to the court as he himself, also participated.

Richard II was indeed obsessed with images of royal power, but his court art tended to express such an obsession not in monumental and permanent aggrandizement, but in that delicate, miniature, portable, "late Gothic" style. The court itself seemed portable, perhaps out of necessity. Among his most memorable artistic projects were interiors, walls, and glazings. The descriptions of the court in transit suggest the air of a travelling fair, not entirely unlike the bon voyage of the Canterbury pilgrims. When Anne died, in a characteristically public expression of profound private grief, Richard ordered her favorite manor destroyed, as if the court itself were conceived as a stage set, meant to impress both ruler and ruled with the illusion of majesty. Nevertheless, a similar theatricality and portability marked Edward III's court. Whereas a totalizing theatrical conception was part of the propaganda of the later Tudor and Stuart courts, Richard's court was marked by a sense of improvisation, and a case could be made that Richard's handling of power itself was improvisational.

Interestingly, in the *Canterbury Tales* improvisation is associated with popular performance. The anarchic and improvisational aspects so often associated with popular discourse turn out in the early poems to be endemic to court life. This inversion is completed by the complex exploration of stability and order in the tales most explicitly associated with the exercise of power, such as the *Knight's Tale*. When Chaucer alludes to his court role in the *Canterbury Tales*, as, for instance, when he has his pilgrim persona recount the *Tale of Melibee*, a typical example of the literature of political advice (Ferguson 1965, Green 1980), he disguises that experimental quality, perhaps because its relativism and skepticism are now socially, and therefore dangerously, imagined.

. . .

It is impossible to pursue my arguments without addressing some overriding theoretical issues, ones that occupy not only literary critics but also scholars in other disciplines. Specifically, the work of M. M. Bakhtin, belatedly translated and interpreted at least partly through his influence on some recent semiotic theory, has provided the impetus for my chief critical metaphor, for Bakhtin's work argues for a continuity between verbal and theatrical expression, between utterance and performance. David Lawton has touched on this connection in the important first chapter of his *Chaucer's Narrators* (1985, ix–16). He criticizes a "persona-oriented criticism . . . that diverts attention from language and styles into a reckoning that is dramatic and psychological" (1985, 7). In fact, using Bakhtin's notion of heteroglossia, Lawton modifies the definition of "persona" to include a range of intercessions of "literariness" into representation of character. From the point of view of theatricality, however, these registers are continually invading each other's territory, resulting in a style finally performative rather than purely narrational.[3]

Nevertheless, the essays that follow do not offer a Bakhtinian reading of Chaucer. Some of Bakhtin's most seductive possibilities for reading Chaucer, such as his identification of the "carnivalesque," are both helpful and limiting. Bakhtin and Chaucer ask interesting questions about each other. On the most basic level, seeking the answers to these questions means pursuing the frequently deceptive relation of some of Chaucer's work to popular literature. On another level, it means the location of Chaucer's work in relation to the contours of "popular culture" as historians have recently redefined that term. Where we might expect to defend a

Chaucer empowered by and in close contact with the force of popular culture and performance, we find ourselves tracing a much more difficult relation between Chaucer and popular understanding, between poetry and power. The result is often a view of the poetry not only as narrative or stylistic expression, but as an expression of the poet's cultural role.

If the fantasy of a primitive Chaucer has been long ago dispelled, at least in academic readings in Anglo-American studies, a powerful myth of his originality remains in some influential romance studies, including Bakhtin's, which admittedly reflect a version of literary history more typical of the earlier part of this century. Nevertheless, since their currency is so high in English studies today, it is worth considering their assumptions at length. According to Erich Auerbach's *Literary Language and Its Public in Late Latin Antiquity and in the Middle Ages* (1965), the triumph of the vernacular was at least partly in the creation of a cultivated public, one that began to resemble the civilized readership of the Roman Empire. For all its historical dynamism, his argument, like the history implicit in his *Mimesis* (Auerbach 1953), envisions not a sense of progress, but an alternation of linguistic possibilities. Literary language may negotiate individual and social differences, or it may exacerbate difference through rigid separations or inscrutable maneuvers of style. Behind the apparent literary subject of the essay lies a humanist vision of Europe. Auerbach's hidden subject is the failed potential of our own century.

It is this vision against which Auerbach's oddly idealized version of English literature needs to be considered. For in his history England (or its literature) is both part of and separate from, almost a laboratory for, *Europa* itself. In the pantheon of texts ("chosen at random") that comprise *Mimesis*, the two English works—Shakespeare's *Henry IV, Part 1* and Virginia Woolf's *To the Lighthouse*—suggest versions of reality that transcend a fragmenting hierarchization. And so with Chaucer and Langland:

> A comparable alertness and racy wit are to be found in the fourteenth century in the literature of another country on the fringe of Europe, namely, England. . . . In the course of the fourteenth century Anglo-Saxon, whose literary tradition had never entirely died out and which had meanwhile developed into Middle English, attained a great literary flowering and with it the beginnings of standardization. And despite the medieval heritage common to all western Europe, despite the ancient, Christian, and French influences reflected in its themes, ideas, and forms of expression, a strong individuality and popular character are apparent from the first, owing perhaps to the fact that English had to assert itself not so much against Latin as against the French of the courts. Another factor is the political, religious and economic awakening of the masses, which, if it did not occur earlier than elsewhere, was more thoroughgoing. Nowhere else during the Middle Ages are profound and var-

ied social currents described with so much concrete truth, so much sympathy and humor as in fourteenth-century England. I am thinking of course of Chaucer's *Canterbury Tales*. (1965, 324–25)

Behind Auerbach's Chaucer lies a complex agenda. Earlier in *Literary Language and Its Public* we learn that England had once before played a role both as a model (in Auerbach's historiography) and as a mission (in actual history). The England of Bede and of Alfred had also integrated a "common language" into its literature and absorbed and transcended invasion and division. However briefly, it exported this vision of its own potential to a Europe literally, according to Auerbach, lacking civilization.

My analysis of Auerbach's motivation is not to call into question his methodology but to point out that his version of Chaucer, which is an example of a larger vision of English literature itself, also implies a social, political, and ethical, interpretation. Moreover, his version is suggested by his early statement of what has since become a critical trope in comparative trecento studies, the response of Boccaccio, Petrarch, and by extension Chaucer, to the challenge of Dante's conception of poetry. The ethical and prophetic weight of such a comparison hierarchizes the writers themselves; the Boccaccio of the *Decameron* is seen as cynically evading poetic responsibility while Chaucer is accorded the saving grace of natural poetry.

If Auerbach's negative critique of Boccaccio and praise of Chaucer is based on a largely Apollonian version of Dante's challenge to language, a similar explicit critique of Boccaccio and implicit praise of Chaucer is available from a more Dionysian perspective, no less informed by the great philological tradition of the late nineteenth and early twentieth centuries. "*The Decameron* is the high point of grotesque realism," writes Bakhtin, "but in its poorer, petty form" (1968, 273). Here Bakhtin contrasts Boccaccio's handling of "popular-festive" forms with their fuller and freer expression in Rabelais. Bakhtin on the one hand seems to be critical of the reservation Boccaccio always expresses and on the other seems to be suggesting that the problem for Boccaccio is historical: he is able to see from a point of view other than the official, but he cannot yet offer a fully celebratory alternative, as can Rabelais. (For Auerbach, the problem is also one of realism, though not of the grotesque sort. In *Mimesis*, he offers an elaborate critique of the circumscribed realism of *The Decameron*.) Oddly enough, in his later years, Bakhtin, according to his American biographers, celebrated Boccaccio's most scurrilous characters (Clark and Holquist 1984).

At least part of the criticism of Bakhtin's interpretation of popular culture has been against his attribution of oppositional status to it. Critics have been quick to point out that by and large festive celebrations such as carnival were tolerated and perhaps even encouraged by institutional authorities, that they represented a safety valve for potentially disruptive behavior. More recently, however, historians have demonstrated that even when officially sponsored, popular festivity could in fact be powerfully rebellious or shaped by unruly specific political and social circumstances.[4] This debate, in which Bakhtin takes, or is given, a place, proceeds at least partly from the stratum of ironies under which Bakhtin's theory labors. For in categorically confronting the very sources of certain varieties of poststructuralist criticism, Bakhtin at the same time predicted some of their conclusions. Nowhere are these ironies more evident than in the important announcement of *Rabelais and His World* in the essays of Julia Kristeva (1980, 64–91). In her stress on intertextuality she offers a sophisticated extension of Bakhtin's obsession with dialogue, partly in order to critique what had been a structuralist consensus. The chapters that follow owe as much to Kristeva's version of Bakhtin as to Bakhtin himself, especially insofar as many of my analyses center upon explicit, implicit, or even "accidental" responses to other texts.

The limitations on Bakhtin's usefulness in describing a writer like Chaucer have been more forcefully addressed by some recent historians than by literary critics. These historians, such as Carlo Ginzburg and Natalie Zemon Davis, have turned to Bakhtin's tracing of popular cultural forms in high literature as a model for identifying the traits of popular mentality within received official documents. These historians quote Bakhtin approvingly, and some of them regard him as a shaping force on their own original contributions to method. It is in regard to method that these historians have much to teach literary critics. In an effort to move beyond the New Criticism, some literary critics have sought to imitate the models of other disciplines. But history and anthropology, most relevant to medievalists, had borrowed the technique of close reading in order to move beyond their own structuralist and narrative impasses. In borrowing from these other disciplines, literary critics are discovering what they take to be the border between history and literature, but which in fact is criticism's own frontier. From the anthropologist Clifford Geertz's crucial essay "Thick Description," to the concern with texts and readings, oral and written, among these historians, one prominent strategy is the very attention to context and use, and to the varieties of possible response among historical actors, that the New Criticism, particularly its English rather than American variety, sometimes in its most antihistorical phase, had articulated (Geertz 1973).

At the same time, concern with the status of documentary evidence has enabled these historians to offer a more compelling critique of Bakhtin's reading of Rabelais than that offered by some literary scholars. Sensitive to the complex "circle" of cultural borrowing and aware of how radically images and ideas change when revoiced or rewritten, they have been able to discriminate between the potential of Bakhtin's theoretical position and his sometimes uncritical reading of Rabelais as a celebration of popular mentality. The tendency of literary historians who have criticized or revised the argument of *Rabelais and His World* is to reject any possible influence of popular culture or to redefine his strongly political analysis as a more or less apolitical "unofficial" tradition, or to use his evidence concerning the "carnivalesque" to support the very "safety-valve" theories he sought to refute. But by thinking about Chaucer's poetry in ways that grow out of the use Bakhtin's work by these historians, we can arrive at a perspective that differs markedly from what one may expect of yet another "carnivalized" text.

The "popular" quality of Chaucer's works can be defined in several different and almost immediately contradictory ways. It can be argued, for instance, that the pilgrim audience is a poetic fiction, because Chaucer could not have addressed his poetry to millers and carpenters. The pilgrims must represent, in some fashion, a "future" audience, an audience of lawyers and doctors and country squires that his poetry seems to call into being.[5] In establishing the variety of interlocutors, Chaucer is permitting the multiplication and variety of responses that mark his perennial appeal. But even in a work like the *Troilus*, Chaucer's address to a courtly audience—qualified by an explicit awareness of posterity—suggests an additional concern, an anxiety about right interpretation and understanding. In this light, it is the address to the court that might be seen as a poetic fiction, a conscious limitation of a possible multiplication of responses that could prove dangerous to the intended meaning and continued significance of the narrative.

Documentary evidence, however, seems to suggest a much less complex and interesting relation between text and audience, or between author and audience, than Chaucer's own text implies. On the basis of libraries, wills, and programs of education in the late Middle Ages, literary taste would seem to have preferred much less difficult, much more explicitly pious, and much more obviously useful poetry than that offered to them in Chaucer, or, for that matter, Langland or the *Gawain*-poet. But the issue is also complicated for historical reasons, for Chaucer, like Dante and Petrarch, and perhaps to a lesser extent Boccaccio, were part of the very process creating a literary public. They did not so much "write for" their readers as invent them.[6] In the narrowest sense, this is literally true. English was only just taking its place as a literary language, not only against the standard of Latin, but also against the dominance of French. But it is also the peculiar quality of the *Canterbury Tales* that each reading of the work is a recreation of the conditions of its creation. This quality is most evident in the tension between teller and tale and in the dialogue between tales and between tellers, but it is also implicit in the details of Chaucer's style, even in the earlier poems. Whereas the same might be argued of all works of art, the art of the *Canterbury Tales* lays bare that process. Chaucer shares with medieval popular theatricality a tendency to dramatize the process of signification itself. The ways in which he plays with the distance between intention and reception have finally become my chief focus.

Chaucer not only comments on but embodies the difficulties of intention. One way to map the distance between intention and reception is to think about what happens when Chaucer resets his earlier work or earlier positions in new contexts, and I have tried to do this in some of the following chapters. But another way is to center on certain passages in which Chaucer's intention seems to be obscure or uncertain. Art historians often concentrate on techniques that compare homologically to textual criticism. Where, for instance, in a corrected section of a painting or a cartoon, where in faded colors, can we locate an earlier, more original intention? Textual criticism finds itself in the same dilemma. Where in an earlier version can we locate the author's original intention, perhaps even his meaning? Like the traces of pentimento, textual cruxes often give us important information. But when we cannot safely date a particular reading or even prove the existence of a particular passage—more difficult to establish than the underlayers of a painting—we find ourselves in a more troubling archaeological situation.

Chaucer's poetry abounds in such cruxes, and earlier scholars have sought to locate his original meaning, his first version, or his development in the evidence they provide. Advances in textual scholarship and a good deal of common sense have obviated many, but not all, of the questions of authenticity or definitive readings. Critical interpretation that aims at clarifying "Chaucer's meaning" must take great care with such problematic passages. This is not to say that criticism that seeks to solve Chaucer's contradictions by envisioning a particular direction—a carefully worked out human drama, a geographically consistent pilgrimage, a theologically correct hierarchy, a reasoned debate on some social and political issues—is without value. But the curious advantage of considering the passages I have centered on here is that it allows us to consider some of the intersections of the vectors that suggest these different possible *Canterbury Tales*. As a result, and this seems to me one of the strong points of Chaucer criticism of late, we can address the most challenging questions of previous, apparently mutually exclusive versions of Chaucer.

Even the form of the *Canterbury Tales* mirrors the sense of constant revision and self-quotation that these accidental passages reveal. What comes later in the *Canterbury Tales* problematizes what comes before. The end of the General Prologue, for instance and even some of its later portraits destabilize the sense of purpose that its opening and earlier portraits claim. Reading backwards, we may, if we wish, locate this destabilization very early on. The tales that follow the *Knight's Tale* call into question its and the Knight's assumptions. As a result, we have begun to read the

Knight's Tale as a discourse that calls into question its own assumptions. Chaucer not only calls into question earlier statements in the *Canterbury Tales* by its shifting context, he also refers, however obliquely, to his own changing poetic role.

The individual chapters of this book, rather than offer interpretative readings, seek to articulate these issues as a set of poetic problems that both take off from and circle back to some traditional Chaucerian questions. The second chapter seeks to articulate and explain some of the issues I have mentioned here, by exploring how Chaucer appropriates the voice of "popular" literary forms such as chronicles and pious collections. The third chapter extends the metaphor of theatricality to the *Canterbury Tales* as a whole, delineating some examples and suggesting Chaucer's equivalence between his own image-making and dramatic performance. The fourth chapter contrasts Chaucer and Boccaccio's handling of the related issues of popular understanding and the creation of illusions, especially in terms of the sometimes discontinuous connection between narrators and tales. The fifth chapter discusses the *Clerk's Envoy* as a comment by Chaucer on his own relation to popular response. The sixth chapter continues this discussion by contrasting Chaucer's theatrical performers, such as the Wife or the Pardoner, with his more selfconsciously literary performers, such as the Franklin and the Squire. The seventh chapter seeks to locate a series of images that run beneath the surface of major tales, conflating popular unrest and "noise." The final chapter concludes by describing the ways that Chaucer both sets up and collapses distinctions between talk and text, between scribally sanctioned authority and orally shared cultural wisdom.

.   .   .

Perhaps in reaction to an Arnoldian condescension to Chaucer's status and a nineteenth- and early twentieth-century skepticism about the unity and coherence of the *Canterbury Tales*, recent criticism has valorized one dimension of Chaucer's poetry: that dimension which asserts its unity and its sense of permanence and mastery, and which proclaims its own monumental and major status. In the following chapters, I seek to alert us to another dimension within the poetry, which exists in nearly dialectical opposition to that first dimension. This second dimension seems almost to celebrate the local, the provisional, the sense of performance and illusion that one also finds in the theatricality and popular culture of the late Middle Ages.

But this celebration is not at all naive enthusiasm. If Chaucer harbored "anxiety" about his poetry, it was not an anxiety of influence or even an anxiety of style. It was much more an anxiety of permanence, of memory. He shared that concern with the other great poets of his day, like Dante and Petrarch, but his solution was different. He makes that concern explicit in the *Troilus*, perhaps because it is the first of his works not obviously occasional in some fashion; the early poems, in their immediate setting and in their odd shifts of tone and action suggest participation in court ceremony, as I suggest above. Even despite extensive glossing, they seem to retain secret meanings, as if commenting on a lost code, character, or events. Despite its appeal to an "audience," the *Troilus* throughout develops its own sense of mastery and permanence; it seems to proclaim an awareness of its own historical significance. Yet that status is announced with some irony, and the *House of Fame* plays even more with these same questions. The *Troilus* becomes exactly the kind of monument its own ideology seeks to question. In turning to a new kind of poetry in the *Canterbury Tales*, Chaucer is not rejecting one set of traditions so much as seeking a different status for the mode of existence of his poetry. In the *Canterbury Tales*, Chaucer does not revert or drop this concern for the permanence of his writing, but he addresses it in reverse, as it were. He seems almost to insist on the ephemeral and minor status of its origins: the *Tales* seem to now proclaim their connection with rumor, now with gossip, now with conversation, games, folklife, flytings, or improvised situations. Forms that seem by nature to assert their secondary status—parodies and anthologies—inform the very center of the work. Even the absence of an authoritative and official point of view in the work, notwithstanding the first and last storytellers, seems consciously contrived. In fact, Chaucer resists the forces that he, and Dante, and Petrarch, feared most as poets—linguistic relativism, the failure of memory, the capriciousness of tradition—by building the symptoms of such forces into the very body of his poetry. He ensures the survival of the *Canterbury Tales* by building into it the possibility of constant reinterpretation, and he does so by making the entire work into a fiction of ephemeral performance and presentation and by including in it structural and formal allusions to the popular, occasional, and temporary forms that I describe in the following chapters.

This sense of the performative nature of Chaucerian voices, whether we ascribe courtly or popular origins to them, complicates one of the most fruitful critical versions of Chaucer to have dominated our readings: a Chaucer who holds together the conflicting tensions of late medieval culture either by placing its antinomies in suspension or by arranging its categories hierarchically. But if we look at even the most quotable speeches in Chaucer or recall the most dramatic moments, we find that the tensions and conflicts, acknowledged or otherwise, are often expressed in the same moments, so that instead of in resolution or even paradox, we find ourselves always in a contested field. It is within the passages of the *Canterbury Tales* and not only in the dialogue between characters or tales that the tensions of its culture are explored, and as a result, neither synthesized nor neutralized nor transcended.

Chapter Two

BAKHTIN, CHAUCER, CARNIVAL, LENT

THE PURPOSE of this chapter is to trace some of the ways in which Chaucer imitates the naivete associated with popular literary forms, particularly collections of various sorts, and in so doing places them at the service of a sophisticated literary enterprise—the self-presentation of the *Canterbury Tales*. That naivete is, however, only assumed or imputed: in fact, it frequently disguises literary strategies that are as self-conscious as the elaborations of courtly literary forms. Chaucer's borrowing, then, alternately depends on the power of popular discourse and distances him from it.

I begin with a passage chosen at random. Sometime in the late thirteenth century, the author of an entry in the *Chronicle of Lanercost* logs a sensational story about a renegade priest:

> About this time, in Easter week, the parish priest of Inverkeithing, named John, revived the profane rites of Priapus, collecting young girls from the villages, and compelling them to dance in circles [to the honour of] Father Bacchus. When he had these females in a troop, out of sheer wantonness, he led the dance, carrying in front on a pole a representation of the human organs of reproduction, and singing and dancing himself like a mime, he viewed them all and stirred them to lust by filthy language. Those who held respectable matrimony in honour were scandalised by such a shameless performance, although they respected the parson because of the dignity of his rank. If anybody remonstrated kindly with him, he [the priest] became worse [than before], violently reviling him.
>
> And [whereas] the iniquity of some men manifestly brings them to justice, [so] in the same year, when his parishioners assembled according to custom in the church at dawn in Penance Week, at the hour of discipline he would insist that certain persons should prick with goads [others] stripped for penance. The burgesses, resenting the indignity inflicted upon them, turned upon its author; who, while he as author was defending his nefarious work, fell the same night pierced by a knife, God thus awarding him what he deserved for his wickedness. (*Chronicle of Lanercost* 1913, 30)

The entry presents all the problems inherent in the use of medieval chronicles to reconstruct political and narrative history, for it is evidence of the sense of scale of such chronicles, in which the most minor incidents are

paired with nationally significant events. For an earlier generation of schol-
ars motivated by the great comparative enterprises of the nineteenth and
early twentieth century, however, the entry really was evidence for the sur-
vival of pagan, pre-Christian agrarian fertility practices. Sir James Frazer
explicitly compiles records such as this (using a secondary source and quot-
ing a different anecdote from the Lanercost chronicle) to establish such an
origin for religious ritual (1966, 286). For E. K. Chambers (1963), who,
we might note, is deeply indebted to *The Golden Bough*, the Inverkeithing
incident would have been one more suggestion of the origins of drama
itself in such pagan ritual, and evidence also of the continuity of folk drama
and quasi-dramatic performances despite the hegemony of the Church. For
slightly later critics, such as John Speirs (1957), this pre-Christian survival
underlies the rhythms of even the most sophisticated medieval works and
even accounts for their literary, or preliterary and mythic, power.

Until quite recently, severe criticisms limited the uses of Chambers and
the implications of Speirs. Chambers's evolutionism had been radically
called into question by the critique of O. B. Hardison's *Christian Rite and
Christian Drama in the Middle Ages* (1965). C. S. Lewis demolished Speirs's
"anthropological approach" in a still important essay (1962). Moreover,
the appropriation as propaganda of folkloric, ritual and pagan imagery ren-
dered the entire enterprise suspect because the manifestations of the enter-
prise at the turn of the century had been associated with social darwinist
and racialist impulses, an association that continued frighteningly through
several decades. In a sense, part of the importance of a work like Northrop
Frye's *Anatomy of Criticism* (1953) was that it sanitized the methodology.

But these questions have been opened anew by a remarkable confluence
of categories in both social and literary history and therefore require atten-
tion yet again. An interest in popular mentality and culture has been rea-
wakened by a generation of historians close to or deeply influenced by the
important French historical journal *Annales*, chief of whom are Natalie
Zemon Davis in America, Carlo Ginzburg in Italy, and Le Roy Ladurie in
France. At the same time, a keen interest in the work of M. M. Bakhtin,
with his fascination with festival and carnival as metaphors for, even
sources or modes of literature, has motivated some of the most intriguing
recent reexaminations of medieval literary texts, suggesting that perhaps
for the first time in several decades the questions raised by medieval texts
are again at the center of literary and cultural theory. Davis and Ginzburg,
most active in reconstructing popular mentality, both explicitly acknowl-
edge Bakhtin's influence. Bakhtin is also quoted in some recent studies of
Chaucer, though usually in support of the applicability of his theories on
genre to the *Canterbury Tales* (Payne 1981; Kern 1980; Andreas 1979,
1984). My own interest in Bakhtin's chief formulations is that they help us

to locate the difficulty of Chaucer's self-presentation as popular voicing, as long as we do not merely apply Bakhtin's notions wholesale.

.   .   .

Bakhtin's most familiar notion is that of the "carnivalesque" (Bakhtin 1968, 1–58). The anarchic holiday celebration in marketplace and square, with its many voices and disdain for the established social order, seems an almost irresistible metaphor for the *Canterbury Tales*. Bakhtin seems to uncover at a stroke an entire social dynamic implicit in monastic satire, popular folklore, and goliardic parody, all of which offer an "unofficial" medieval comic tradition for Chaucer's tales and frame. His location in medieval humor of what he delicately calls "the lower bodily stratum" in Rabelais highlights yet again the "parts" in Chaucer that sometimes have loomed large in modern critical discussions. Bakhtin's "carnivalesque" would again crown Chaucer's comic tales and "low" characters as the rulers of his work.

In a sense, then, Bakhtin would return us to materials—popular culture, folklife, London life and lore—that fascinated scholars of nearly a century ago. But we cannot simply take the attractive, apparently historically motivated metaphor of the carnivalesque and apply it to Chaucer without taking Bakhtin's other theoretical concerns seriously. Otherwise we risk ignoring the problematic and reading Chaucer in a celebratory or mimetic relation to a particular strain in "medieval life." Such a version of Chaucer, which grew up in the wake of romantic theories of poetry and peaked in late nineteenth- and early twentieth-century studies, perhaps most beautifully articulated in Virginia Woolf's essay on the Pastons (1925), is the version against which later scholarship has taken aim, stressing instead the learned, academic, and institutional, even hermetic, sources of Chaucer's art.[1] Far from promising a revolution in our conception of Chaucer, the possibility of a carnivalesque Chaucer returns us to a pre-Kittredgian Chaucer. An understanding of Bakhtin's notions of language and cultural interchange are necessary to supplement the appealing metaphor of carnival.

Oddly enough, given the great effort Chaucer criticism has made to free itself from the hegemony of the novel, it is in fact Bakhtin's theory of the novel that provides an adequate formal description of the *Canterbury Tales*. In the period before the novel, he says, older genres find themselves parodied, comically criticized, in Bakhtin's term, "novelized" (Bakhtin 1981, 295–315). For Bakhtin, the novel's particular shape is inextricably related to its situation in relation to language itself, particularly the rise of what Bakhtin calls "polyglossia." This term seems to indicate a historical situation in which the authority of a single dominant dialect or language breaks down. His historical location of such situations is demonstrated by his preference for Alexandrian literature, late classical literature in general, and those situations traditional literary history might regard as decadences of various sorts. For Bakhtin, these moments encourage the rise of "novelizing" forms because older, hierarchical relations between discourses no longer hold, and the "novel," whatever that may be, can develop in its most characteristic fashion, as developing, renewing, or recreating rather than merely reflecting or describing reality. For Bakhtin, then, "novelization" is something distinct from the novel. Bakhtin finds "conversational" folk forms particularly keen sources of this multivoiced and parodic discourse. The art of the novel is to let voices other than that of the author speak. It is paradoxically an art with its roots in artless forms.

The irony of Bakhtin's most apparently fruitful argument being potentially the most reductive and regressive suggests yet another irony of his uses for Chaucer scholars: his most helpful contribution may not be to help us reinterpret Chaucer, but to reorient the chief issues of Chaucer criticism. He can help us rewrite some of its traditional questions by replacing their controlling metaphors. The slight shift in angle of vision, I think, may help us see that some of the traditional questions of Chaucer scholarship, which we sometimes feel "hop alwey behind" may well be at the center of critical inquiry.

We might consider the *Canterbury Tales* as a demonstration of what Bakhtin calls "border crossings," not only between genres and reportage and fiction as he uses that term, but also between apparently independent parts of Chaucer's work. Dialogue interrupts narrative, lines are echoed and reechoed, no—or precious few—statements are accorded final authority. This sense of "mixture" of styles is arguably one of the constants of the best Chaucer criticism of our time, but the model of Bakhtin's poetics suggests that the synthesis or concord or hierarchy that we seek as the end of interpretation should not be so easily assumed. We may be forced to think of both the drama and the unity of the *Canterbury Tales* in a new light.

Moreover, the context of popular and folk culture, with its communal and participatory nature, conditions the place of the reader vis a vis the *Canterbury Tales*. The interchange between audience and performer, the provisional and ironic attitude towards the efficacy of the illusion before us, the peculiar jostling of high and low forms, which Chaucer shares with the popular and urban theatricality of his time, are precisely those elements which touch upon his "modern" appeal. What Bakhtin says of the place of the participant in carnival—and as a result the reader of carnivalized literature— has important consequences for one of the most obvious and underemphasized qualities of the *Canterbury Tales*, the place of the reader vis a vis the text: "Carnival is a pageant without a stage and without a division into performers and spectators. In the carnival everyone is an active participant; everyone communes in the carnival act" (Bakhtin 1973, 100). While obviously true of the pilgrims as participants, and their attempts to answer and correct each other, we as readers are similarly involved.

More comprehensively, and perhaps most important, let me suggest that we borrow from Bakhtin's stress on polyglossia and rewrite the entire metaphor of "framing" and "framed fiction," with its pictorial and architectural (and nineteenth-century) heritage. In place of a metaphor based on "framing," with its concomitant stress on stability and placement, I suggest we rely on a metaphor of "quotation," which suggests more forcefully the dialogic and self-generating style of the work. The purely linguistic nature of action in the *Canterbury Tales*, the way in which themes and words are quoted and parodied from speaker to speaker, the sense of dialogue rather than of drama or of set narrative is thereby emphasized.[2] In contrast to Dante with his vatic stance, Chaucer has to rely on more ironic and unsteady possibilities and at best would perhaps lay claim to the less lofty appellation, "grant translateur," which itself reveals the relative authority of a single voice or even a single language. We are familiar enough with obeisance to "mine auctor" in medieval texts. Yet it must also be pointed out how the actual construction of poetry, as well as the place and role of the narrator, is conditioned by this sense of quotation, by a constant echo and reecho of another's words.[3]

Bakhtin's stress on polyglossia should lead us to a consideration of texts not as a collection of sources or images, but as the embodiment of a set of relationships between author and audience, though we may perhaps want to discriminate at the outset between a public whom the author addresses directly and an audience that hears that story but for whom it may not necessarily have been intended. The oral fiction of the *Canterbury Tales* is not that it is heard, but that it is overheard. Part of the "overheard" quality of the work is also implicit in its dependence on forms of village communication such as gossip, or in Chaucer's conscious play with the possible disparity between a public culturally and socially prepared for the interpretation of a particular text and an audience without that context or with a totally different one. Quotation and polyglossia are also matters of cultural fact.[4] The General Prologue itself is filled with a whole set of languages, subcultures, and specialized discourses, many of which find themselves parodied by the narrator's attempt to voice them. Beneath the English "native" soil itself are layers and mixes of specific cultures, marked more by mixture than by purity.

．　　．　　．

To illustrate the difficulty of this cycle of cultural borrowing, we return to the passage from the Lanercost chronicle with which I began. I want to proceed by describing some qualities of voice and style in this passage and suggest how those qualities wend their way into more self-consciously literary forms. I want to locate, that is, some of the complexities involved in what historians have identified as the "circle" of popular and elite cultures. But to do that one must first admit that this little episode already has a definable literary form and literary voice. Chronicles, while not sources for content or even for form, reveal a great deal about the voice and style of romance and other genres. Like sermons, they represent a characteristic discourse, one that finds itself echoed in the chambers of other forms.

One's first reaction may be that the passage is an example of the sort of gossip and hearsay that invalidates the documentary veracity of so many chronicles. But it is equally possible to read the passage as an echo of another chronicle with wide circulation, the famous history of Bede, who at one point laments the return of the English to their pagan customs in a time of despair and uncertainty. There is nothing of the epic tone of Bede's passage in Lanercost. In fact, the stress on the offended sensibilities of the disciplined burgesses and the relative lack of stress on mental anguish suffered by the dancing girls lend the passage an unconsciously comical note. Probably this quality derives from the actual source of the passage, which one suspects is not hearsay or the chronicler's repressed imagination, but a legal procedure, with suspects, motives, and the record of the attitudes of the village and the personality of the deceased. Two centuries later, the incident might be the occasion for hysteria and claims of witchcraft. It is in fact pleasing how the chronicler ascribes activities on all sides, except for the justified murder, to human motives and drives, not least of all John himself. This is especially so in contrast to other marvelous episodes in *Lanercost* in which it seems almost as if the chronicler had intruded a folktale as an actual fact. The passage is also amusing in the social attitudes it expresses—the disgust at John's abuse of his position, the sense of a little power struggle between him and the burgesses, the touch of admiration for the force of his personality, and the surprising fact that anyone has put up with him for this long. In fact, the priest has a personality more often found in wicked nobles in such monastic chronicles. But what exactly did the parishoners think they were doing in following John? The various social forces implicit in the episode seem at odds with the paltry moral the chronicler provides. It shares in this lack with another few examples I want to cite, from Robert Mannyng of Brunne's *Handlyng Synne*.

Handlyng Synne is particularly interesting because it includes within itself—in the famous sequence of the Dancers of Colbek—a meditation on the uses of various sorts of poetry, if we take carols as a form of poetry and if we take seriously the work's own tension between narrative and doctrine. Moreover, it frames such a meditation in terms of a dichotomy between piety and indulgence in a way that suggests some of the weaknesses of such a dichotomy. The priest Robert, who commands the twelve dancers in the churchyard to stop their revels ("Why stonde we? Why go we nought?" translates Mannyng from their ironic Latin song), seems to suffer as much as the dancers who are left in their magic dancing circle for a year and a day. His attempt to undo his act when he realizes his daughter Eva is one of the dancers is equally tragic, for her arm comes off in the hands of his son Azone, whom he has ordered to rescue her. In a sense, the tale is as much an emblem of the conflicts in the author's own materials as it is a moral tale. Out of season perhaps, but Carnival battles Lent here in a Pyrrhic victory.

For instance, Mannyng tells the story of two hermits, one of whom leaves to become abbot of a nearby monastery. The other hermit grows extremely lonely (Mannyng's sympathy for loneliness in a hermit is touching) and pines away. God takes pity on him, and in a marvelous inversion on a plot like *Yvain*, awards him a bear who becomes his best friend, even watching his sheep without eating them. Unfortunately, some of the brothers in the monastery dislike the idea of the hermit's bear attracting more attention as a miracle than anything their new abbot has done, and they murder the bear (*Handlyng Synne*, 1901, 1903, ll. 4000–156). (Mannyng adds that envy is the vice of the English as lechery is that of the French, and in that it comes from the soul rather than the body is much worse!) Typically, the story is supposed to be about envy—the brothers are punished by God in such a way that their bodies begin to decompose while they are still alive—but the stress of the story is on the hermit's loneliness and his profound desire for friendship.

This human sympathy, obvious in nearly every one of Mannyng's tales and not always highlighted in his source, the *Manuel des Pechiez*, is accompanied by a creatural obsession with bodily corruption so common in sermon literature. In the same sequence as the Dancers of Colbek, to illustrate the sin of sacrilege, Mannyng recounts a tale of a nobleman who lives next to a parson. The nobleman's cattle wander into and of course defecate in the graveyard. When a bondman forthrightly complains to the nobleman, the lord answers, with marvelous haughtiness, that the bodies of such churls ought to be honored. But the bondman has the composure of, say, the old woman in the *Wife of Bath's Tale*, and points out that God made earls and churls of the same earth. The nobleman, suitably chastised, builds a fence. In a dozen lines, the lesson runs off in as many directions. What is its moral? That noblemen should be more gracious? That the bondsman is a good servant? Where has the parson been all this time? Its import seems more along the lines of the democracy of death so frequent in sermons. Like the *Parsons's Tale*, *Handlyng Synne* points out the common creatural existence and end of all of us, yet the images of the sanctity of the burial ground on the one hand and the cattle doing their cattlelike business on the other (Chaucer's Parson's obsession with dung is in fact quite different), which might be made to make the same point, are opposed.

As if aware of his audiences' predilections, Mannyng condemns popular superstition and contrasts it with more authoritative (if imageless) faith in providence (ll. 340–602). We should, for instance, abstain from witchcraft, especially calling on the devil to locate property that has been stolen from us. We should not make children stare at the blade of a sword or in a basin or at a thumb. The chattering of a magpie does not necessarily mean that you will have a guest. If you should meet someone on going into town, and if your business does not work out while you are in town, do not curse that person, who certainly had no intention of wishing bad luck upon you. The folk imagery of such remarks provides the power of Mannyng's most extended narratives. Yet even when Mannyng stays closest to his source, the *Manuel des Pechiez*, he demonstrably achieves a marked change in tone that sometimes compromises the very meaning of the tales he retells. *Handlyng Synne* offers what is in some ways an inverse version of Chaucer's ironies and suggests the complex cultural layering of apparently popular or learned or courtly texts.

Robert Mannyng's explanation of his title after Raymond of Waddington's *Manuel des Pechiez* is typical of his stylistic and generic accumulations:

> "Manuel" ys "handlyng with honde";
> "Pecches" is "synne," y undyrstonde.
> These twey wurdys that beyn otwynne,
> Do hym to gedyr, ys "handlyng synne."
>
> (ll. 83–86)[5]

Although closely translating from the French, Robert Mannyng has a way of making such explanations sound like nursery rhymes or popular sayings. This shift in tone—making what has no such resonance sound homely or popular—is one Chaucer uses again and again to arch advantage.

> Handlyng yn speche ys as weyl
> As handlyng yn dede every deyl.
> On thys manere handyl thy dedys,
> And lestene and lerne whan any hem redys.
> Thou darst never recche where thou bygynne,
> For every-whare is bygynnyng of synne;
> Whedyr thou wylt opon the boke,
> Thou shalt fynde begynnyng overal to loke:
> Overal ys bygynnyng, overal ys ende;
> Hou that thou wylt turne or wende,
> Many thyngys mayst thou theryn here;

With oft redyng, mayst thou lere;
Thou mayst nat, with onys redyng,
Knowe the sothe of every thyng.
Handyl, hyt behoveth oft sythys,
To many maner synnes hyt wrythys.
Talys shalt thou fynde therynne,
And chauncys that hath happed for synne;
Mervelys, some as y fonde wrytyn,
And other that have be seyn & wetyn;
None ben thare-yn, more ne lesse,
But that I founde wryte, or had wytnesse.

(ll. 115–36)

The form of *Handlyng Synne* itself has a peculiar historical origin (not unrelated to, say, the *Parson's Tale*), a "manual" made necessary by the Fourth Lateran Council's decree that parish priests would henceforth take confession on a regular basis and must therefore be instructed in the taxonomy of sins. Part of the unintentional aesthetic interest of *Handlyng Synne* is in the ways in which the examples struggle against the structure imposed on them. The implicit audience of such manuals, at least as they filter into the English tradition, seems to have broadened to include a lay audience. Whatever the reasons, a work like *Handlyng Synne* encyclopedically includes a great variety of voices in a manner that seems to raise more questions about the authority of any single point of view than it synthesizes. In so doing, without the same level of self-consciousness, *Handlyng Synne* predicts some of the qualities of the *Canterbury Tales*. Robert Mannyng's informed style suggests a speaking voice, at the same time as he makes us aware again and again of the uses of this written "manual." He (and this includes only to some extent his source) tells us precisely how the book is to be read. Indeed, he explicitly tells us that one reading is not enough, and that one may only learn with many readings. These readings allow us to endure temptation vicariously. The book becomes a substitute for experience itself and saves us from the constant pitfalls and dangers—the new beginnings—of everyday existence. As with the beginning of sins, so too with the beginning of the book. One can find its origins everywhere, in all the stories, just as the stories themselves make the book begin anew each time. This claim is not unsophisticated theologically, and someone like Chaucer could also have seen how it was full of formal potential.

Throughout *Handlyng Synne* a conflict between official and unofficial culture goes on and takes the shape of the conservative populism of sermons, inveighing at the same time against the pride of nobles and "wasters" and against popular superstition. In the dangerous fashion of sermon literature, there is a slight tendency to make the worldly excesses it seeks to condemn seem rather glamorous. One of the interesting things about Chaucer's *Pardoner's Tale*, for instance, which uses the exemplum in a much more complicated way than is usually acknowledged, is that the Pardoner pretends to the sort of moral recklessness he has his "riotours" embody, but the representation of the immoral life in the tale is more tawdry, thread-bare, and depressing than even Chaucer's Parson is able to make it. This is part of Chaucer's daring, and I am not especially modernizing the effect of the *Handlyng Synne*, where the power of the inset narratives does destabil-ize the moralizing framework. What Chaucer does is to call into question the solidity of his moral context and yet allow the implicit power of the narrative imagery to prevail. In a sense, a tale like that of the Pardoner suggests a narrative context not unlike that of *Troilus and Criseyde*, in which the narrator finds himself at odds with and disturbed by the direction and impact of his story. But in the *Handlyng Synne* we find, if not a more com-plex, a more unresolved and multilayered tension between official and un-official cultures. Whereas Chaucer exploits such a tension, Robert Man-nyng's collection illustrates it.

William J. Brandt (1966) distinguishes between two sorts of medieval chronicle writing, a dichotomy most easily located in "aristocratic" chroni-cles on the one hand and "monastic" chronicles on the other. In "monastic" chronicles, the "ground of being" is historical stasis, and any disruption is regarded as bad and framed in the most disastrous imagery. History pro-ceeds intermittently, by the intervention of God, historical action therefore acquiring the status of a sign rather than a series of events with conse-quences. A certain determinism, however, is accorded in the "aristocratic" chronicles, although action there proceeds from the will of the noble hero, whose biography spans the frame of the events under question. With his death, and before his birth, unformed and inconsequential randomness reigns. The purity of Brandt's dichotomy may be open to question, but it addresses directly the connection between social and narrative disruption. However remote this historiographic model may apparently be from Chaucer, the comparison with these discontinuous genres may illuminate some formal problems of Chaucer criticism, for it can be argued that Chaucer recognizes and articulates the connection between social and liter-ary disruption that is latent in texts such as chronicles and manuals, where moral vision and narrative illustration are almost always in conflict.

For comparison, we may briefly look at what Alfred David (1976, 93–94) identified as Chaucer's most obviously carnivalesque moment, the *Miller's Tale*. The famous self-description of the *Canterbury Tales* both in the General Prologue and in the prologue to the *Miller's Tale* is often taken as a defense of the poet's art and even a defense of originality through attribution of that originality to traditional variety or to characters. We are most likely to immediately to think of the sophisticated defense of the *De-*

cameron's earthiness in Day 4, but there is also a less sophisticated tradition that Chaucer exploits, in which authors of collections, particularly practical collections, instruct their readers in the uses of a book, as Helen Cooper (1984, 69) has shrewdly noted.

> What sholde I moore seyn, but this Millere
> He nolde his wordes for no man forbere,
> But tolde his cherles tale in his manere.
> M'athynketh that I shal reherce it heere.
> And therfore every gentil wight I preye,
> For Goddes love, demeth nat that I seye
> Of yvel entente, but for I moot reherce
> Hir tales alle, be they bettre or werse,
> Or elles falsen som of my mateere.
> And therfore, whoso list it nat yheere,
> Turne over the leef and chese another tale;
> For he shal fynde ynowe, grete and smale,
> Of storial thyng that toucheth gentillesse,
> And eek moralitee and hoolynesse.
> Blameth nat me if that ye chese amys.

(I.3167–81)[6]

Thanks to Donald Howard (1976, 66), we now read this passage as an articulation of the "bookness" of the *Canterbury Tales*. But it is also an inversion of the awareness that we observed in *Handlyng Synne*. Whereas the danger of those earlier texts is almost certainly that of making game out of earnest, Chaucer warns us against the opposite, the result being an arch defense of playfulness. Character again intrudes upon moral categories, confusing the issue further. By assuming the tone of voice of conventional piety, Chaucer displays the helplessness of that piety in containing explosive, often amoral forces. In *Handlyng Synne*, the lesson of the book helps us deal with the problems of life. In the *Canterbury Tales*, our simple versions of experience are called upon to help us deal—quite impossibly—with the text.

There can be no question of these passages influencing each other in an explicitly textual way, which is partly why I have chosen them. A case could be made that Chaucer read *Handlyng Synne* but all I would insist on is that he be familiar with the voices we find articulated in these examples, and that we recognize that these voices, despite the best efforts of their compilers, are many rather than single, that the implications of the exemplum destabilize the moral point.

I do not ascribe this conflict to naivete or stupidity. It is, rather, dependent on the author's awareness that the material is itself potentially dangerous, that one must frame it exactly right in order not to move too far under

its own seductive spell, and yet at the same time one must draw a recogniz-
able outline. The odd restraint we find in the framing of these exempla is
the result of moral and theological perplexity, which Chaucer converts to
hermeneutical perplexity.

Robert Mannyng recounts the startling incident of a man who is exiled
to a neighboring area and takes refuge in a dwelling on church ground
(*Handlyng Synne*, ll. 8937–86). Loneliness and desire overcome his prom-
ise not to do so, and he has sex with—in Mannyng's example—his wife.
The result is that they are stuck together, "like dogs." They are able to
uncouple, after some public display, and much regret, only after a much
stronger resolve and a minor miracle. The story is close to something we
may want to call an anti-fabliaux and is narrated in that tone. Interestingly,
the tale immediately precedes the story of the Dancers of Colbek, with its
articulate and elaborate explanatory context, which forbids in the church or
churchyard:

> Karolles, wrastlynges, or somour games,
>
> . . . .
>
> Or entyrludes, or syngynge,
> Or tabur-bete or other pypynge
>
> . . . .
>
> Karolles to synge, and rede rymys.
>
> (*Handlyng Synne*, ll. 8987–9000)

Chaucer also does not frame his fabliaux as expressions of sophisticated
and self-conscious farce, as Nykrog (1957) would have us read them. In-
stead, he borrows something of the voice of narrators like Robert Man-
nyng, and the resigned puzzlement of chroniclers, quite desperate to inte-
grate exempla into their frame. Yet with this tone of voice he releases the
anarchy these other writers seek to control. It is as if in parodying the most
characteristic forms of popular culture, Chaucer releases their real power.

.   .   .

By proclaiming the identity of fiction-making with humbler pursuits,
Chaucer is constructing a skeptical, almost modern version of creation,
while at the same time allowing the comforting, almost naive connection of
art and popular culture. It is more likely, for instance, for the storytellers of
the *Decameron* to be telling their stories than for the pilgrims to be engaged
in the stories they are assigned, or that they apparently respond to. From
its earliest proposition in the General Prologue, dramatic illusion itself be-
gins as a daring, almost self-defeating enterprise.

By highlighting the fiction of performance—by making it the very sub-
ject of his art—Chaucer both achieves the sleight of hand of rendering his

art and ensures its public, rather than private, character. Thus the frame becomes enormously important, not as drama, but as a context for each tale and as a model of reception. These two functions sometimes conflict, and the model becomes an anti-model. The context serves to disturb rather than place the meaning of a story. By constantly contesting the settled character of its own written existence, the *Canterbury Tales* also insures its own permanence, the need for its constant reinterpretation.[7] It appropriates the subversiveness of popular culture as a condition of its own survival.

Despite the trappings of engagement and participation in the *Canterbury Tales*, the work mutes its own connection with ritual. It contains only a fiction of improvisation and festival, in the same way that *Troilus and Criseyde* suggests its own performance. Even the General Prologue, which contains overtones of primitive renewal celebration and even the healing and rejuvenating images typical of folk ritual, ends up asserting its existence as artificial community, a socially accidental construct, and the world in which it finally finds itself is one grown old, rather than a brave new one. Primitive communal images underlie the urban processional of the pilgrims, so that high art, local culture, and the rhythms of natural life coexist uneasily. In the very process of drawing life from popular culture, the work reveals its own artifice, its existence as historically and socially located art, and not timeless and natural ritual. The *Canterbury Tales* pretends to be "natural poetry," but the act of pretense asserts the dominance of culture over nature.

Written into the *Canterbury Tales* is an allegory of its own production, a double-edged commentary on the power of popular sources. The critique of purely aristocratic values in the tale may be obvious, if ironically stated, but Chaucer's verse also embodies the traces of its origins in popular culture. This strikes us initially as redundant, for at least one traditional reading of Chaucer has been as popular literature, as naive poetry. But if the criticism of the past century has taught us anything, it is how far from these forms, or at least mediated by elite forms, the *Canterbury Tales* is. One function of my argument here has been to trace the outline of this allegory, to delineate the complex and ambivalent relation that Chaucer's poetry bears to one of its richest sources. By extension, this allegory is an emblem of an entire cultural shift, the invention of bourgeois culture itself, with its appropriation of traditional, oral, conversational, folkloric forms to new and highly specific uses.

Without arguing from either a biographical or sociological reading, I still want to assert that the relatively unique class status of Chaucer and his perspective on, even connection to, the center of power in England leaves a mark on the poetry. It is a mark most clearly traced in a concern with both status and power, however transformed in literary images. And however disguised, the poetry everywhere articulates a story of its own cultural making. In his secular and class status, in his vernacular materials, even in his own official life, Chaucer is himself evidence of new, barely precedented literary and social possibilities. It may seem strange to evoke the usual comparison in reverse, but compared to Gower, Chaucer seems to have been more ambivalent about those possibilities. In some ways (linguistic, formal) more daring than Gower, Chaucer seems hemmed in by reservation and qualification in others, social and political. It would be easy enough to explain this difference as a matter of income or temperament. But even on a sheerly literary basis the complexity is there. Gower seeks avowedly to unify the voices of the common weal. In the *Canterbury Tales*, the embodiment of that society, those voices are revealed to be speaking on very different levels, asking for different things, and responding in ways not intended by each other. Part of Langland's uniqueness, to continue this contrast, is his effort to accomplish the same goal as Gower with the realization of something close to the reality revealed in Chaucer's divergent voices.[8]

Chaucer's poetry, that is, is both haunted by and depends upon an instability of context. He is a poet who in his most explicit philosophically oriented statements, such as his shorter poems, inveighs against instability and change. With Boethius, he would probably say that instability is a symptom of the illusory nature of earthly reality, and that it is our own foolishness to trust in the stability of earthly things.[9] But his poetry, even the early poetry, but especially the *Canterbury Tales*, builds a certain instability and indeterminacy into its very fabric. Partly it is a matter of editorial difficulty, of ascertaining the final order, if any, of the manuscripts. Partly it is a matter of completion, of an uneasy sense of links and sometimes entire poems unfinished. But these negatively phrased larger problems are in fact evidences writ large of exactly what this or that tale means, of whom we are to trust to make sense of the tale for us, of how we are to take the responses of pilgrims or even of characters within those tales. This is not just a matter of the ambiguity that the American New Criticism liked about Chaucer or the indeterminacy more recent critics have found in him. Poetic statement in Chaucer is in fact generated by dialogue among the characters and within the text. As a result, meaning is redefined as a process, as an act of intended instability. As a result, his poetry becomes less a poetry of image, moral, and paraphrasable message, and more a poetry of action, gesture, and stance.

This chapter has argued that in the self-presentation of the *Canterbury Tales*, fictional instability and process are imputed to be a result of the illusion of popular voicing. Chaucer both draws his power from and places ironically what Bakhtin would call the "dialogic" and "carnivalesque" aspects of his work. The next chapter explores these tensions between "carnival" and "lent" as a function of some underlying identities between Chaucer's fiction and medieval drama and theatrical performances.

Chapter Three

THE POETICS OF THEATRICALITY

IN CHAPTER 1, I suggest that the style of Chaucer's early poems owes something to the pervasive theatricality of the late medieval court, that, indeed, it was part of that theatricality. I want to suggest here how the *Canterbury Tales* also includes versions of theatricality dependent on urban and popular and folk culture.[1] Again, part of my point is to suggest that we replace the notion of the "dramatic" in Chaucer with the more pervasive notion of the "theatrical." The result may dissolve the thorny problems of character and realism and dramatic unity that bedevil the discussion of "drama" in the *Canterbury Tales* and may alert us to another dimension. Rather than providing a dramatic setting, the *Canterbury Tales* internalizes and appropriates certain dramatic structures within itself. Most alternate suggestions for discarding the idea of "roadside realism" have stressed the radically narrative character of the work. But in fact that narrativity is everywhere subverted and transgressed, in much the same way as dramatic realism is violated. That spirit of transgression and subversion is especially typical of the popular theatricality of the late Middle Ages. This chapter will argue further that Chaucer's apparently light-hearted and satirical references to medieval popular dramatic performances disguise a concern about some serious issues of poetics and the difficulties of representation.

Social historians have long emphasized the highly dramatic quality of late medieval life in general, and I do not want to dwell on such commonplaces here (Huizinga 1954; but see Aston 1979). Of course, the Mass itself had an implicitly dramatic form; pulpit delivery must have approached a nearly histrionic state; much rhetoric, despite the frozen quality of late medieval literary style, stresses the importance of delivery and impersonation. For our purposes here, I align myself only with those historians of the stage who point out that we ignore processions, disguisings, festivals, and tournaments only at the peril of missing a large area of medieval theatrical art (Chambers 1903; Wickham 1959). Although I suspect that most members of a medieval audience made some distinction between pure ceremony and spectacle on the one hand and some kind of narrative action or extended impersonation on the other, I shall not here so discriminate.

Even Chaucer's treatment of his sources is not always so dramatically coherent as we sometimes assume. The *Troilus* admittedly represents an expansion of the dramatic quality of his source, and in most cases Chaucer deepens and complicates character. But to take one familiar example, the compression evident in the *Knight's Tale* does not emphasize the considerable protodramatic quality of Boccaccio's romance, but rather develops elements of spectacle and ceremony, of medieval theatricality rather than of realistic drama (Muscatine 1950). Nor did Chaucer's versions of his stories lend themselves to dramatic treatment in other hands. It is not clear whether a fifteenth-century Griselde play had any basis in the *Clerk's Tale* nor whether Grimald's *Troilus* was a play at all. Chaucer wrote the *Clerk's Tale* before the appearance of a dramatized French version in the late 1390s. The one dramatic text printed in *Sources and Analogues* (Bryan and Dempster 1941, 423–39), an Italian play from the fifteenth century, bears some striking parallels to the *Pardoner's Tale*, not only in its wording, but in stage business, exits and entrances, and a lively, mordant humor missing from English fifteenth-century analogues. A play by Hans Sachs is also printed there. The records of the building of Milan cathedral indicate that in 1389 the ladies of the Porta Vercallina district performed a version of Jason and Medea complete with such props as imitation bones to raise money for the building fund (Larner 1971, 164–65), an activity that makes bingo seem like the purest spirituality. The performance is too late for Chaucer to have stumbled across it, and, in any case, the *Legend of Good Women* impresses one with the radically narrative character of its stories. The spectacular death scenes in those stories may owe something to the tradition of saints' plays epitomized in the plays of Hroswitha, but whether anyone saw such scenes mounted is a question. Certainly the description of miracles played in Chaucer's lifetime do stress the sufferings of the protagonists, and the famous Passion sequences of the "York realist," for instance, attest to the technical possibilities. But in any case such moments more nearly resemble the theater of Artaud, say, than that of psychological and social realism. It may have been a fairly common misapprehension, certainly as far back as Trivet and as late as Lydgate, that classical tragedy was performed by a narrator reading the text while the action was mimed on a platform behind him. Lydgate not only described, but wrote scripts for such performances. A famous description of such an activity can be found in the beginning of the *Troy Book* (Lydgate 1906, ll. 862–906).

Indeed, what we conceive of as drama in modern terms is much too narrow a conception to encompass the broad range of performances and improvisations that comprised the medieval theater.[2] There have been some very helpful studies that have divided *Troilus and Criseyde* into acts and scenes or discussed the use of dramatic gestures in Chaucer's narratives, for example. But these studies end up underlining Chaucer's formal artistry. From the point of view of the conventions of the nineteenth- and early twentieth-century realistic stage (which we now see in revival as it were), most forms of medieval narrative actually manifest a good deal more "dramatic realism" than the medieval theater. The mechanistic world of the fabliau, with its sometimes slapstick physical comedy, requires a mastery of certain dimensions not needed or acknowledged by the mystery plays, except for those few sequences that modern criticism tends to accentuate. The sophisticated conversations and rendezvous of high romance indicate a complexity, if not a depth, of character much more advanced than the theater of the Middle Ages can display. The anachronism of our critical terminology, particularly that of dramatic metaphors (as in Dempster 1932 and Lumiansky 1955), by no means invalidates their usefulness: these labels do indeed describe something absolutely central to the poetry, and I am perfectly aware that this critical terminology is not exclusively generic. But while the analogy to modern dramatic technique highlights the mimetic and psychological dimensions and the qualities of unity and self-conscious permanence in Chaucer, the analogy to medieval theatrical devices highlights a quite different set of qualities: the provisional, improvisational, and occasional, a sense of invention that responds more to the pressures of performance than to unity or classical standards of coherence.

· · ·

We have gotten used to thinking about the General Prologue either in terms of its character analysis, that is, the largely realistic and psychological dimension of Chaucer's art, or in terms of its reference to literary, particularly allegorical or courtly texts. These frames of reference are by no means mutually exclusive. The collocation of typical and specific elements seems common enough in many forms of late medieval art; moreover, Chaucer can be shown often to conflate literary sources with observed details. In such a fashion, it might be argued that the General Prologue, at least in its form, alludes to that predominantly civic form of art, the pageantry and procession of the late medieval city.

We have spent so much time scoffing at the nineteenth-century notion of the General Prologue as a tableau vivant that we have forgotten how much it literally resembles one. Chaucer would have been more than familiar with the custom of drawing costumed and posed figures through the streets of the city, even if the secular version of this practice was more common on the continent. Such a resemblance explains more about the peculiar spatial organization of the General Prologue than the phrase "portrait gallery." In addition, the order of the pilgrims becomes less important in such a context. Indeed, the rhythm of the General Prologue suggests instead the drift, randomness, confusion, and arbitrariness that lie behind the initial and apparent order of such parades, as of parades today. The very form of the portraits captures the peculiar combination of physical reality and illusion found in such processions.

It is impossible to separate images of medieval theatricality from the more anarchic world of popular festival (Bakhtin 1968, 7). The city processions, to which I suggest Chaucer alludes in the form of the General Prologue, in large part impose a vision of an elite on the celebration. Their order was hierarchical in spirit if not in fact; their imagery was lofty and idealistic. Civic processions themselves operated against the peculiarly centrifugal quality of sizable cities, where the differentiation of social groups and the division of neighborhoods tended to contrast with the centralizing imagery of official functions. We find official city governments often attempting to use celebrations and festivals as mechanisms of control, or at least controlled release. But the carnivals of market towns and villages represented an unhierarchic view of the social world, sometimes accomplished by outright disruption of hierarchy, but more often by parody of hierarchy. Whereas the imagery of civic processions tends to be historical, the imagery of carnival tends to be nonhistorical, earthly, naturalistic, and animalistic. One can locate such a regeneration—or degeneration—in the action of the first sequence of Canterbury Tales.

A specific analogue to the figure of the Knight in the General Prologue, to take the first image arbitrarily, is the popular custom of the riding of St. George. Perhaps the clearest and earliest description is that of the Norwich riding, which dates from 1408, although the guild of St. George in that town certainly dates from 1385. Here, the warrior-saint seems almost to have stepped out of a tournament, an aristocratic pageant, and stepped into a civic pageant. In the Norwich riding, St. George is accompanied by his club-bearer and other assistants (Withington 1918, 23–37; Chambers 1907, 118–224; Nelson 1974, 181). The guild was required not only to choose a "George," but also a man to bear his sword and "be a kervere before him." In later ridings, these assistants are described as having the aspect of foresters or wild men, dressed in leaves, an interesting parallel to the Yeoman, who, dressed in green and armed with his hunting equipment, accompanies the Knight. In some later ridings, St. George is accompanied by a much younger figure supposed to be St. Christopher, an odd coincidence considering the St. Christopher medal the Yeoman wears, although in fact the St. Christopher figure in some much later descriptions rather resembles the Squire. Lydgate wrote a poem on St. George, probably for some such performance. St. George was the patron saint of the Order of the Garter, so that his image recalls both courtly and civic symbolism. Much of this is coincidence, of course, especially since most of this evidence comes from the fifteenth century, and since St. George in these performances is not much more than a knight on horseback, hardly a rare occurrence. I am not arguing for a Spenserian reading of the Knight as St.

George, though worse things have happened to Chaucer's character recently. What I want to emphasize is that certain parallels to even the one "noble" member of the pilgrimage exists in contemporary civic pageantry. This theatrical and public dimension suggests that some of Chaucer's images might have been less learned and hermetic than has sometimes been assumed. The theatrical images of the *Canterbury Tales*, that is, involve the world of civic order and disorder. In this sense, the *Tales*, although they do not take place in London except tangentially, and though most of the examples I have located are far from London in provenance, suggest the experience of the poet in the city. In its kinship with sideshow rather than main event, the *Canterbury Tales* becomes a species of marketplace theater.

Perhaps the chief example of medieval theatricality that would have involved Chaucer as an observer and participant would have been court ceremony. Tournaments, disguisings, and elaborate spectacles approaching the scale of stage sets were central to the ritual of court life. We have no record of Chaucer, as we do of Lydgate, actually taking part in the design or script of such ceremonies, but an important dimension of the early poems is lost if we do not regard them as part of the distinct court style that Richard attempted to foster. When the courtly "theatrical" images that dominate the early poems are recalled in the *Canterbury Tales*, they are recalled, as it were, in quotations, set off and balanced by other versions of performance and celebration. Thus, it may be argued that as part of court ritual, Chaucer's early poetry manifests an implicitly adaptive, celebratory, and elitist quality; even its ironies are consistent with the uses of its aristocratic audience. But in the *Tales* we find such moments placed in contrast to more popular, parodic and subversive versions of performance. It is no accident that the first two tales, following upon the "procession" of the General Prologue, borrow heavily from other forms of medieval theatrical performance, in the case of the *Knight's Tale*, the spectacle of the tournament and its accompanying festival, in the case of the *Miller's Tale*, references to, and inclusion of, the stagecraft of the mystery plays. Such dichotomies are among the commonplaces of modern Chaucer criticism, but I am not sure that the synthesis and balance so often the conclusion of such criticism can be assumed.

There is a literal analogue to the place of the *Miller's Tale* and the *Reeve's Tale* and, more tangentially, the *Wife of Bath's Tale* and the *Merchant's Tale* as part of the carnival strata within the *Canterbury Tales*. For in French medieval villages, there is evidence of associations of young bachelors who made it their business to harass newlyweds with pranks and songs and charivari—modern bachelor parties and wedding pranks are thin inheritors of this custom.[3] They could be silenced only by gifts of drink and coins. Apparently, the intensity and cruelty of the charivari became especially intense when there existed a disparity of age between husband and wife. The sexual highjinks of the charivari reveal the resentment of the community as a member of the village young is taken away from the available group. Interestingly, this particular variety of charivari is recorded with more frequency as ecclesiastic prohibitions against marriage weakened. In some, the dead husband is present as an effigy. In a sense, fabliau might be regarded as the literary expression of the spirit of charivari, but that spirit more than occupies the tales of the "marriage group." The considerable cruelty and violence of these celebrations often is expressed in muted or comically subdued forms in Chaucer.[4]

.   .   .

Although I cannot offer any specific parallel, it might be worth considering the peculiar role of the narrator at the end of the General Prologue as akin to the master of ceremonies in popular folk plays such as the mummer's plays, in which a character who is both participant and stage director clears a space for the production and comments on the action for the audience, as well as taking part in the action (Chambers 1907, 205–27; Doran 1858). Interestingly, the Fool historically has a similar function in court festivities, able to take advantage of his protean place in the order of things to speak on many different levels of reality (E. Wilson 1936). Much apparently modern criticism concerned with the narrator may well have an analogue in the theater of folk and folly, although, again, documented parallels are regrettably late.

The Fool provides an unacknowledged source even for Chaucer's narrator in the earlier poems. His desperate desire to please is one that has most persuasively been ascribed to Chaucer's own experience as a commoner in the service of his noble betters. In a typically sophisticated way, Chaucer throws his own relative lack of sophistication in an ironic and slightly comic light. The place of the Fool in some folk plays suggests an uncanny analogue to the *Canterbury Tales'* narrator. "I'll do my duty to please you all," says the Fool in the Waterstock play, and a number of other Fool plays echo the same line (Weimann 1978, 43). Indeed, the Fool steps outside the fiction of his own place in the play: he provides a link between audience and play, not unlike the role that Chaucer himself plays. In a movement that is as old as the satyr plays of the Greek dramatic festivals, the Fool allows a transition from the more ritualized to the more secular aspects of the form. There is no concomitant shift in the *Canterbury Tales*, unless we regard the narrator (and Harry Bailly) as directing us from the highly stylized, even ritualized General Prologue to the entertainment of the tales themselves.

There is, of course, only a touch of this foolish quality in the narrator's self-presentation. By managing the storytelling contest, which itself has a folkloric quality to it, Harry more directly assumes a role akin to the master of ceremonies. Indeed, what is partly amusing about Harry's own attitude towards his function is his attempts at restraint and respectability. Despite his sense of amusement and recreation, he bristles at and seeks to control the very sorts of anarchic explosions that his stress on festivity almost by nature releases. His restraint may be more than merely burgher-like respectability: popular rituals, even when filled with festive qualities, are often performed with a certain dignified awareness. Between them, Harry and Chaucer the narrator share the mediating function of the Fool and the clown: a comic, parodic, sometimes self-frustrating link between audience and performance; they assume the role of stage manager or "director." At the same time, they lend the *Canterbury Tales* the air of performance, by recreating the conditions of its "creation" each time we read it. It is at least partly in this sense that the *Canterbury Tales* is dramatic, or theatrical. Despite their presence as characters—and this may be true of other pilgrims such as the Miller and the Reeve and the Cook in the fabliaux sequence— their function is least as much to enact the spirit of festivity as to create a mimetic illusion.

Folk theater and popular performances inform another typically Chaucerian problem. The Fool, and other characters in these performances, have an uncanny self-consciousness about their own place in the performance. As a result, their language alternates and mediates between impersonation and interpretation. They are aware, simultaneously it seems, of the reality of the play action itself and of the audience that observes it. So too do the speakers in some of Chaucer's tales (such as Justinus warning January to heed the Wife of Bath's advice) playfully indicate their narrator's awareness of the pilgrim audience; more directly, those who seem to be speaking to that pilgrim audience, such as the Wife of Bath, often indicate an awareness of speaking to a larger audience than the pilgrims. Those who have criticized the conception of organic unity in Chaucer have a point well taken, though I think we must become aware of the alternations and fluctuations between the mimetic and interpretative moments among which Chaucer's narrative style plays. Popular theatrical performance also manifests these alternations and fluctuations.

But there are of course several levels of fiction operating in the *Canterbury Tales* above and beyond our reading of them: the tales themselves and the frame. At certain points, the frame itself is broken, and the illusion of the pilgrims telling the stories is called into question. At other points, the frame intrudes into, even controls, the tales, so that the fictional and traditional quality of the stories becomes personalized, specific, and mundane in regard to the pilgrims and their own relations among themselves. At times, we are even made aware of the gap between the role the pilgrims assume on the pilgrimage and their behavior in "real life." At other times, we are aware of a marked contradiction in their ability or suitability to a particular tale or discourse. This sophisticated metanarrative awareness, which seems so redolent of modernist literature, again has an analogue in the popular theater, in which characters call into question other actors' suitability for their roles and mediate between the everyday experience of the audience and their consciousness of watching a play, often doing so by literally joining the audience, leaving the play area, or questioning the fiction of the performance (Weimann 1978, 45; Chambers 1907, 205–227).

.   .   .

It is, of course, the great mystery cycles that immediately spring to mind when we think of extant Middle English drama. The most notable explicit mention of the mystery plays in Chaucer is in the *Miller's Tale*. The most common explanation for these allusions are either mimetic (the plays prepare the reader for the reaction of John to the cry of water or contribute to Absolon's character portrayal) or iconographic (we are meant to see parallels to Joseph and Mary or the Flood itself). Of course, these allusions also suggest a structural analogue: the action of the fabliau itself is very much dependent on "stage" technique, and Chaucer is indicating his dependence on another generic form entirely.

In asking for some attention to Chaucer's relation to the mystery plays and to medieval theatrics in general, I am well aware of insurmountable obstacles. Except for agreement about a few texts or the records of a few likely productions, we do not know exactly what part of the body of medieval drama we now have would have been available to Chaucer.[5] London was by no means the chief dramatic center of England. Certain provincial cities had more fully developed civic drama, and many rural localities had more uninterrupted traditions of folk drama. Although Chaucer's official position as clerk of the works might have involved the administration of the building of structures for some plays and tournaments, no direct connection between him and the authors of the mystery plays can be assumed. Nor were English pageants and processions as highly developed as those of the continent, although some English court records are admittedly incomplete. As a result, we are forced to rely heavily on fifteenth-century evidence, a dangerous procedure for deducing literary attitudes.

The evidence for Chaucer's borrowing from the mystery plays in the *Miller's Tale* was established in an article by Kelsie B. Harder (1956) that argues that the tale is a parody of the mystery plays. Harder cites three chief parallels: between the Miller and Pilate and Herod, between the ending episode and the Noah plays, and between Absolon and Herod (Absolon is described as actually playing Herod). Moreover, argues Harder, "Chaucer works in a burlesque, joking manner, making fun of the uncouthness of the plays, a fact which he is well aware of in his small retraction at the conclusion of the *Miller's Prologue* where he says, 'put me out of blame' for the story of the coarse Miller" (I.193).

Harder's argument remains important, but I would offer a few revisions. First, Chaucer's use of these elements is not so thoroughgoing in a structural sense that the mystery plays can be called a source. Second, although Chaucer treats Absolon's theatrical narcissism and John's permanent suspension of disbelief in regard to the plays with some irony, I do not think that Chaucer is treating the mystery plays dismissively. Third, it may be that Chaucer's debt to the mystery plays, as to many forms of popular literature, is more pervasive than local borrowings in the *Miller's Tale*. Indeed, I should like to suggest that Chaucer's allusions to the mystery plays (and I think some such case could be made for *Sir Thopas*) comprise an acknowledgement of his own difficult relation to popular literary forms, a relation not merely of disdain. Moreover, the allusions to such works as the plays raise some serious aesthetic issues belied by the lightheartedness of Chaucer's references to them.[6]

Nicholas's plan (I.3560–76) appeals to John's skill as a carpenter, but it is also a stage set, with the entire community as its intended audience. Indeed, he asks John to put together the set just as the directorial committee in charge of the mystery play of Noah might have approached their own carpenters. But this backstage quality is lost on John, for whom it is not an illusion. He can imagine Nicholas's plan, as has been noted, because he has seen such plays as the flood, and even with his technical knowledge of how the set is built still accepts the dramatic illusion. There is a touch of Hamlet talking to the players in Nicholas's speech. Just as Polonius is the "official" moralist of Shakespeare, John is the great defender of mimesis in Chaucer.

Gestures and actions in Chaucer, such as Absolon's preparation for his first contact with Alison ("This Absolon doun sette hym on his knees /And seyde, 'I am a lord at alle degrees' " [I.3722–23]), often have the air of stage business about them, though it must be admitted that such actions usually have their origins in the exigencies of narrative setting rather than dramatic action.[7] The *Miller's Tale* is unusual in that it includes as well as refers to numerous examples of medieval theatrical practice. Absolon has already been described as an actor on the medieval stage: "He pleyeth Herodes upon a scaffold hye" (I.3384), traditionally, as Shakespeare's remark indicates, not the most understated of roles. Here, however, the lines not only echo Herod's ostentatious love of his own status, but Lucifer's brief moment of ascent in, for example, the York *Creation*, when he sits on God's throne. His Herod-like language continues when he seeks to revenge his humiliation: "My soule bitake I unto Sathanas, / But me were levere than al this toun" (I.3750–51). All of creation is imaged in this "toun."

One of the ironies of this analogy is that if Chaucer had anything to do with the production of plays at Clerkenwell, the chief site for the London plays, it would have been with the larger aspects of production. He would not have regarded it from the aspect of the private, solitary activity of writing, but from the aspect of public performance: sets, audience access, costs, revision. He would have been concerned, that is, with the business of it all being set up and taken down again, activities that might have been part of his duties as clerk of the works. Chaucer the administrator would have been as concerned with backstage as with frontstage behavior, but certainly this concern would have preceded his possible involvement in theatrical arrangements. But if the drama of the *Canterbury Tales* does have a modern analogue, it is one of those plays about the theater, with its attendant intrigues and conflicts.

Moreover, for reasons of common aesthetic culture rather than influence, the structure of the drama itself is a striking analogy to the *Canterbury Tales*. The plays are filled with a broad spectrum of characters and types, types whose general characteristics must have been altered or enhanced by the actors to the best of their ability. The only other comparable source is biblical, of which the plays themselves are a representation. While certain narrative works, such as the *Romance of the Rose* and Ovid's *Metamorphoses*, also contain a great many characters, the plays have the advantage of displaying characters in a social and historical context. The anachronism that sometimes calls into question this historicity must also have appealed to Chaucer, who had a more profoundly developed sense of history in the humanist sense than some of his contemporaries. The various biblical episodes lent themselves to different kinds of representation and dramatic style. A striking alternation of serious purpose—high theology as high art—and of comic interlude—interludes that might have suggested their own version of truth as well as reinforce the chief message—is shared not only by the plays and by the *Tales* but by many other medieval works as well. They have an enormous cast of characters, include varieties of mimetic and nonmimetic modes, and depend heavily on "serial" form. The interplay of gesture and speech evident in such characters as the Wife of Bath or the Pardoner is shared not only by the mystery plays, but also by some of Shakespeare's characters.

But it must have struck someone who in other respects (recall the poem "To Adam") took care for the preservation of his lines, that certain kinds of poetry and perhaps poetry itself were subservient to another purpose. Such a problem would have been commonplace from the point of view of much medieval moral teaching, but here, in the mystery plays, was evidence of real conflict between the material fact of sacred source and the revisionist tendency of its representation in performance. Chaucer and the authors of certain medieval theatrical works, especially mystery cycles, had to face certain contradictions about the nature of representation, and they resolved those contradictions, to the extent that they could, in ways that are surprisingly similar, given the different natures of their enterprises. In both, there is self-criticism within the work. There is, as a corrective and realignment of moral purpose, a constant address to the audience. There is also anxiety expressed about the connection of particulars in the mundane world and hence about the efficacy of narrative form, though this last concern is more prominently displayed in the *Troilus*. The mystery plays express an acute consciousness about their own limits and sometimes approach the condition of "metatheater." It is no accident that the aggressively self-conscious theater of our own time should borrow stage techniques from the mystery plays. Chaucer shares with the mystery plays a constant awareness of the fictive nature of his work and constant reminders of its constructed quality to the audience.

What I would like to suggest is that Chaucer's allusions to the mystery plays, especially in the *Miller's Tale*, alert us to a larger, less thematic concern that Chaucer shares with the authors and promoters of these exceedingly popular performances: an anxiety about the moral impact of certain kinds of representation. The *Miller's Tale* features these allusions because there, both in its parodic quality and the "excuse" for the tale in its prologue, Chaucer plays in a comic fashion with issues that are from a certain point of view serious. It could also be argued that the mystery plays, for all their naivete, also include within themselves a certain awareness, if not a defense, of the very qualities that their detractors criticized. Chaucer's allusions to the mystery plays are akin to what I believe is an underlying point of his parody of popular romance in *Sir Thopas*. In both cases the parodic note is not only a criticism of the other form—popular romance or popular drama—it is also an indication of awareness of the aesthetic possibilities and dangers, for the sophisticated poet, of these naive forms.

That the authors of the mystery plays had some awareness of the dangers of mimetic representation has been established in an important article by Robert Hanning (1982). Hanning argues that the sense of "game" in these plays is actually a way of avoiding the danger of seeming to imitate Creation. Lucifer in a sense "imitates" God in the "Fall of Lucifer" plays; following Kolve, Hanning develops a certain identity between playwrights and the Devil himself. As a result, these playwrights, according to Hanning, differentiate their version of mimetic action from the subversive action of Lucifer. Drama itself only becomes possible when God leaves the stage, an act itself so improbable that it suggests the highly metaphoric quality of that stage, and the angels themselves turn from being an included audience to being participants—hence, irony and conflict result, as Lucifer indulges his self-willed creation. Indeed, Lucifer's impulse is itself a dramatization of a version of Augustinian theodicy. By its historical, providential completeness, the mystery cycle itself overarches this local and unselfcon-scious creation. I would also add that dramatic technique itself becomes an important part of this process—something Hanning does in fact stress—by constantly addressing the audience's understanding of how the action is to be interpreted, and, significantly less integral, by reminding the audience of the original purpose of certain scenes and actions.

The mystery plays constantly interrupt their historical narrative in order to reorient their audience, sometimes by the voice of God, sometimes by a "Doctor." One function of this orientation is to stress how transhistorical forces and eternity are at work in the apparently discrete episodes that con-stitute human history. But another function of these interruptions and ex-planations is to correct our potential misunderstanding of the action. The dramatists implicitly acknowledge that they may be more of the Devil's party than they would like to admit. That is, the cycle plays do not entirely escape the danger that Hanning outlines and that the Lollard attacks on "playing," for instance, bear out. Indeed, the Lollard pamphleteer may turn out to be a very perceptive literary critic, whose concerns other poets and artists may ignore at their peril.

Hanning points out that such dramatic staples, admired by earlier gener-ations of scholars, as realistic detail, low comedy, the very invention of "lies" and half-truths as a constituent of irony, are generated by Lucifer's fall. It is the sense of heaven's overarching control, largely achieved by the dramatic space itself and the division into mundane and supramundane fields of existence, that allows this lower action to play itself out, to indulge in chaos and disruption. The central point of the "Fall of Lucifer" plays, says Hanning, is "that the success of perverse mimesis is its failure" (1982, 156). By highlighting the "blasphemous confusion" between creator and creature in these plays, the playwrights successfully defend themselves against the charge of blasphemy they level at their own art.

Contemporary criticism of the mystery plays as presented in the "Tretise of Miraclis Pleyinge" is much less subtle; nevertheless, its Lollard author indicates awareness of the defenses of dramatic representation offered by the defenders of the drama. Of these arguments, the ones least of issue to the plays themselves are of most interest to a more general justification of aesthetic imagery. Some people may not be converted by the "ernestful doing of God. . . . Thanne now it is time and skilful to assayen to convertyn the puple by pley and gamen as by miraclis pleyinge and other maner mirthis" (Davidson 1981, 39). Another related argument apparently is that since people seek some kind of refreshment after their work, "bettere it is (or lesse yvele) that they han theire recreacioun by pleyinge of miraclis than by pleyinge of other japis" (39–41).

Given the often satiric tone of the attack, it is likely that the refutations of these defenses is more or less polemical. It is worse, says the author, "than though they pleyiden pure vaniteis" (44). The notion that recalcitrant men may be converted by the plays draws forth a more interesting response. The affective quality of the plays elicits a misplaced reaction, for "the weping that men wepen ofte in siche pley comunely is fals wittnessenge that they lovyn more the liking of theire body and of prosperite of the world than likinge in God"; they have "more compassion of peine than of sinne" (43). The author here sounds like a stern Virgil chastising the sentimental sympathy of the overwhelmed Dante for the damned. Indeed, the worldliness of these plays encourages a concern with earthly suffering and loss, "as don dampnyd men in helle" (44). A number of the points raised by the author specifically concern the representation of Christ's suffering and its affective quality; another is the striking force of visual representation for evangelical purposes. The defense of these aspects has a strong basis in Franciscan thought, and the attack and debate can be traced in other tracts and sermons.

One more general defense of the plays as recounted by the Lollard author also has some applicability to narrative. The spectators can observe "the devul by ther aray, by the whiche they moven eche on othere to leccherie and to pride, makith hem his servauntis to bringen hemsilf and many othere to helle, and to han fer more vilenye herafter by ther proude array heere than they han worschipe heere" (39). That is, part of the defense of the mystery plays must have been that they functioned as morality plays. As such, they are defended as akin to exemplary and cautionary tales and share the apparent function of such tales, as, for instance, Chaucer's *Pardoner's Tale*.

It must be emphasized that one cannot simply transfer the interpretative traditions of sacred texts to secular texts, which often have their own purposes and justifications. Nevertheless, in the absence of a coherent secularized literary theory, such a translation is often one of the few external pieces of evidence we have for literary understanding. Indeed, medieval poetics apparently did just that. And it is in any case difficult, except on the extremes, to draw the line between secular and sacred narrative. Even the most avowedly secularized narratives from the later Middle Ages have at their core at least an analogy to sacred cultural and literary forms.

But the defenses of the mystery plays attacked by the Wycliffite author are not unique to sacred literature. At least some of the arguments in favor of the plays are arguments that poets and writers could offer for virtually all medieval fiction, even the most outrageous. The arguments are particularly intriguing because they concern an avowedly popular form, both in its sense of participation and its audience. The moral difficulty of representation and illusion on which the pamphlet centers is thrown into relief by the problem of representing biblical episodes and the life of Christ, but it could be extended to all sorts of literary forms. The implicit defense of poetic representation that we find in some of Chaucer's "moral" works seems also to address some of the same issues.[8] The *Canterbury Tales* ends with a rejection of dramatic illusion—or illusion of any kind. If the *Parson's Tale* is not without a possible theatrical analogue, the paternoster plays in which virtues are held up to admiration and vices to scorn, no contemporary texts of those plays are extant. In any case, the real source of the *Parson's Tale* lies in the most sober tradition of confessional manuals, the least public and the least dramatic corner of the exercises of faith.

As with other serious issues, Chaucer addresses the question of heresy both comically and metaphorically. The Parson is the butt of the nameless pilgrims' imprecation in the *Man of Law's Epilogue*, "I smelle a Lollere in the wynd" (II.1173). The creatural image itself has an echo in the discourse of the Parson: he does not attempt to avoid the smell of corruption. Indeed, the scatological proverb in the Parson's portrait in the General Prologue, although it has no direct parallel, imitates the direct and earthy language of the Wyclif Bible and sermons. It is, after all, the profoundly serious Parson who is in fact explicitly accused of unorthodox ideas. The critical sense of social reality we find in the General Prologue, the consistently anticlerical theme we find throughout the *Canterbury Tales*, even the connection with John of Gaunt, protector of Wyclif, by no means marks Chaucer as a Lollard, but it does suggest that in appropriating the energies of popular discourses and languages to the uses of his fiction he also incorporates some destabilizing and dissident attitudes, if only in quotation. Moreover, it is perhaps time to regard Lollardy as only the most intellectually visible and perhaps relatively restrained version of a range of unorthodox attitudes and popular pietistic trends. It served as a convenient umbrella term for the opponents of the unorthodox or for any dissenting voices. However playfully, Chaucer regards the making of poetry or at least his own poetic development as akin to heresy.

Chaucer implies a certain relation between art and heresy in the comic context of the *Legend of Good Women*. This is not to say that Chaucer was a Wycliffite or a Cathar or a Waldensian.[9] Instead, it suggests at least one of the chief problems of medieval literary art and medieval art in general: its proclivity for allowing elaborate misinterpretation. Not only late medieval allegory but much late medieval fiction and commentary threatens to wreck itself on the rocky shore of the literal. For Chaucer, the image of heresy is a metaphor, suggesting the various ways in which the poet might well be misunderstood by his audience or the ways in which his own material might follow a logic not entirely of his own conscious intent. Much of his work consists of rewriting and translating in such a way as to transform the original intent, to insert the unorthodox into a received text or to insert orthodoxy in the most unlikely places.

But in so doing Chaucer also proclaims the kinship of his poetry to unofficial and unorthodox culture. He never defends anything like Lollardy, but he does celebrate the process of resistance to or willful misunderstanding of oral tranmission, which constitutes not only much of the poetry but much of unofficial and popular culture in the Middle Ages. Literary history itself can be read as a process of heretical reinterpretation, as is clear to anyone who has looked at some recent hermeneutic theory and its appropriation of theological rather than philological assumptions. The idea may not have been all that new to Chaucer; after all, his rewriting of stories often changes the immediate direct source as if to recover how it really was—to return to origins, however fictional, at the same time as he includes the history of interpretations of that source. His version of literary history, that is, seems to be modeled on the history of theological controversy, especially as it entails the dialogue, the frequent ventriloquism, of orthodoxy and heterodoxy. The inclusion of various interpretations as commentary within the text itself has two effects: one to suggest, albeit tentatively, the relativity of all interpretation, and the other to protect his own interpretation from its apparent, or hidden, deviance.

·   ·   ·

I think I can illustrate this nexus between heresy and theatricality as poetic modes by pointing to a series of peculiar associations in what seem to be Chaucer's unerased revisions. One of the most puzzling moments in Chaucer is the beginning of the *Shipman's Tale* and its remarkable confusion of gender. Says the narrator of husbands in general:

> Swiche salutaciouns and countenaunces
> Passen as dooth a shadwe upon the wal;
> But wo is hym that payen moot for al!
> The sely housbonde, algate he moot paye,
> He moot us clothe, and he moot us arraye,
> Al for his owene worshipe richely,
> In which array we daunce jolily.
> And if that he noght may, par aventure,
> Or ellis list no swich dispence endure,
> But thynketh it is wasted and ylost,
> Thanne moot another payen for oure cost,
> Or lene us gold, and that is perilous.

(VII.8–19)

These lines are usually cited as evidence that Chaucer originally intended the *Shipman's Tale* for the Wife of Bath, but later devised her own tale as a more appropriate fit.[10] As a result, the tale has been relegated to a corner of most Chaucer criticism and has usually only been commented upon by those concerned with Chaucer's developing plan for the pilgrimage. There have been a few attempts to take the tale seriously, usually in terms of Chaucer's handling of the fabliau. Only a few critics have pondered the implications of even Chaucer's possible original intention to assign the tale to the Wife of Bath.[11]

Given the troublesome placement of the lines before the *Shipman's Tale*, however, a number of intriguing problems rise.[12] One is the appropriate-ness, if any, of these lines to the narrator of the *Shipman's Tale*. Keiser (1977) has made a good argument that the materialism implied in these lines is consistent with the materialism of the *Shipman's Tale* itself, the nar-rator becoming implicated in the moral bankruptcy of the tale itself. This is an appealing argument, though it depends at least partly on minimizing the "Alisounian" imagery we have just noted. Indeed, as appropriate as the lines are to the narrator of the *Shipman's Tale*, they raise a larger submerged theme in Chaucer's poetry.

The other apparent slip I want to mention in this regard is in the *Man of Law's Epilogue*, which occurs in over thirty manuscripts, with its impas-sioned outburst of the pilgrim who interrupts the Parson. The passage is also usually cited as evidence that the present *Shipman's Tale* was originally meant for the Wife of Bath. Some editors follow the *Man of Law's Epilogue* with the *Shipman's Tale* itself. A good deal of the imagery in this little speech ("glosen," "joly body," even the oddly intellectualized viscerality of "litel Latyn in my mawe") are typical of the Wife. There are compelling reasons to consider the outburst voiced by the Wife, although it is not impossible to assign the lines equally to the Shipman, mentioned in four manuscripts, or even the several other speakers to whom the lines are as-signed in various manuscripts, although it has hard to imagine the lines voiced by the Squire, who is the speaker in some manuscripts. These other assignments, however, probably were scribal means of justifying the order of specific manuscripts. My point is that there is an ambiguity about the identity, including the gender, of this speaker, and there is an interesting accusation of heresy.

The problem can be phrased as a series of related questions. Why does this speaker specifically object to the Parson speaking, why is the Parson vilified as a Lollard, and why does the speaker so insistently argue against interpretation and difficulty? The first question has been elegantly an-swered by Alfred David, and the tenor of the answers to the other ques-tions have been implied in his answer: "Ostensibly the objection is to heret-ical doctrine that a Lollard might preach. . . . But the more probable desire is to restore the gay mood of the company. . . . But the sermon has only been postponed, and when the moralists were put in their place in the epilogue of the *Man of Law's Tale*, Chaucer probably realized that he was only delaying the hour of their ultimate victory" (1976, 130–31). The *Man of Law's Prologue* and *Epilogue*, according to David, comprise a meditation on Chaucer's development as a poet, and answer, on several different levels, the criticisms of some in his audience. If in fact the charges of heresy against the Parson here are unfounded, what is the purpose of the accusation? I agree that it forestalls the more serious turns that the tale-telling might take, and thereby stakes a claim for Chaucer's artistic breadth and freedom at this point in the tales. But we might extend this observation to point out that Chaucer playfully associates charges of heresy with the proper or improper realms of art several times in his poetry, and the *Man of Law's Epilogue* stands as only one, if the most crucial, of these comic meditations. The epilogue apparently returns us to the festive world of the *Miller's Tale* and its consequences, but it is no accident that it finds itself in sober company, for the workings of the tale reveal a mordant rather than a festive view of human nature and limits. In one sense, from the point of view of poetic freedom, it enacts the heresy against which it asserts itself.

If we skip ahead to the poetics of the *Shipman's Tale*, imagining it as Chaucer's possible early plan as the next tale, the moral atmosphere becomes murky, for, like the *Merchant's Tale* and the *Manciple's Tale*, the *Shipman's Tale*, despite, perhaps even because, of its quality of fabliau and its "realism", comprises what we might regard as "dark" Chaucer. Like those other tales, the *Shipman's Tale*, for all its professed amorality, forces upon us questions about the limits of language in defining reality and the limits of sympathetic affect in relation to others—questions at the heart of artistic creation itself. These questions are raised by the language and workings of the tale, but it is not impossible that the *Man of Law's Epilogue* predicts some of them. For it addresses directly an association between poetry and heresy that Chaucer has made before, in the *Legend of Good Women*, and that he will make again, perhaps finally answering it, in the *Wife of Bath's Prologue*, which in some ways can be read as a rewriting of the *Shipman's Tale*.

The *Man of Law's Epilogue*, I would argue, can be read as an inversion of the accusations of the God of Love. Here it is the ambiguously named pilgrim, with no moral or other authority except a "joly body," who accuses the one pilgrim with any sort of definitive moral authority of "heresy." The charge is sweeping, because "heresy" is here defined as all interpretation, by extension, all readings or frames of perception that would make things difficult. It may be argued that it is precisely that lack of moral framework which makes the *Shipman's Tale* itself so disturbing, but in keeping with the challenge of pilgrims like the Miller and the Wife of Bath, the tactic of the speaker is apparently to turn things upside down. But the real force of his charge is to separate things rather than reverse them: interpretation and representation are severed. In the *Wife of Bath's Prologue*, this is not so; there, interpretation is shown to be representation and vice versa. She implicitly defends herself against heresy, largely by celebrating heterodoxy in her own way.

If we regard the *Shipman's Tale* as another case in which Chaucer rewrites his own materials, we discover a microcosmic example of one of Chaucer's most characteristic moves in the *Canterbury Tales*, the conversion of narrative into performance. The *Shipman's Tale* is especially interesting in this regard because a number of its images and themes return in more powerful form in some of other Chaucer's other tales. These revisions are nowhere more evident than in the *Wife of Bath's Prologue* and *Tale* itself, which, more than a replacement for, is a revision of the *Shipman's Tale*. Although it would seem clear that the Wife's prologue was in fact written later, the *Shipman's Tale* itself is relatively late Chaucer, and matters of dating are not my chief concern here, except to point out that as with much mature Chaucer, references to and images of his other works are frequent in the *Shipman's Tale*. The contrast between the two, moreover, is not one of Chaucer's "development." It suggests rather the range of possibilities Chaucer could call upon in his most inventive period. The tale can be read as a laboratory, uncomplicated by matters of an assigned narrator with a distinct personality, for the testing of themes fully explored in other of Chaucer's fabliaux-like tales. In its assertive narrativity, the tale offers a lesson to those who would in fact exclude matters of narrator and Kittredgian dramatics from a critical frame of reference, for the result is cynicism verging on nihilism.[13]

Moreover, the shift represents an interesting comparative problem, for the more purely narrative and schematic quality of the tale resembles more nearly the fabliau as found in the Italian tradition, particularly in the analogues in Boccaccio and Sercambi. In some ways, the world of the *Shipman's Tale* is more frighteningly modern than that of the Wife's performance, a point that by no means invalidates Fradenburg's (1986) premise about the nostalgia of romance.[14]

Even the rich puns of the *Shipman's Tale* suggest a level of incisive wit that the Wife, though she is not lacking in wit, lacks.[15] Her turnabouts are dramatic and reflected in the surface of things, not hidden away. Chaucer allows her a variety of meaning that is enacted rather than stated. But the question of wordplay is not one of character alone, for it calls upon what some have recently argued is at the very center of the fabliau as genre, questions about the moral status not of sexuality but of literary language itself. Chaucer himself suggests at times a dark and disparaging view of the potential of language to uncover truth; indeed, he stresses its more powerful ability to dissimulate and distort. But he does so largely in contexts that can be considered separately from or in contrast to the great body of tales:

in the *Pardoner's Prologue*, the *Merchant's Tale*, and the *Manciple's Tale*. The *Shipman's Tale* makes these questions more problematic, if no more disturbing, because of its lack of an anchor in personality or even a clear position vis a vis other tales. As a result, and in spite of the vexed relation of the tale to its analogue in the *Decameron*, the *Shipman's Tale* comes closer than any other to a Chaucer working in a Boccaccian mode.

From the beginning of the tale, nothing anyone except for the merchant himself says is close to the truth. Moreover, except for the merchant, the statements of the characters are inevitably contrasted with conflicting evidence, evidence available immediately or shortly to their interlocutor. One example of this is the wife's complaint to the monk, which contains within it a striking image much more developed in the narrative of the *Wife of Bath's Tale*:

> Myn housbonde is to me the worste man
> That evere was sith that the world bigan.
> But sith I am a wyf, it sit nat me
> To tellen no wight of oure privetee,
> Neither abedde, ne in noon oother place;
> God shilde I sholde it tellen, for his grace!
> A wyf ne shal nat seyn of hir housbonde
> But al honour, as I kan understonde;
> Save unto yow thus muche I tellen shal:
> As helpe me God, he is noght worth at al
> In no degree the value of a flye.
> But yeven me greveth moost his nygardye.
> And wel ye woot that wommen naturelly:
> Desiren thynges sixe as wel as I:
> They wolde that hir housbondes sholde be
> Hardy, and wise, and riche, and therto free,
> And buxom unto his wyf, and fressh abedde.

(VII.161–177)

As the monk very well knows, most of these criticisms have no justification whatsoever, and we eventually learn that the rest do not. Of the criticisms his wife levels against the merchant, the only one with any basis, as Gardiner Stillwell (1944) long ago pointed out, is his considerable seriousness. Stillwell was concerned largely with Chaucer's accuracy in thus representing the demeanor and general ethic of a medieval businessman. But more disturbing are the literary and semantic implications of this portrayal. The merchant is the only character in the tale who takes things literally, who takes people at their word. His literality is such that he never notices the sinister and subversive shifts that sweep beneath him, and the words around him. One may argue that this literalness is itself problematic, that one ought to be able to interpret more profoundly, to see beyond the surface, but this is hardly the lesson of the tale. For this literalness (combined with his quantitative obsession, which suggests some values in common with his wife) is tied to his trust, a trust that, unlike the nearly superstitious mentality of the carpenter in the *Miller's Tale*, is a functioning set of values. Trust for the merchant is in fact a commercial necessity. Nevertheless, his surprising concern with values, as well as value, extends to all aspects of his life, and combined with his heroic description of the perils of commerce, suggests at least an ethical awareness lacking in nearly all the other characters of all of Chaucer's fabliaux. The self-delusions of January, the suspicious wariness of Symkyn, the foolish gullibility of John—none of these implicate, though they may signify, larger social values.

There is then a semantic nexus in the tale between commercial and ethical values. Such a connection is, of course, one of the starting points of modern sociological analysis, and we may ignore how striking it is within the world of the tale. But the connection is, moreover, parodied in another nexus expressed by the wife, the nexus between sexual and financial values. Such a connection, of course, is to be also expressed, even demonstrated in a richer and more dialectical way by the Wife of Bath. Indeed, part of the process of "rewriting" here is the replacement of the equations of the *Shipman's Tale* with the dialectics of the *Wife of Bath's Prologue*.

But the parody has a double edge. For the merchant's wife and the monk call upon or are described in images and activities that are analogous to the fabliau form itself. In contrast to the serious merchant, they invoke images of festivity and decoration. She is "compaignable and revelous" (4), qualities the narrator seems to suggest are extravagantly displayed at "festes and at daunces" (7), "in which array we daunce jolily" (14) and which cause us, apparently, to happily run up a bill. Fine clothing and dancing run through the tale like a motif, especially noteworthy because in the aristocratic *Sir Gawain and the Green Knight* or the *Squire's Tale*, for example, we have remarkably spare descriptions of both. This display of finery and movement is in the tale oddly divorced from its apparently obvious function of sexual attraction and display. It is more like the "payoff," to borrow the narrative's own association between commerce and sexuality. But what is the point of this mild perversity beyond its illustration of the shallowness of the merchant's wife herself? Certainly the imagery of sexual reward is part of colloquial stereotypes. Even as unlikely a text as the last tale of the *Decameron*, an analogue to the *Clerk's Tale*, uses it to put into perspective the relationship of Gualteri and Griselde: "It might have served Gualteri right if he had run into the kind of woman who, once driven out of her home in nothing but a shift, would have allowed another man to shake her up to the point of getting a nice-looking dress out of the affair" (1983, 681). But such images run throughout the tale at large. The monk also is left by the narrator to "ete and drynke and pleye" (73). The first thing the wife does after their deal is arranged is order the cooks to hurry dinner (210). Festive imagery is then driven out almost entirely by commercial imagery until they spend the night together, and even then sex is described, conventionally enough, as "myrth" (which has an explicitly sexual meaning in its two appearances in the tale) and "busy." This conventional pairing now takes on the tone of dichotomy: "In myrthe al nyght a bisy lyf they lede" (318). When the merchant returns, his business deals (to him at least) over, the images of festivity return, although they now ring as hollow as the narrator: "he maketh feste and cheere" with his wife, although his idea of small talk is of more business deals. Don John also "maketh feeste and murye cheere" (342) at the merchant's return. The merchant completes his dealings, "and hoom he gooth, murie as a papejay" (VII.369) at his profit. Refreshment and release, the sense of free festive joy, is sharply limited in the world of the *Shipman's Tale*, for it is shown to have been achieved, like the compliments and attraction mentioned in the narrator's first comment, at too high a cost. Yet it is precisely these qualities of festivity and refreshment that have been convincingly shown to be among the chief qualities of the fabliau and related forms in the Middle Ages. In *Literature as Recreation in the Later Middle Ages* (1982), Glending Olson describes an overlooked area of medieval aesthetics, one that found a place for pure entertainment as a justified virtue, analogous to the contribution of play to health. The quality of play, however, in *The Shipman's Tale* is strained.

The end of the *Shipman's Tale* is a pun that summarizes the sexual and commercial connections made through the tale. "Thus endeth my tale, and God us sende / Taillynge ynough unto oure lyves ende" (433–34). Like the flexible recording of expenditures in accounts, so too language in the *Shipman's Tale* can serve two purposes at the same time. Moreover, as in accounts, reference is not only to an external reality, but to the very process of accounting itself, which proclaims its own abstract reality. With this in mind, it is not impossible that "taillynge" also includes a shade of meaning registered in some manuscripts, where the form of the word is "talyng." Although certainly not Chaucer's form, this modification returns us to the very process of the *Canterbury Tales*, which is itself telling tales, and in some cases telling tales as a form of reckoning, with all the implications, from revenge to salvation, implicit in that word. This is of course a positive construal. On its debit side, the equivalency suggests also the very problem of telling tales, with its attendant danger of getting things wrong or leading us wrong. In the fleeting possibility of this lost pun, the *Shipman's Tale* points to what R. Howard Bloch (1986) calls "the scandal" of the fabliaux, but which might be called the embarrassment of fiction itself. Bloch makes the claim that the real scandal of the fabliaux is not that they deal in obscene matters and questionable morals, but that they reveal the more profound failure of literary language in the Middle Ages, its failure to accommodate truth and its notorious unreliability vis a vis fixed meaning. Through a close analysis of puns and other linguistic manifestations, through a reckoning of significant images (such as clothing as a self-reflexive metaphor), Bloch makes a case for some fabliaux, at least, as emblems of the problems of medieval literary art as a whole. The very lines that complicate the placement of the tale and call into question the gender of its speaker also indicate that its major themes are implicated in this "scandal." The *Shipman's Tale*, unlike Chaucer's other fabliau tales, including, I believe, the *Merchant's Tale*, functions partly as such a disturbing meditation. It levels an accusation against literature, even against language, that is difficult to answer, and it is, I believe, the function of the *Wife of Bath's Tale* to seek to answer it. Even that answer, the defense of meaning as enacted, even performed, in the self, is a problematic one, but it is Chaucer's best defense.

The Wife of Bath enacts Chaucer's own defense of poetry, which is that far from being heretical, that is to say misleading, representation is a form of truth. Chaucer earlier articulates his position in his ironic self-portrayal in the *Legend of Good Women*. Accused of heresy by the God of Love because of the *Troilus* and other works, Chaucer is made to offer penance, at Queen Alceste's suggestion, by telling officially sanctioned stories that slander neither women nor love. Nevertheless, his rehabilitation, in the form of the narratives of the *Legend of Good Women*, seems not to have been entirely successful. His confession and contrition subvert the accusations made against him. Love cannot be constrained by the official forms that the God of Love proposes, and woman cannot be defended by the rote pattern that Alceste inscribes. What Chaucer had tried to say was that the relations between the sexes were more complicated than either commandment allowed. This was the lesson of the *Troilus*, and this was also the point of his "translacioun" of the *Romance of the Rose*. Sexuality and love are akin to dialogues among differing points of view, sometimes, as the *Romance of the Rose* suggests, within the same person. What both his defender and accuser agree on here is that Chaucer's poetry should speak with one voice. Their own "dialogue" is thereby rendered false: what they seek is an official point of view, one enforced by coercion and power, as they themselves demonstrate. Were the poet allowed to speak, he might have pointed out that it is precisely such behavior that condemns the "good women" to their fate. What both speakers define as heresy is in fact a matter of interpretation. However inelegant and misguided, that is the point of the *Wife of Bath's Prologue*. And in a sense, the last and best "Legend of Good Women" is her tale. It is in the contrast between these comments on heresy that we observe Chaucer coming as close as possible to a dialogue with himself as to the nature and sources of his poetry, and defining its coordinates by reference to the very different points of sexuality and theology.

Such bizarre forms of interpretation as the Clerk's envoy to the Wife of Bath, Harry's reaction to the *Melibee*, and the willful twisting of meaning in the Wife of Bath's quotations and summaries of books must be taken as more than the sly jokes they certainly are. At the end of the *Wife of Bath's Tale*, one is left with the impression that the magic of the old hag is at least partly an antidote to books, which thereby acquire the status of male magic, the "magic," the power, of official authority. It is the *body* that the Wife's tale opposes to books. Indeed, the books themselves are described as having been written by clerks who can no longer serve the body, to do "Venus' werkes." The "joly body" in the *Man of Law's Epilogue* is related to these assertions, though denatured of gender and individuality, precisely the obsessions on which the Wife of Bath plays, it strikes only an overture to its larger development in her prologue. The *Man of Law's Epilogue* rejects traditional interpretative apparatus but does no more than suggest an alternative other than the celebration of surface and material.

Indeed, the Wife seeks constantly (though not always consciously) to accomplish the reversal of the carnival world: she converts images into impulses, and impulses into images. This is exemplified by the most overriding image of her entire discourse, that of the text itself: "that gentil text kan I well understonde" (III.29), "But in oure bed he was so fressh and gay, / And therewithal so wel koude he me glose" (III.508–9), and the constant reference to books and texts within the prologue (Patterson 1983, Hanning 1985), both as allusions and actual narrative images. Her own body becomes, magically, a text with its own authority. Of course, "glose" is not entirely metaphoric; it meant to flatter and seduce, in the modern sense of "smooth talk." To "glose" seems also to require knowing very well, almost interpreting in order to convince. Troilus says to Criseyde that Calchas can "glose" her and convince her to marry one of the Greeks (IV.14–71).

Part of the Wife's strategy, although I think it is an aspect of mentality rather than strategy, is to question whether abstract and general laws are to be regarded as appropriate to all.[16] She not only pleads special cases and exceptions. She accuses the propounders of the rules as generalizing from their own position or preference or experience: "He mente as in his bed or in his couche" (III.88). As the Wife finally realizes, the Apostle speaks not only of the "couche," although it is not entirely clear that she acknowledges that her own generalizations are partial. Even clerks later on in her story are revealed as not behaving according to their own absolute standards. Only when they are old and not capable of "Venus' werk" do they resort to the rhetoric she so strongly opposes—at least according to her. In her insistence on the relativism of apparently official ideology, "Who peyntede the leon, tel me who?" (III.692), the Wife is not so much being "modern" or "skeptical" as she is embodying the very mode of popular culture and of carnivalized literature: the privileging of the individual and idiosyncratic over the official, the representation of authority as partial and self-serving rather than objective, the appeal to interests rather than to logic, and the sense of fixed positions—even naturally ordained ones such as sexuality—as reversible (rather than as negated). The Wife does not so much offer a critique of sexual politics as a parody of it.

The Wife throughout her discourse alternates between rather direct reference to her "queynte" (although Benson [1984] reads that too as a euphemism) and genteel references to her "bele chose," perhaps symptomatic of a larger alternation between her challenge of social norms and her acceptance of them. Even her threat when the Pardoner interrupts her, "thou shalt drynken of another tonne . . . shal savour wors than ale," which is completed a few lines later (III.170–71) as a version of Pandora's box—you don't know what kind of barrel you're opening here—is a nearly scatalogical image. "Wors than ale" sounds suspiciously like her recounting of the story of Socrates' wife Xanthippa, who "caste pisse on his heed" (III.729). There is no way to prove this, but it is consistent with the kinds of associational logic on which the Wife, and some others of Chaucer's characters, depend.

The Wife conflates even more conventional imagery. She calls upon two sets of images, which, although both are no doubt profoundly traditional, have about them the air of a confluence of old and new notions. On the one hand, she refers to marriage and sexuality in terms of bread, vessels, and food, extremely old, folk-derived images that have mythic as well as scriptural roots. On the other hand, she calls upon legalistic and economic language, currency, precious metals, debts, hard work, agreements, images that probably have equally old origins but in the context of the tale, seem new, "bourgeois," urban.

One conclusion one would like to draw from the uses of the new historiography is that Chaucer sexualizes popular knowledge. For instance, the Wife of Bath or Pertelote in the *Nun's Priest's Tale* represents a form of popular knowledge particularly related to a naturalistic, almost physical interpretation of things as they are, while ideal, abstract, and official knowledge is represented by male characters. But a bit more scrutiny reveals the case to be more complicated, an issue of genre rather than gender. It is in the comic and explicitly satirical tales that Chaucer matches popular knowledge and female voices. In the serious and religious tales, such as the *Second Nun's Tale* or the *Man of Law's Tale*, the ideal, fixed, official, religious interpretation is represented by female protagonists; "official" culture and pagan powers are revealed as only temporarily in authority, an authority limited by conversion, resignation, or gruesome accidents. In the *Second Nun's Tale*, for instance, despite the frenetic efforts of the prefect Almachius to suppress, torture, and finally execute St. Cecilia, it is the saint who possesses inner authority, and the more desperate Almachius grows in his persecution, the more her spiritual power seems to dominate. In the *Man of Law's Tale*, Constance turns her physical beauty into an instrument of conversion, however implemented by hair-raising adventures and by appeals to the kings and sultans who wish to marry her. Interestingly, it is the spiritual power of these pious women, sometimes reflected in their appearance, rather than their verbal agility that fulfills their mission. Nevertheless, the association of comic truth and earthly female knowledge is there in the *Canterbury Tales*, and that association is based on an intimate connection between language and experience, precisely what the *Shipman's Tale* so frighteningly questions. By performing rather than merely narrating, the Wife at least temporarily overcomes the limits of poetry.

Chapter Four

CHAUCER, BOCCACCIO, LONDON, FLORENCE

SACCHETTI, writing towards the end of the fourteenth century, recalls the story of a driver reciting Dante to his mule:

> As Dante went out for a walk one day . . . wearing armor on the neck and arms in the fashion of the time, he came across an ass driver who had some loads of garbage in front of him, and this driver walked behind his ass singing from the work of Dante. And when he had sung a bit he hit the ass and cried out, "Arri." Dante went up to him and with his arm-covering beat him about the head and shoulders, saying, "I did not put that 'arri' in!" The man did not know who Dante was nor why he had hit him, so he struck the ass hard again and shouted, "Arri! Arri!"[1]

The story continues with much ado about how the poet outwits the mule-driver, which Sacchetti seems to have found excruciatingly funny.

If the mule-driver had not existed, other late fourteenth-century Italian writers would probably have had to invent him, for at least part of their poetics consisted of defining an idea of poetry against such circumstances. The use of poetry, Petrarch writes in a letter, is not for "necessity," or it would be inferior to the trade of "the shoemaker, the baker, and the humblest mechanical arts."[2]

Petrarch denies that he is jealous of the "hoarse applause" that Dante receives "from tavern-keepers, fullers, butchers, and others of that class," and in so doing predicts some elements of Chaucer's pilgrim audience.[3] Chaucer seems to be calling into question Petrarch's rarefied version of reception at the same time as he offers a radically new perspective for his own audience. But Chaucer seems to consider quite seriously the real danger that Petrarch elsewhere outlines. Petrarch's contempt for "usefulness" is dealt with in a complex fashion in the *Tales.* For at various moments Chaucer underlines the vacuity of literally useful and moral fiction while suggesting that baking and carpentry may have within them some potential for poetry. The dichotomy between autonomy and utility is seriously debated by the pilgrims, and Chaucer at many points seems to make us aware of our own prejudices on the uses of fiction.

The issue of popular understanding is a problematic one for Chaucer, perhaps because the aesthetic issues are not as clear as for Petrarch or Boccaccio (Howard 1979). As much as the theme of marriage or the comedy of human existence, the question of literary understanding forms a central motif in the *Canterbury Tales* and sometimes subsumes other themes within itself (Ferster 1985). The question of literary understanding and reception becomes particularly crucial for Chaucer as he seeks to appropriate the model of Italian literature. There is no doubt that Chaucer knew French and French poetry intimately; he may have even composed in French, as did Gower. Although he certainly knew Italian, it was by no means the intimate relation he had with French. What Chaucer learned from the French was style; he could absorb and parody the sounds and nuances of the language.[4] But both early and late his debt to Italian literature lay elsewhere. French literature may have been a tradition for Chaucer and his contemporaries, but the new Italian literature must have seemed like a revolution. It was partly a matter of the invention of character and the control of narrative line—this Italy had mastered with more freedom and breadth than elsewhere. But his most important lesson was in the very idea of poetry and the conception of the poet that the model of Italian literature offered, which Chaucer seemed to understand more profoundly than his English contemporaries. Indeed, Chaucer's "English" period is less a period or a matter of Englishness than his nearly career-long attempt to answer the questions raised by his reading of Italian poetry. The obsession with popular reception so starkly articulated by the Italian writers offers a useful focus on Chaucer's apparently clear but in fact complex relation to unofficial culture and popular understanding.

If Chaucer's relation to French poetry has been gauged with more accuracy, it is partly because the conceptual and critical apparatus for determining that relation is more highly developed, in an earlier period of scholarship by the study of explicit sources, and later, by the analysis of stylistic detail. But in determining Chaucer's relation to Italian literature, we are forced on more general categories: the modulation of voice between author and audience, the creation and defense of new literary materials, and the means to integrate noncourtly and popular materials into the framework of major literary enterprises.

In pointing to some of these qualities in Chaucer's poetry, I want to call chiefly upon Boccaccio's *Decameron* for illustration, partly because the creation of an included audience of tale-tellers provides a point of comparison with the *Canterbury Tales*, and partly because the literary culture of Florence itself provides a useful contrast with Chaucer's London. But my hidden agenda is one that rests on the uncertainty of Chaucer's knowledge of the *Decameron*, and I am interested in considering the ways in which Chaucer's poetic project constitutes a reading, or a response, to Boccaccio's.

.   .   .

I want to locate Chaucer's equivocation by comparing the Pardoner's performance with Boccaccio's tale of Ciappelletto in Day 1, Story 1, of the

Decameron.[5] Both examples concern themselves with the nature of belief and in particular with the relation of the "lewed folk" to meanings and performances of various kinds. I want to suggest that both represent meditations by the author on his relation to popular culture as a "source" for his art.

Ciappelletto, in every way unattractive, has led as unholy a life as possible, but in his deathbed confession presents such an extreme posture of holiness that the Friar who hears him preaches to the multitude of his singular virtue, so persuasively that he is extolled as a saint. The two Lombard merchants who house him, who had been at the point of throwing him out since they assumed that no one who knew of him would give him a Christian burial and it would reflect badly on their enterprise, overhear the confession in the manner of an included audience. They know of his previous reputation and are simultaneously delighted and appalled at his contempt for damnation. The "contexts" of the story consist of revised versions of Ciappelletto's previous life. The first is of his "real" life as the narrator has presented it to us. Then we have his blatantly fabulous confession, overheard by the two merchants who know of his real life. Finally, we are offered an idealized version of his life and character in the Friar's eulogy. These revisions are also performances: the obvious performance by Panfilio in telling the story, the fabulous confession, staged like a play, and the performance that constitutes the Friar's eulogy, so powerful that it moves people to religious ecstasy. In the fraudulent confession, as in the Friar's later eulogy, one of Boccaccio's favorite themes, the foolishness of gullibility, is immediately established, but in the context of hearing and listening. A moral frame of reference is reinvoked, but only as an unlikely possibility, as the appearance of appearance itself is called into question, when the narrator wonders who is to say that Ciappelletto has not at the last minute repented.

The similarity between Ciappelletto and the Pardoner is so striking that I hardly need explicate the similar scenario of the *Pardoner's Prologue* and *Tale* more than briefly. The Pardoner, too, courts damnation, and does so by implicating the salvation of others in his scheme: "I rekke nevere, whan that they been beryed, / Though that hir soules goon a-blakeberyed" (VI.405–6). He puts on a performance of sorts for the delectation of his pilgrim audience, who become, momentarily and unwillingly, akin to "lewed peple." The power of his story attests to the power of belief, however cynical he may be about it.

Throughout his prologue, the Pardoner gloats over the stupidity of popular gullibility, and the imagery of rural and village life, used for more joyful but not uncomplicated purposes in the *Miller's Tale* and the *Nun's Priest's Tale*, here acquires a mean and pathetic quality, as it is reflected in his own language:

If that this boon be wasshe in any welle,
If cow, or calf, or sheep, or oxe swelle
That any worm hath ete, or worm ystonge,
Taak water of that welle and wassh his tonge
And it is hool anon; and forthermoore,
Of pokkes and of scabbe, and every soore
Shal every sheep be hool that of this welle
Drynketh a draughte.

(VI.353–60)

Although the sacramental and pentecostal parody that underlies the language is of course part of its art, its immediate impact is to denigrate rural life as it calls up its image. Chaucer's sources for the Pardoner's monologue do not necessarily single out the poor and the simple for special attention. Moreover, the very processes of the *Canterbury Tales* are implicated in the Pardoner's definition of his audience, "for lewed peple loven tales olde; / Swiche thynges kan they wel reporte and holde" (VI.437–38). Significantly, it is Harry Bailly who takes the Pardoner's comments most personally (of course, he is the first one called forward), just as he offers autobiographical readings of the *Clerk's Tale*, and, interestingly, Chaucer's own *Tale of Melibee*.

There are other confidence men in Boccaccio worthy of comparison with the Pardoner. The story of Cipolla (Day 6, Story 10) is one of those that pretends to be about events turning out better than could be expected, but it is equally concerned with the nature of irony, of what an audience understands of what it sees. That it can play with the theme of appearance and reality is evident from the moment we are told that the protagonists are mummers. Again we have a series of audiences: the townspeople crowding around the bier bearing the miraculous body, the actors themselves almost becoming an audience as a result of their own curiosity, and the "play" that the townspeople do not realize they are watching as an arranged performance. The art of reading the tale is at least partly in the rapidity with which audiences become actors and fiction becomes truth, in a way that could easily reverse itself at any time. Yet the rhetoric of the tale depends on our knowing the ruse. We are not first presented with a cured cripple who turns out to be an actor. We are told immediately that the actor is pretending to be crippled. We are not so much asked to be fooled as to observe others being fooled, and this protects us from the shock or unbalance of surprise. Again, Boccaccio includes a certain analogy between belief implicit in faith and the species of belief necessary to fiction, so that we find a peculiar distance on both.

One could explain away this parallel between Chaucer and Boccaccio easily enough. The Pardoner, after all, can hardly be said to triumph.[6]

There are enough antidotes such as the *Miller's Tale*, the *Wife of Bath's Prologue*, and the *Nun's Priest's Tale* to counter this dark moment. Moreover, there is a profound difference between these portraits. It matters that the mob that Cipolla addresses exists within the fiction itself; it matters that the two merchants exist as a surrogate audience within the story of Ciappelletto. Part of the wit of these stories is to suggest that even the reaction of a sophisticated audience does not differ in some ways from more apparently primitive beliefs, but it makes that point indirectly and by means of parable. Part of the "miracle" of Ciappelletto's vita is that it seems to have genuinely devout results, however cynically portrayed; part of the magic of the Pardoner's story, if we adhere to the most convincing interpretations of some ambiguous lines, is that it seems to move even the cynical Pardoner. But the *brigata* can take a perspective of distance and superiority to the stories, even if they are moved by them and learn from them and disagree about them, and in this fashion they represent models of ideal readership. No such distance is permitted the Canterbury pilgrims, who because of the Pardoner's address are implicitly asked to enact the part of the "lewed folk" who love old stories. By pretending to go through his act, he asks them to pretend to be his usual audience.

The relative obviousness of the Pardoner's ploy, then, compared to the wit and ingenuity of Boccaccio's characters, is complicated by the operations of the included audience: the pilgrims are forced to react. In their stress on verbal ingenuity and on the creation of relatively convincing illusions, characters such as Cipolla and Ciappelletto suggest a connection between art and some more scurrilous occupations. Chaucer also seems to have an obsessive interest in the less-than-respectable pilgrims, and it is perhaps an accident of rhetoric, though noteworthy nonetheless, that the General Prologue seems to refer to the narrator in the same breath as the less savory members of the pilgrimage. In any case, the *Pardoner's Prologue* is at least partly an essay on the efficacy of fiction and the peculiarities of intention. Like some of the late *Canterbury Tales*, it meditates on the difficulties of language in a fallen world. Although more frightening, it achieves through the reaction of the pilgrims, and perhaps the reaction of the Pardoner himself, a certain redemption, as the cheap illusions of the *Canon's Yeoman's Tale* and the cynical demythologizing of the *Manciple's Tale*, which is terribly concerned with language, do not.

.   .   .

Both Chaucer and Boccaccio, however, find themselves obsessed with the irreducibly social nature of language, and, as a result, its capacity for changes in meaning and willful or random misinterpretation. Always above and beyond their fictions is the model of communication as an ideal sign, but within their fictions, they are much more concerned with articulating, in ways that themselves might be misunderstood, the means by which we understand or misunderstand each other.

If the introduction to the fourth day contains the ostensible defense of art by Boccaccio, the beginning of the sixth day, for all practical purposes the middle of the work, contains an even less varnished celebration of its own existence. Here, too, as in the "author's" apology, the story is barely a story and therefore draws attention to itself as statement. Oretta is accompanied by a knight, who promises to entertain her on a journey by telling her stories. But the knight is not a very good artist. He stops and repeats himself and complains that he is not telling it right, until the lady has to stop him. The emphasis on the aesthetic pleasure of the tale, in its telling, its timing, and its presentation, is enormously socially conscious. It underlines the articulateness that is part of the self-definition of the noble life. To speak well is as important for the late medieval and early Renaissance courtier as to fight well.

The most obvious import of the tale, however, and perhaps of all those linguistically conscious tales of the sixth day, is to comment on the process of the *Decameron* itself, to call attention to itself as an act of storytelling and to call attention to our own role as an audience. Especially notable, however, in this little piece, is the justification of its own existence and the right of a work of art to take its own existence as its subject. We are reminded of other such moments in the *Decameron*, of the minor drama and self-incrimination of fiction that we find in the first tale of the first day. There is an obvious echo of this concern in Chaucer, most notably in the inability of Geoffrey the pilgrim to tell a proper tale or the debate on the proprieties of fiction entered into by such characters as the Reeve or the Man of Law.

The peculiar relation between art and such qualities as truth and beauty is explored later by Boccaccio when we meet Giotto, who turns out to be rather less than beautiful himself and whose art is praised in the story not because it imitates life or inculcates right action, but because it successfully creates an illusion. Boccaccio suggests art's alignment with the sinister underground, where it merges with magic and confidence men and miracles. Not only the Pardoner but some of the unsavory members of Chaucer's pilgrimage are also members of the same fraternity.

Boccaccio's urbane malice is also directed partly at his public. After all, the first story is about a Florentine away from home, as is our included audience, although not very far away. It concerns the appearance of virtue, which is so strongly emphasized in the beginning and ending of the frame. Its technique includes a naive auditor, who accepts all he hears at face value. It also includes another audience, the two usurers, who hide behind a screen and hear the false confession, responding much as we might.

The first three stories of Day 1 set up situations in which we share more or less in the suspense, not only of the included audience of tale-tellers, but of another audience within the tales themselves. The two brothers wait in a state of crisis for Ciappelletto's potentially damaging confession; Gianotto, in despair that Abraham has gone to Rome of all places to learn Christian behavior, assumes that he will never convert, and awaits his return; in the third tale, we are more or less in the position of Saladin. But as our interest in the narrative proper parallels that of these "audience" figures, our sympathies with them are limited by divergence in class, grace, or character.

The next tale (Day 1, story 7) continues this series of included negative models, this time in the guise of a historical personage, Cane Della Scalla, who, given his class situation, is susceptible to the grace imparted by the quick tongue of the fictional "storyteller," the courtier Bergamino. The joke of the next tale (Day 1, story 8) is a sign, the idea of painting "Cortesia" in the miser's hall. But as with many of Boccaccio's images, the important thing is not the sign or the idea, but the reaction of characters within the story and the dialogue that ensues. The point is the transaction and process of communication, which we, with the narrators, observe and remark on, but are not involved in, for the adjustment that these negative models of audiences and readers provide is only an adjustment, asking us to return to the original pose with which we began.

For Chaucer, it is our perception that is problematic; indeed, language itself, our chief medium of literary perception, is subject to not only a defense, but a searching examination. From the very beginning of his career, as in the *House of Fame*, to the last tales of Canterbury, Chaucer reveals a nearly Jacobean obsession with the deceptions worked by the human tongue, an obsession obscured, as are many of his darker themes, by an apparent geniality and good humor. The "tydings" of the *House of Fame* are a compulsive though less than impassioned statement of charges; in the *Troilus* there are a series of more disturbing references to speech and silence; the theme culminates in the sardonic talking crow of the *Manciple's Tale* and the poet's own retraction. This difference between the two writers is not one of imagery alone, for it is implicit also in one of the chief similarities between the two works, what is usually described as the "frame." I want to contrast Boccaccio and Chaucer's use of their superstructured narration to locate Chaucer's theatricality in contrast to Boccaccio's.

However intriguing and subtle the metaphors for response within the tales, the most powerful means of inviting or distancing the reader from these "framed fictions" is the frame itself, the "cornice" of Boccaccio's *Decameron*, the pilgrims and their interrelation in the *Canterbury Tales*. The frame of the *Decameron* continually returns to the patrician calm of the storytellers as they move from villa to villa. It is as if the frame were a bulwark against the anarchy of the tales. Our perspective, then, is realigned after each tale; the equanimity and balance of an ideal world is reasserted. Certainly its concord is fragile, highly selective and in reaction to the horror of the plague. But the frame never involves us in the comic but ultimately disorienting experience of the "roadside drama" of the *Canterbury Tales*, in which each move requires a new strategy, sometimes a new set of rules, and a new perspective, in which the ostensible ideals of each "reader" among the pilgrims are contrasted with less attractive motivations. The cornice of the *Decameron*, as much as it liberates the possibilities of narrative, also functions as a screen. The stories create a separate reality that does not often intrude on the world of the storytellers, except in the larger sense that it has the same effect on them as it does on us. Much more starkly, the worlds of tales and tellers in the *Canterbury Tales* intertwine. The result is a more "grotesque" style in the original sense of "unfinished" and "provisional," and it suggests further a conception of reality more incomplete and dynamic than that of Boccaccio, a sense of reality moving towards a purpose and meaning always slightly beyond our horizon. In this sense, the pilgrimage itself is an epistemological metaphor.

Although Boccaccio may appear to be more modern, his frame allows him to retain the role of the love-poet, the characteristic voice of the medieval secular poet, which probably finds its origins in Ovid. In Chaucer, we are made to feel part of a public of varied and nonexclusive backgrounds and tastes. In reality, that may have been more true of Boccaccio's audience, but the frame there almost seems to protect us from the implications of that fact. Aware that he is speaking to a public, Boccaccio articulates his rationale for reading in a courtly register: we are to model ourselves on the young tale-tellers, appeal is made to the young ladies in the audience (which is to say the most refined, civilized, and socially sophisticated parts of ourselves), and our chief interest is assumed to be in matters of love. He retains the social pretense of a courtly adviser. It is almost as if this tone were necessary to allow the considerable range of experience embodied in the tales. Indeed, this traditional appeal is part of the process of balance and recovery that the frame of the *Decameron* is meant to cultivate.

Both the beginning and the ending of the *Decameron* make clear the purposes of its tale-tellers' literal "retreat":

> As you know, it will be fifteen days tomorrow that we left Florence to find some means of amusement, to preserve our health and our lives, and to escape the melancholy, suffering and anguish which has existed continually in our city since the beginning of the plague. This goal, in my opinion, we have virtuously achieved; for, as far as I have been able to observe, even if the stories we have told were amusing, and possibly of the sort conducive to arousing our carnal appetites, and though we have continually eaten and

drunk well, played and sung (all things which may well incite weaker minds to less proper behavior), neither in word nor in deed nor in any other way do I feel that either you or ourselves are worthy of criticism. Constant decorum, constant harmony, and constant fraternal friendship are, in fact, what I have seen and felt here—something which, of course, pleases me, for it redounds to both your honor and merit and mine. And therefore, to prevent an overly practiced custom from turning into boredom as well as to prevent anyone from criticizing our having stayed here too long, I now think it proper, since each of us has, with his day of storytelling, enjoyed his share of the honor that still resides in me, that, with your approval, we return to the place from where we came. (1983, 682)[7]

Whatever the apparently frivolous concerns of either the *Decameron* or the *Canterbury Tales*, their frames place their stories in a context that must be regarded at least partly political or social, even given the distance of their authors' distinctive voices from those of Dante or Langland. For both place their storytellers in a specific time and a specific place with a common goal and thereby implicitly raise certain questions about the nature of social ties, the necessity of order and degree, and the meaning and basis of community.

Both openings link their images of community to images of disease and regeneration, a trope at least as old as Sophocles. The more starkly opposed images of Boccaccio's cornice, whatever the literary sources of his description of the plague, certainly reflects the mood of Tuscan culture after the Black Death. It is sometimes implied that because his description is based on an earlier model, an earlier plague, it is somehow less accurate, but all images of doom and disaster must be based on other "literary" analogues; even those of our own century, in their insistence on incomprehensibility, reveal a dependence on earlier imaginings of disaster. This makes them no less powerful, terrible, or "accurate." In Chaucer, this corruption is more individualized and humanly scaled. A number of pilgrims are ostensibly making their journey to thank St. Thomas for helping them when they were sick. Even the order of society in Chaucer seems somehow degenerated from an ideal, perhaps imagined, order. Yet Chaucer's suggestions (and they remain only suggestions) of corruption form a soil in which the stories and characters can intertwine. Boccaccio's social order is more immediately threatened, and we are asked to regard the retreat and the fictions as a kind of treatment, a purge. When it is over, storytellers and listeners can return strengthened to the larger community. Herein lies a primitive element of an otherwise sophisticated literary experience.

There is also a sense in Boccaccio's farewell to his included audience that the stories have been a kind of test: "Who doesn't know that wine is good for the healthy . . . but harmful to anyone suffering with a fever. . . . A corrupt mind never understands a word in a healthy way! And just as fitting words are of no use to a corrupt mind, so a healthy mind cannot be contaminated by words which are not so proper" (Boccaccio 1983, 686).[8] This may be dismissed as a way of excusing some of the less-than-pious fiction in the collection: by being able to regard the stories as stories, the listeners have built up resistance against the pervasive breakdown of moral order that infects the world after the plague (G. Olson 1982). The explanation bears a strange resemblance to some late medieval heresies, whose proponents supposedly indulged in extremely worldly excesses in order to demonstrate how their purely spiritual natures were unaffected by such excess.

It is characteristic of Boccaccio to acknowledge that this utopian contract could not last forever and that isolation would eventually result in discord. It is almost as if Chaucer were beginning the *Canterbury Tales* with the mood of the end of the *Decameron*, for Chaucer's pilgrims, admittedly more socially heterogeneous, achieve this concord only for a moment. Part of the problem is that Chaucer's storytellers take their stories very seriously indeed. Boccaccio's more sophisticated group are always aware of the artifice of their creations. Indeed, here the crown prince of their adventure seems to be aware of the danger of art being taken in other ways. It is one thing to deal with our passions by observing them objectively in art; it is quite another to have them incited by art, which happens a few times in Chaucer's work.

Interestingly, Boccaccio's conclusion also directly addresses two themes implicitly included in Chaucer's General Prologue, and which play a large role in the *Canterbury Tales*. Boccaccio's closing infers that hearing about love has helped the patrician storytellers get along with each other. The individual goals of the tradition of courtly romance are here subsumed to a public, almost civic definition of community (Boitani 1982, 246), along with a note of parody of the goals of the great monastic ideal of perfection. Indeed, the relation between love and governance is at the very heart of the theme of marriage in Chaucer. The second theme of the conclusion is that of memory and the importance of recollection and anticipation to human consciousness. Chaucer similarly builds this great medieval concern into the very structure of his work.

Despite the apparently more conventional moral concerns of many of Chaucer's tales, then, the two works share a certain decentered quality. Both are deliberately explicit, even obsessed, with their own making, and both "lose control." In Boccaccio, the materials of the tales themselves are potentially disarming, even nihilistic. But the frame allows us to take a relatively measured and even stance, one that allows an immersion in disorder, but which promises a return to the gentle equanimity of the beginning and ending. If Chaucer ever had a sense of closure and containment, he must have abandoned it as the tales themselves opened up a multiplicity of perspectives.

The measure and balance of the frame of the *Decameron*, meant as a defense against the corruption of the *città*, exemplified in the anarchy of its tales, is dependent everywhere upon the social perspective of its audience, on sharing the patrician calm of the ladies and gentlemen moving from villa to villa. The class perspective of the frame is reemphasized in Boccaccio, no matter how high or low it has gone in the tales. In Chaucer, the consonance between the class origins of a particular tale or genre and its explicit or implicit reception by the pilgrim audience is not always as clear. Indeed, frequently in Chaucer the class origins of a tale and its teller differ. The *Knight's Tale* is appropriately told, but who among the pilgrims can provide us with a model of aristocratic response? Indeed, part of the process of reading the *Canterbury Tales* is a constant readjustment, as each tale introduces a new fictional world, and as the pilgrims themselves offer response and correction, which we ourselves must correct. Just as we are forced to rely on our own perceptions rather than the judgments of the narrator in apprehending the portraits in the General Prologue, so are we often forced to construct the meaning of the tales almost negatively, by reacting against the reactions of the internal audience. For the class basis of that audience is not only broad; it lacks an authoritative center. The theoretical social order cannot contain the social forces among the pilgrims. If the *Decameron* purports to offer its readers a protective exposure to the disorder of the world, the *Canterbury Tales* engages us in that disorder. If we watch games and play in Boccaccio, we engage in them in Chaucer.

· · ·

The imagery of sexuality and desire, so apparently part of Boccaccio and Chaucer's employment of popular motifs, and their obsession, alternately misogynist and sympathetic, with female characters, is something other than the return of the repressed. For in both writers, sexuality and sexual difference is accorded an intimate relation with poetic creation and literary understanding. The passionate engagement of late medieval poets with female characters and antifeminist topics is a passion that suggests projection. Like the woman in the medieval court or household, medieval poets were also subject to a list of impossible prescriptions and conflicting demands and held up to an ideal only utter sanctity could achieve. The fascination in so many medieval plots with the convolutions of erotic experience, its dangers and its momentary rewards, suggests an analogy with the process of poetry itself. The art of love for the medieval heroine, courtly or not, is literally an art and derives from a skillful balance between competing and sometimes mutually exclusive desires and a working out of dangers, revenge, and resentment. The conventional address of the audience as "lovers" is only the surface of a more secret and subversive analogy.

The preface to the *Decameron* as a whole places the metaphor in an apparently historical and realistic setting:

> And who will deny that such comfort, no matter how insufficient, is more fittingly bestowed on charming ladies than on men? For they, in fear and shame, conceal the hidden flames of love within their delicate breasts, a love far stronger than one which is openly expressed, as those who have felt and suffered this know; and furthermore, restricted by the wishes, whims, and commands of fathers, mothers, brothers, and husbands, they remain most of the time limited to the narrow confines of their bedrooms, where they sit in apparent idleness, now wishing one thing and now wishing another, turning over in their minds a number of thoughts which cannot always be pleasant ones. And because of these thoughts, if there should arise within their minds a sense of melancholy brought on by burning desire, these ladies will be forced to suffer this terrible pain unless it is replaced by new interests. (1983, 2)[9]

The witty and poignant sympathy for women in love contrasts radically with the bare assumption of the *Canterbury Tales* that curiosity and the fascination with experience are enough reason for the reader, if not the pilgrims, to be listening to the stories. Boccaccio's address to his audience resembles more the address of the *Troilus*.

Another address to the audience, as "women," may have been equally metaphoric, despite the apparent actual increase of women readers and audiences. The most famous of these is Boccaccio's preface to the fourth day in which he steps forward to defend his art against attacks by means of a tale. The tale itself is wittily self-explanatory. A man leaves Florence and lives as a hermit with his son, whom he protects from all worldly images. One day, since the man is getting along in years, the son suggests that he too go along to town for supplies. Reluctantly, the man agrees. The boy is impressed but nonplussed by the buildings, gardens, and crowds. But he is more than a little taken with the beautiful creatures whom he sees everywhere. When he asks what they are, the father, in a doomed attempt to protect the boy, says that they are geese, at which the boy replies that he would very much like to take them home and feed them.

The preface to this story is addressed to women, and it implies that his readers need to be protected much more from their protectors than from Boccaccio himself. More accurately, he suggests that they can hardly be kept from their own nature, which the author, unlike his censors, sees as fine and gentle. However true that may be, the preface takes its place in the long medieval tradition of including a defense of art within one's fiction. What is remarkable about Boccaccio's defense is its squarely secular basis. When Chaucer turns to similar lines of defense, in the *Legend of Good*

Women, or in the *Troilus*, there is a nervous touch of moral seriousness, and that seriousness is dramatized, comically, in the *Man of Law's Prologue*.

Boccaccio's appeal here, then, is a metaphor for artistic freedom. It is significant that his tale-tellers must leave the city to carry on their narration, free, that is, from the weight of social obligation to carry a great deal of moral baggage. The escape of the frame, like the escape of all popular romance, is an antidote to the boredom and enclosure of everyday life. The address to women is by no means unrelated to this, for everyday life in the *città* for most wealthy Florentine women was a pattern of unrelieved boredom. As a communal act, the telling and hearing of stories in the *Decameron* is an antidote to the plague, a way of holding together the social fabric in the face of the dissolution that the pestilence has generated, so powerfully described in the preface. As an individual act, the stories represent a gesture towards freedom, a parody and often a travesty of the social bonds that the city represents.

The closest analogue in Chaucer to Boccaccio's defense via the ladies of his audience is the prologue to the *Legend of Good Women*. In a characteristically self-deprecating fashion, rather than calling upon women as allies, Chaucer arranges to be accused by the God of Love of slandering women. The defense against such uncourtly behavior is something of a feint. For the stories that follow offer less satisfaction to either party in his audience, and the entire enterprise finds Chaucer exhausting the possibilities of the courtly forms with which he had been working. Debates about similar topics, such as love, marriage, and the relations between the sexes, continue in the *Canterbury Tales*, but there they are placed in a context that provides its own justification.

Chaucer's real defense against the explicit accusations of the God of Love is not the list of writings about women that show them in a good light. It is rather that his case is made by a woman herself, Alceste. A transformation of the daisy, she seems almost an emblem from Ovid. As in the similar scene in the *Knight's Tale*, Alceste is able to temper the immoderate fury of the God of Love with mercy. In so doing, she has already defended our poet, who in the very presentation has created a "good woman" even if, as I suggest above, he finds her defense limiting. The technique is also familiar from the *Book of the Duchess*. There, Chaucer solves a problem of social tact by having the Black Knight himself sing the praises of the lost Duchess. In writing such a script, Chaucer closes the ironic gap between text and voice.

In both Chaucer and Boccaccio, there is a trend away from medieval certainties, though in rather different directions. The effect in Boccaccio might be taken for cynicism, but it is an attempt to inculcate worldliness. Unless we are already women unhappy in love, there is no reason to pretend to be. There is a touch of distance in the portrayal, perhaps also condescension, an attitude we are asked to take towards more than a few of Boccaccio's characters. Such a tension is created by a paradox in the stories themselves, where their measured tone, the consistent length, and highly conscious style conflict with abandoned anarchy, comedy, and violence that inhabit the tales themselves. Moreover, in Boccaccio, tale-telling is represented, strictly by the number of participants, as a female pastime, and with a special justification, if only as a defense, to female experience. Hence, plots that depend heavily on the popular, the folkloric, gossip, and hearsay, are associated, as if naturally, with female speakers, as if that were their normal conduit into polite literature. In Chaucer, however, such un-official sources leak into high cultural forms from all directions and through the voices of both genders, so that the separation between levels and their relative hierarchical authority are obscured. In Chaucer, obsessive narration is represented as a generally human, rather than specifically fe-male, need.

.   .   .

One could point to the many differences between Chaucer's and Boccac-cio's art and explain those differences by the historical and cultural devel-opment of Florence and London. Even after the plague, Florence was at least twice the size of London. Villani's description of education in his chronicle implies that eighty percent of the pre-plague population was lit-erate. There is nothing like the urban patriciate of Florence in Chaucer's London, nothing to compare to the mountains of diaries, records, and letters produced by the merchants of Florence. "Never," the aspiring Flor-entine merchant was told, "never stop using your pen" (Larner 1971, 188–89). Notwithstanding the banking crises of the fourteenth century (coinci-dentally precipitated by heavy loans to the English crown), Florence had amassed enough wealth to assure a cultured elite with sufficient leisure to support its sophisticated literary and artistic culture. Boccaccio's storytell-ers are not "unreal" in that social sense.

Even though London may be regarded as the seat of a substantial Eng-lish literary culture, with an incipient literary public, the development of that public and of the vernacular was comparatively retarded. On the one hand, literary language suffered under the yoke of French feudal forms; on the other, language itself had the advantage of a more direct connection to everyday reality. A poet like Chaucer, then, could not count on the culti-vated public that Boccaccio could claim but had a more direct connection to a more popular and fluid literary tradition and could, at the same time, count on enough intelligent avant-garde readers connected with the court to allow his experiments to succeed with those who would appreciate them and yet not offend those who would not notice them. Hence the difference between the radically relativist process of the *Canterbury Tales* and the constant return to patrician balance of the *Decameron*. Hence the radical discontinuity of style in the various *Tales*, and hence the elegant subordination of potentially anarchic motives in the *Decameron*. On some other levels, particularly the peculiar relation of elite and urban and popular and folk culture that marks much late medieval literature, there are enough similarities between these two literary situations to call into question the adequacy of this model.[10] The culture of their day was simply not as polarized in terms of city and country as it was to be later. As Auerbach (1965, 239) argues in his definition of a literary public, too strict a line between popular and elite culture cannot be drawn. Access to popular and high culture even in Italy resulted in a peculiar amalgam.[11] The urban poor in general shared a culture with the countryside, and records of Florence at least indicate a considerable ebb and flow of population from urban to exurban status. There is no reason to think that London did not partake of the same pattern.

Certainly fourteenth-century London resembled a continental city more than it did York or Chester, but even its cosmopolitan qualities were almost against its own will. Although there were, for instance, members of the European international community in town, they were in large measure confined to what amounted to merchant ghettos. Even some of the provincial cities hosted foreign merchants, particularly Italian bankers. That Chaucer saw more of the world than military service alone would have allowed marked him as exceptional, while the travels of young Florentines of a certain class would have been the norm.

Despite the considerable pride in the polis and the distinctiveness of Tuscan urban culture, public display retained a distinctly aristocratic veneer. As Becker (1967, 15) describes it, "Businessman, banker, merchant and industrialist took delight in both the fantasy and the reality of the knightly world and venerated such aristocratic organizations as the Guelf party. Pageant, ceremony and tournament were the hallmarks of *civiltà* in Florentine society until the 1340s. With their full consent the place of honor in communal processions was accorded to high clergy as well as to magnates." Of course, the political system underlying this expression was markedly different in London and Florence. The similarity suggests instead the relatively limited means of civic and public expression. In interpreting the significance of such public forms, we should be alert to the placement and context of particular elements rather than their generally similar outlines. The political and social messages of these urban displays were often very different. More often than not, the civic processions of Florence have the quality of an articulated and conscious expression of the unity of the polis, the special place of Florence in history and the moment. The civic expressions of London, less rich and frequent, have the quality of conditioned assertions, statements in a dialogue between countervailing forces in the city and the nation. Whereas London's political style was a series of statements loosely hinged together, Florence's was a conscious program.

Despite the striking image of a specific and historically specifiable event, the plague, the world of Boccaccio's storytellers seems consciously and artificially timeless. Even its idealism is a version of life consistent with the existence of the urban patriciate, who did have villas in the hills around the city. Yet the stories they tell, for all their variety, return again and again to their own origins, to the history of the city itself. The portraits of the pilgrims, despite their obvious indebtedness to conventions of estates literature and such allegories as the *Romance of the Rose*, seem paradoxically to assert their historicity and individuality. The peculiar combination of individuality and typology in the General Prologue also has an urban context to which I have pointed earlier—the processions and ridings of late medieval urban celebrations. Yet taken as narrative alone, the stories lack the immediate and obsessive concern with urban origins that we find in the *Decameron*'s tales. The only tale that makes much of its city origins is the *Cook's Tale*, lost in its own backstreet-and-alley existence, while the *Shipman's Tale* and the *Canon's Yeoman's Tale* give us only glimpses of urban life.

In comparison, the "realism" of the *Canterbury Tales* is in large part a result of the variety of its style and not its attempts at verisimilitude. Even as realistic a confession as the *Wife of Bath's Tale* limits its present historical description to its introduction, while the tale itself is set in a mythical past. The world of the tales often impresses with its faraway and abstract character, in contrast to a narrating voice that is equally often palpable and present. We meet the pilgrims across the river, outside the city, and it remains a silhouette. It is as if the poet were indulging in an act of poetic exile. Yet as a fictional community, for all its faults, the world of the pilgrims temporarily forms an urban world, right down to its language.

Indeed, it is in its style that the *Canterbury Tales* reveals its urban origins, not in clear pictures of city life or the startling images we find in Langland or Hoccleve. In their way of talking and interacting, the pilgrims themselves capture the energy and expansiveness that is finally a distinctively urban style. The pilgrimage is on its way out of the city, and no tale seems to be recited in a town—we seem always to be on the edges of towns, not in them, as Howard (1976) points out. Chaucer does imitate the texture of urban life, chiefly in crowd scenes, in ways that recall not "everyday" life, but special occasions, such as festivals or mobs—highly qualified or unusual occurrences in city life. The most famous such scene is the chase in the *Nun's Priest's Tale*, with its explicit reference to the Peasant's Revolt, but the form of that chase more resembles a hunt. The most striking version of a city comes when Troilus wanders through Troy and recalls the places that remind him of Criseyde. It is a peculiarly ghostly city in that passage and in any case has about it the spaciousness and plan of an Italian rather than an English city.

In scenes such as the deliberations in the *Parliament of Fowls* or the assortment of figures milling around the Temple of Fame, we find urban images in other—parliamentary or court—contexts. When Chaucer does picture a city, it is likely to be in the form of a parade, as when Troilus rides his horse through the streets of Troy and the crowd cheers him, or in the portraits of the General Prologue, which resemble a parade or procession and an urban quality. The network of gossip and association in the *Miller's Tale* or the *Wife of Bath's Tale* depends strongly on town and village life, not urban life as we would think of it. For all the pastoral, bucolic, and natural imagery in the *Canterbury Tales* and the *Decameron*, then, in contrast to the dominant tradition of medieval narrative, they bear an unmistakably urban stamp. Chaucer's and Boccaccio's management of crowds and scenes of life, their fascination with towns, suggests a new literary fascination with the possibilities of life in urban settings—a fascination perhaps most starkly featured in the fabliau, but not limited to that genre. For all their feudal and rural associations, the Canterbury pilgrims convert fields, forests, and streams into streets, halls, and market squares.

One of the most famous observations on the *Decameron* in our time has been Branca's description of the work as a "merchant epic" that looks back to the great age of Florentine mercantile expansion, not of Boccaccio's generation itself. Even its geography is that of the circuit of commerce of the Italian city-states. The tales themselves often take place on the route east, or the northern outposts of Italian banking and trade. The daring and risky adventures of those earlier generations must have contrasted with the economic operations of late fourteenth-century and early fifteenth-century Florence, which, while at the height of its wealth and power, had already begun to turn inward, to force its local markets, and to rest on its accomplishments rather than explore new paths. In a sense, then, the material energy and dynamism of the tales, although it reflects certain aspects of Florentine life, also offers a critique of urban mercantile values from their own perspective, just as the frame seems to review its history from yet another perspective—the sense of largess, generosity, and gentility modeled on an aristocratic vision of life. The criticism that the *Decameron* offers of its social context is very different from that offered by *Piers Plowman* or the *Canterbury Tales* or even the *Divine Comedy*, all of which contrast medieval social reality and medieval social ideals.

The tales both document and reflect a confidence and arrogance that verges on a kind of conquest, which belies the respect paid to natural forces in the tales. Even the treatment of human character nowhere receives the respect Chaucer allows it. Nor is this a matter of Chaucer's "modernity," for it is in fact the plots and situations of Boccaccio that, although they are borrowed in some cases from medieval themes, are freed from the controlling and mitigating structures of medieval social values and thus release a control and mastery of the world that verges on rapacity. Boccaccio's recoil at his own invention thus has a dimension beyond a retreat to medieval certainties. In his very retraction of his work he completes a cycle of alternating celebration of untrammeled energies and a pessimistic rejection of a consequent nihilism that will mark Western literature in the following centuries.

. . .

We are thus led to a crux in the theoretical framework that Bakhtin builds around the notion of "carnivalized texts." It is a difficulty because Bakhtin is very hard on Boccaccio and seems to exclude him from the underground tradition that his new version of literary history seems to promise. Far from celebrating the world of festival and carnival that Bakhtin sees as representing "unofficial culture," Boccaccio only allows us to "pose the problem" (Bakhtin 1968, 273). Bakhtin's stricture addresses what I have tried to locate in my remarks, the appropriation, rather than celebration, of popular culture in Boccaccio. But if Bakhtin is right about Boccaccio, what then do we do with Chaucer? For Chaucer also appropriates the styles and operations of popular culture to other purposes but accomplishes this by even more intimately including its workings in his fiction.[12]

Each writer includes a defense of "poetry"—I use the term in its widest sense—within his fiction, and popular responses are an integral part of such defenses. Boccaccio's defense, reduced to its simplest level, is that all of phenomenal reality is subject to the same qualities of illusion, false belief, and distortion as art. For all the sophistication of his tone, Boccaccio leaves himself open to the very questions that he himself eventually asks about fiction. The play with reality and the equation of art and lying that is a virtual leitmotif of the *Decameron* asks of us not so much a suspension of disbelief as of moral judgment.

One check against these problems of poetics is to be ironic about one's work, and both writers include more than a measure of irony about the efficacy of their fiction. But such sophistication and irony, while dangerous weapons, are also dangerous defenses. The uses of irony in either writer are, however, quite different. The result of Boccaccio's ironies is to strengthen the urbane perspective that his style everywhere inculcates, for the author of the *Decameron* reveals everywhere an impenetrable worldliness that the narrator of the *Canterbury Tales* only pretends to. We become aware of the performances in the *Decameron* as artifice, and this distance results in a feeling of superiority to the human need that impels the enter-

tainment and our interest in it. Certainly the stories themselves have a
breadth of appeal that ensures their popular reception not only in Italy but
elsewhere, if only because they play upon, and ironically legitimize, many
of the themes common to popular literature. To do otherwise, for Boccac-
cio, would mean a reversion to the pitfalls of naive belief that his skepticism
and his plots everywhere oppose. There is always the danger that we join
the mob clambering around Ciappelletto's bier. One senses in Boccaccio's
style, his urbane humor, and his very emphasis on the sheer entertainment
value of story, a kind of education against an absolutism of truth and mo-
rality. Hence, we are put always on guard in the *Decameron*, as eager not to
lose a sense of graceful ease as are the storytellers themselves. In Chaucer's
work, we are forced to lay aside our defenses and our interpretative precon-
ceptions time after time.

The first few tales of the *Decameron* seem to instruct us in the pitfalls of
listening, understanding, and misunderstanding—the ways, that is, of
being an audience. In general, this is accomplished by holding up for our
observation the image of an included audience, whose reaction tends more
often than not to be partial or incorrect. We are called upon to correct such
responses in our own apprehension of the narrative. Out of the experience
of life, nature, and multiplicity on which the *Decameron* ostensibly draws,
we are expected to learn a pose of gentility and tolerance, qualities inextri-
cable from the social perspective of an urban patriciate, observing life, as it
were, from a balcony above the world from which they sprang. In compar-
ison to Chaucer, the tone of these stories assumes rather than leads us to an
awareness of the relativity of memory and worldly truth. Indeed, the tone
and the frame itself assume concord, even about the discord of nature.
Hence, the stories, even when they correct each other, do so organically
and through consensus.

In a famous essay, Singleton (1944) has argued that the frame of the
Decameron liberates the stories from the tyranny of meaning. They are ele-
vated to a species of pure narrative, art for its own sake. It is interesting to
consider the analogous implications for Chaucer's idea of the *Canterbury
Tales*. There, stories that might well in another context be buried under the
freight of their own meaning and moral purposes are freed by being tied to
specific speakers, whose often conflicting motives reveal the values implicit
in the stories to be conditional and relative rather than absolute.

One of the most fertile modern obsessions with medieval fiction has
been the notion of game and play. It is a topic, after all, that Chaucer makes
relatively explicit in the General Prologue. Tales are told to "quit" one
another. The entire conception of the tales told on the pilgrimage is to win
a game, with a specific prize. Indeed, the very holiday spirit of the General
Prologue is a kind of play world, suspended from the rules of everyday

existence. It comes then, as a kind of surprise, to find Boccaccio's storytellers making a peculiar rule:

> Here it is cool and fresh, and, as you can see, there are games of chessboards with which all of you can amuse yourselves to your liking. But if you take my advice in this matter, I suggest we spend this hot part of the day not playing games (a pastime which of necessity disturbs the player who loses without providing much pleasure either for his opponents or for those who watch) but rather telling stories, for this way one person, by telling a story, can provide amusement for the entire company. (1983, 20)[13]

Again, it is almost as if Chaucer is filling in an absence left by Boccaccio's comment here. Of course, in a sense Boccaccio's tales are themselves a replacement for the world of games, but his stricture holds. His tales are replete with games, play-acting and the evening up of odds and are filled with "distressed personages." Perhaps because the world within the tales allows the planned chaos of games to explode with such merciless and random energy, the storytellers themselves must exercise a kind of restraint. Like some of Mann's artist figures, the chaos of their fictions contrasts with the discipline of their lives, however mild that discipline remains here. Such decorum, of course, is as much social as literary, for in a sense they retreat to the countryside in order to continue to be able to regard the world from their patrician frame of reference, almost as much as to flee the plague itself.

The stress on "game" as a metaphor for the performance and invention of these works has become fashionable recently, at least partly as a way of describing this freedom, but such a metaphor masks a deeper problem for the writer. It describes the process of telling the tales; it describes the workings of the tales themselves; it also helps us to read these texts as literature. But for the writers themselves, the notion was more difficult. To equate the making of poetry with the stylized dramatization of life common to the late medieval court was a conception on which both writers depended, but which they were also struggling to leave behind, in the same way that they were wrestling with the vatic stance of Dante. Their challenge was to create an art that justified itself neither by its numinosity nor by its triviality.

Inseparable from this quest was the notion of the importance of literary creation as serious work, a notion that owes more to almost bourgeois notions of humanism than it does with the court's conception of the poet as talented amateur. Both poets seem to acknowledge this in one way or another, Boccaccio, for instance, by his academic career, as well as by the concern of both with reputation and self-development, as if they were aware of their work as spanning a career, as constituting an opus, a canon, rather than pieces tossed off here and there. The very span of their literary plans, the idea of writing so many tales, is in fact a denial of amateurism.

Both writers owe this new seriousness in some part to Petrarch, though both seemed aware—Boccaccio briefly, Chaucer throughout his career—of the crushing weight such a calling could impose.

Chaucer establishes the seriousness of his endeavor by a characteristically comic means, by a kind of anti-spezzatura, woefully aware of the work his narrator has to put in. Indeed, all of his narrators, even his most drunken and tedious, take their task with admirable seriousness of effort. We need only point to the enormous amount of work that goes on in the tales of Boccaccio and in the descriptions of work in the General Prologue to see that, unlike the ideal courtly performer, these writers equate work and being in a rather explicit way that inevitably spreads to a vision of their writing as serious work, too. They suggest that their writing is to be admired even at its most frivolous moments as an exactingly produced artifact, and it gains substantial dignity therefrom. Such a conception may not be totally unrelated to the class origins of these writers. In both cases, at least part of the defense of poetry is a demonstration of the work itself, that such frequently unpromising and unregenerate material could be made into something. This point lies at the heart of the performances as various as that of the Pardoner and the Wife of Bath and is made time and again in the *Decameron*.

The poet, said Petrarch, is not merely a craftsman, like a cobbler or a mason, but someone chosen. He had in mind a secularized version of the prophetic calling of a Dante. Petrarch was, of course, creating a new mythology of poetics, one of great importance for the calling of poetry in centuries following, but not necessarily distant from the concerns of his contemporaries. In fact, Chaucer and Boccaccio reveal a secret anxiety about being regarded as "cobblers," an anxiety Chaucer displays by his display of learning and information on one hand (its "use value"), and on the other hand by his delight in the sheer entertainment value of his work, its dimension as a sideshow to the center of existence. The note of presentation of the *Canterbury Tales*, especially in the General Prologue, its emphasis on its variety, its ability to suit every taste, is less in the manner of the exalted maker offering a book to his patron than in the manner of a merchant displaying his goods. In Boccaccio, a similar note of anxiety is expressed in an almost self-conscious elegance, a distance from the less-than-pleasant portrayal of artisans in the *Decameron*. Chaucer nearly chooses to imitate effort, even when he can write effortlessly in the Italian style. The vatic poet who speaks for the inspiring power beyond his control has a kind of prelapsarian gift. The poet who speaks for himself must work at it.

Implicit in the fictions of both writers, then, is a rejection of the vatic stance devised by Dante, and there is also evident a certain anxiety about that rejection. For having forsaken the quality of vision that allows the apprehension of past, present, and future in a single instant, they are left with the humility of narrative, which, like the humble understanding of mankind in general, proceeds from the beginning, moment to moment, to a given end. Without prophecy, they are left with invention. If we agree with Frank Kermode (1967) that fiction represents the displacement of myth, notably the myth of apocalypse itself, it is far from accidental that the two most inventive medieval masters of fiction should also be the most skeptical about the efficacy of apocalyptic as a way of making sense of the world. They are both poets of the "middle," and it is significant that the beginnings and endings of their works should cause the most trouble or elicit the most controversy, partly because they are themselves divided or troubled about the relation of their poetry to absolute belief and are constantly involved in inventing provisional images to justify that relation.

Rather than a pose of superior sophistication, Chaucer chooses one of naive belief. The result is that the stories themselves are marked by an incomplete and provisional quality, and he can easily manipulate our sense of complicity. In his apparent artlessness, Chaucer generates a series of questions about art and about our own ability to interpret or learn from it. I have argued elsewhere that the progress of *Troilus and Criseyde* uses conventions of listening, of audience reaction, to draw us deeply into the fiction and to turn such devices against our own ways of making sense of the world (1983, 79–102). It moves from rhetoric to epistemology. In a less programmatic way, such a result is also achieved in the *Canterbury Tales*. Even in such details as the portraits of the General Prologue, the moral frame we might expect of such a convention is missing. We are forced to orient ourselves, much of the time in reaction to the naive enthusiasm of the narrator, which calls up in us not sophistication or superiority, but an acknowledgement of our own capacity for prejudice.

What marks Chaucer as a bourgeois poet, if I may be permitted the phrase if only for heuristic reasons, is not his skepticism and pragmatism—for these are also the hallmarks of popular culture—but his shrewd use of these qualities and his ironic smile at the tender and vulnerable tendency towards naive belief. Although Chaucer may seem to be more genially disposed towards the processes of popular reception, and not as exploitative and sardonic as Boccaccio, he is in fact implicated in much the same process of appropriating popular culture as Boccaccio. In a sense, the Pardoner's self-portrait contains in it a faint reflection of Chaucer the artist. One of the chief functions of the frame audience—as with Boccaccio's gentile—whatever their "modern effect," is to assert the most traditional genesis of poetry, to create the illusion of collectivity, and to identify fiction-making with nearly all other medieval arts and sciences in so doing. Such a collectivity in the case of written and individually invented literature is itself a fiction. Part of the fiction of the *Canterbury Tales* is that it is a communal, orally created, collective event: it is an attempt at precisely the version of *gemeinschaft* that the finely observed fissures and contradictions of the General Prologue would seem to have rendered impossible. In embodying his fiction through a series of amateur but identifiable voices Chaucer further complicates the matter of collectivity as he seems to celebrate it, for one of the themes of the *Canterbury Tales*, tales and prologues together, is how collective, public, and traditional schema are appropriated to private and momentary ends. How this contradiction is addressed, and converted into a literary theme, is the subject of the following chapters.

Chapter Five

CARNIVAL VOICES IN THE *CLERK'S ENVOY*

IF THE MOST apparently festive or innocent of Chaucer's tales address serious poetic problems, if not in the most serious way, some of his most "official" tales are undercut, or at least rendered problematic, by the theatrical or festive gestures on which their tellers feel compelled to call. Whatever purpose one wishes to ascribe to the unofficial impulses in any late medieval writings (revolt, satire, subversion, refreshment), Chaucer's comic tales at least initially fit the categories of festive literature. If these categories have any value other than comic relief, however, their relation to the tales of "sentence" needs to be accounted for in some way other than polar opposition. In brief, I wish to argue that the effort at clarification and intelligibility sought by Chaucer's most serious narrators opens the way to poetic difficulty. The *Clerk's Tale* is the first of a series of tales I wish to consider in this light, but I will also briefly discuss the Franklin's and the Squire's performances in the next chapter.

If there is a paradigm to the problems of Chaucer criticism, it is revealed most clearly in the ending of *Troilus and Criseyde*, and in the notoriously various commentary that has grown up around those lines. Another famous passage, the envoy to the *Clerk's Tale*, has also divided critics, but the clarity of the debate has been obscured by more pressing issues such as the significance of the *Tale* itself, the editorial integrity of the lines surrounding the envoy, and the fact that it is the status of the envoy and its dramatic appropriateness to the Clerk that inspired Kittredge's famous essay on the Marriage Group (1911–12). The authority of James Sledd's "The *Clerk's Tale*: The Monsters and the Critics" (1953–54) has been such that the problematic of Kittredge's specific reading, although not the "dramatic" thesis itself, has been suppressed, but Sledd does not dwell on the envoy.

In *Chaucer and His Poetry*, Kittredge repeats his argument that the envoy is "a masterpiece of sustained and mordant irony" (1915, 199–200). He writes, "It is a marvelous specimen of technical skill in metre, in diction, and in vigorous and concentrated satire. None but the Clerk, a trained rhetorician, could have composed it. None but the Clerk, a master of logic and a practiced disputant, could have turned upon an opponent so adroitly." Kittredge by no means settled the matter. Malone could still argue that "the new ending does not fit the character of the Clerk, into whose mouth it is put. . . . This ending is Chaucer pure and simple, naked and unashamed" (1951, 222). More recently, the uncertainty of who speaks these last lines has been stressed, and the textual problems have been reintroduced into the critical controversy (Covella 1970). Although the critical consensus is that the Clerk himself speaks these final lines, the question remains troubling to some critics. My own position is that the Clerk is articulating a poetic problem for Chaucer, and therefore speaking for him.

The stylistic or rhetorical appropriateness of the envoy to the Clerk is of course related to the moral or philosophical appropriateness of the Envoy to the *Clerk's Tale* itself. Tatlock (1907, 162), who also contributed to the debate over the *Troilus* "epilogue," reads the envoy as a "frivolous and ironic" turn after the "obvious mediaeval moral" of the *Tale*. Partly because irony is no longer considered a frivolous Chaucerian issue, attempts to integrate the envoy into the tale have accounted for some of the most interesting critical explorations of the *Clerk's Tale* in the past few years.[1]

Without denying the importance of these questions, I want to focus attention on the envoy not as a dramatic device or mere aside, but as a particular kind of discourse within the *Canterbury Tales* as a whole, a discourse marked by its grotesque, highly personalized, exuberant, and often satirical qualities. Furthermore, I want to consider the envoy not only as an "answer" to the Wife of Bath, but as a comment, admittedly parodic, on the problems of interpretation and understanding. The links and prologues, I believe, are designed as much, perhaps even more, to contribute to a consideration of such problems as they are to create the human comedy or serve dramatic consistency. As much as the theme of marriage or the comedy of human existence, the question of literary understanding forms a central motif in the *Canterbury Tales* and sometimes subsumes other themes within itself.

The evidence seems to indicate that the envoy was added after the tale itself was originally written, perhaps much later. I shall assume, however, that the envoy and the ending were intended by Chaucer and are part of the meaning and context of the tale.[2] The exuberant style of the envoy and some of the lines surrounding it are typical of Chaucer's late style, a style marked not only by a lively feeling for the grotesque, the comic and the creatural, but also by an uncanny sense of what he has already written. As a result, this style manifests a remarkable degree of self-parody and self-quotation, which taken together perhaps reflect a keen awareness of reactions to his writing and his concern about the place of his work in history. Interestingly, this discourse finds its most characteristic expression in performance and festivity rather than narrative or dramatic coherence. The envoy offers a form of discourse typical of unofficial culture and student subculture as opposed to the official doctrine of the *Clerk's Tale* and its moral.[3] It calls upon a parodic and subversive discourse to parody and subvert an already "carnivalized" voice, and the result is problematic both for the Clerk who ostensibly utters it, and, more consciously, for Chaucer himself.

Studies of the *Clerk's Tale* often read the tale as if the envoy and ending were a mere afterthought, and it might be perversely instructive to reverse the procedure and focus attention on the envoy first. What happens if we read the envoy as a poem, separate from its narrative context? It immediately assumes the quality of epistolary lyric, akin to the casual and witty performances of Chaucer's own lyrics. Here, it is addressed to "Wives" and to the Wife of Bath herself by indirection, but it is obviously not a private communication. As in Chaucer's lyrics to Scogan or Vache, the apparent literal statement is less important than the tone, and what that tone communicates about the playful and intelligent relation between speaker and audience (Pace and David 1982, 4).

The change takes place on lines IV.1163, and everything—diction, tone, humor—changes, everything except the control that marks the Clerk even in this moment of relative abandon. The line has about it the air of afterthought or interrupted climax that complicates the ending of the *Troilus*. We simply do not know where we stand. "But o word," he asks. There are many words that follow and not all exactly in the tone of moralization that preceded. Moreover, the very language of the plea suggests entirely another sort of poetic voice, one against which the Clerk has in fact placed himself implicitly, as has his master Petrarch. "Lordynges" is a fairly conventional, perhaps slightly flattering form of address to the audience in romances and narratives of all sorts. But "lordynges, herkneth er I go" recalls the breathless pace of the minstrel, the performance anxiety of the popular romancer. It is precisely that voice which Chaucer the Pilgrim assumes in *Sir Thopas* almost as a comic way of exorcising the pressure of a performance dedicated to pure entertainment, of distinguishing himself from a less sophisticated kind of poet, at the same time as he contrasts his own enterprise, more marginal than that of a poet such as Dante.

"But o word, lordynges, herkneth er I go" is colloquial enough to capture the rhythms of everyday speech. It is difficult to tell whether "lordynges" is merely a polite fourteenth-century appellation, as "ladies and gentlemen" has recently been, or whether it then had the glib and oily quality that it acquires in Chaucer's pilgrims' conversations. Certainly the most notable use of it is in Harry's remarks, and there it is inseparable from Harry's own social assumptions. But the one line in Chaucer that the Clerk's change of voice most clearly resembles is spoken by the Pardoner, "But herkneth, lordynges, o word, I yow preye" (VI.573). The Pardoner in his prologue (VI.329) is engaging in much the same sort of play, with a good deal of malice, suggesting a resemblance between the "lewed folk" before whom he ordinarily performs and the pilgrim audience. The Clerk, too, is outlining the gap between what his story ought to mean and what untutored readers will almost certainly take it to mean. The Pardoner plays upon our fascination with evil, bizarre aberrations, and superstition, which is often embedded in and inseparable from discourse that ought to be pointing us to higher things. It is a "sideshow" performance. The verbal echo is too flimsy as evidence to argue for direct intention, but it does suggest an incongruous resemblance.

The very insistence and flattery of "lordynges" and "herkneth" parody the language of the Host, much as the Host has parodied the language of the Clerk's profession in the Prologue to the *Clerk's Tale*: "I trowe ye studie aboute some sophyme / But Saloman seith, 'every thyng have tyme' " (IV.5–6). Solomon seems to stand throughout Chaucer for a sort of popular wisdom, rather than official doctrine, not only in the *Wife of Bath's Tale* but also in the *Miller's Tale* (I.3524). The Clerk had declared his obeisance to Harry as if Harry were a stern classroom master: " 'Hooste,' quod he, 'I am under youre yerde' " (IV.22). "Yerde" is both rule and stick; the Clerk, a teacher, alludes to himself as a rambunctious schoolboy only unwillingly assuming good behavior. And in the song that follows, the unruly student, playing rather than working, returns. The sense of reversal between master and student is entirely appropriate to the festive nature of the envoy. The envoy is filled with such comic sexual reversals, also typical of festive behavior. Here Harry's mastery of the proceedings and his sense of how stories are meant to be understood, is made fun of, certainly as much as the Wife of Bath's ideas on marriage are ironically praised.

The ending of the *Clerk's Tale* might be read as a comic debate with and accession to Harry's values as he reveals them in his original instructions to the Clerk:

> "Sire Clerk of Oxenford," oure Hooste sayde,
> "Ye ryde as coy and stille as dooth a mayde
> Were newe spoused, sittynge at the bord;
> This day ne herde I of youre tonge a word.
> I trowe ye studie aboute som sophyme;
> But Salomon seith, 'every thyng hath tyme.'
> For Goddes sake, as beth of bettre cheere!
> It is no tyme for to studien heere."
>
> (IV.1–8)

Harry's image predicts the story of Griselde, since both Griselde herself and, in the denouement of the tale, her daughter either are or are about to be "spoused." We know from his outburst at the end of the *Tale of Melibee* and at the beginning of the *Monk's Tale* and the *Nuns' Priest's Tale* that Harry prefers strong and clear definitions in such matters as sexual appearances. His comment may therefore be taken as an arch judgment of the man of practical affairs upon the scholar. He shares with John the carpenter of the *Miller's Tale* a suspicion that too much learning is literally a dangerous thing. It is dangerous here, of course, because it threatens to break the playful mood of the storytelling contest.

As in many of the prologues, Harry seeks both to impress the pilgrims with his knowledge of their calling and to create an intimacy with them in order to encourage their performance, a combination of both psychology and courtesy. In the case of the Clerk, his hearty coaching alludes knowingly to certain university practices, at the same time that it conflates unwittingly two meanings of the word "study." The subtle joke is a play upon an important word for the Clerk, since it constitutes in essence both his work and his thought, which come to much the same thing. Chaucer plays upon two distinct meanings of the word "study," which are not unrelated. The first is literal and uncomplicated. "I trowe ye studie aboute some sophyme," he says. Here, however, he stumbles upon the connotations of "sophyme." He means to imply that the Clerk is involved in some complex university exercise, some feat of logical ingenuity far removed from the practical logic of everyday life. But the word also has shades of meaning not far from our use of "sophism." The technical and popular connotations of the word collide.[4] His second use of the word calls upon meanings not very different from the phrase "to be in a brown study." From Harry's point of view, intellectual activity and the demeanor popularly associated with it are identical and certainly not appropriate for the pilgrimage. His rousing of the Clerk in the General Prologue is almost certainly a reference to the mood, rather than to the activity of study: "And ye, sire Clerk, lat be youre shamefastnesse, / Ne studieth noght" (I.840–41). "What sholde he studie and make hymselven wood?" we are asked in the portrait of the Monk in the General Prologue (I.184). The association between madness and study, which I take to be made by the narrator rather than the Monk here, or, rather, the narrator speaking as if for the Monk, is also one held by John in the *Miller's Tale*. "This man is falle, with his astromye / In some woodnesse" (I.3451–52), concludes John when Robin reports to him Nicholas's state, "He shal out of his studiyng, as I gesse" (I.3467). For John, the line between psychological disorder and study is very thin indeed. Harry realizes the difference, but despite his knowing reference to the *studium*, he displays a similar popular suspicion in his attitude toward "study." And in the envoy the Clerk plays with the implications of such an attitude as they bear upon the uses of fiction.

The *Clerk's Tale* does, as Harry requests, put aside "youre termes, youre colours, and youre figures," the apparatus of learning that someone like Harry might confuse with learning itself:

> Keepe hem in stoor til so be ye endite
> Heigh style, as whan that men to kynges write.
> Speketh so pleyn at this tyme, we yow preye,
> That we may understonde what ye seye.
>
> (IV.17–20)

But stylistic difficulty is not the same as conceptual difficulty, and the Clerk is aware at the end of his tale, as he must be throughout, that his "playn" speaking demands a more difficult and rarified attention than Harry, or many of the pilgrims, are prepared for. His shift to the sort of performances I have indicated—song, minstrelsy, student prank—dramatizes that failure. We simply cannot understand ideas or experiences without personalizing them, without converting them into models or lessons or autobiography. There is a certain pique to the Clerk's comic dramatization of the problem, but his own responsibility for this failure is considerable. The story itself has vacillated between allegorical purity and narrative compromise: the Clerk has sought to achieve the elegance of parable by uniting a fairy-tale plot with a severely abstracted philosophical and theological point, but he seems not to have trusted his audience enough to manage the synthesis (David 1976, 167–69). It is difficult to tell whether Chaucer meant this difficulty to reflect upon Petrarch's version, but the humanist in the Clerk and the scholastic in the Clerk do seem to be at odds.

The next two lines call up a theme typical of monastic and learned satire, the difference between the ways things were and the way they are now (Dean 1977). Here the Clerk contrasts the "past" of his own story, which despite the "tyme of fadres olde" (IV.61), is presented in a relatively timeless, but peculiarly modernized landscape, one localized perhaps excessively with the present. But the present becomes a relatively casual "now-a-dayes," and the place becomes the "toun" that is so often the setting of fabliaux. However serious the point, it is presented with a colloquial casualness. It would be "ful hard" to find "now-a-dayes / In al a toun Grisildis thre or two" (IV.1165). Even Walter would be willing to admit the uniqueness of Griselde. To replicate exemplary figures is to call into question their exemplary qualities, and to reduce the image to a notably unsymbolic quantity like two or three continues the deflation.

This deflation of the signification of Griselde is continued in the explicit monetary image of the next four lines:

> For if that they were put to swiche assayes,
> The gold of hem hath now so badde alayes
> With bras, that thogh the coyne be fair at ye,
> It wolde rather breste a-two than plye.
>
> (IV.1166–69)

Not least of the ironies of the image is that Griselde herself can hardly be said to "plye." The lines recall other lines in Chaucer. Pandarus refers to a similarly proverbial metaphor in encouraging Troilus to be more flexible and patient. The mighty oak may seem admirable, but when it falls, it falls all at once. "And reed that boweth down for every blast, / Ful lightly, cesse wynd, it wol aryse" (II.1387–88). It is rather Criseyde who turns out to be like the reed. Her flexibility, from a realistic and worldly point of view such as Pandarus's, is rather natural and from another point of view marks her distance from an ideal model like Griselde. Most pointed of these lines are the images in the *Wife of Bath's Prologue* about the uses of common vessels. "For wel ye knowe, a lord in his houshold," she says in an image that sounds like an inspiration for the *Clerk's Tale*, "He nath nat every vessel al of gold" (III.99–100). Some can be made of wood. But perhaps more disturbing is the peculiar association with the image of a newly minted coin that Chaucer uses in the portrait of Alisoun in the *Miller's Tale*: "Ful brighter was the shynyng of her hewe / Than in the Tour the noble yforged newe" (I.3255–56). Certainly that the *Miller's Tale* associates Alisoun with a relative measure of money is revealing, as is the choice of the coin, a "noble." But that the envoy chooses such an archetypal monetary image is itself interesting, for it forces us to think of Griselde as part of a continuum that arrives at Alisoun, unless we understood the previous narrative in such a way as to preclude such association. The replication of Griseldes in the previous lines ironically recalls counterfeit—or at least deflated—currency (Dean 1977, 405–6). Merely on the level of imagery, the lines make explicit the implicit relation of this tale to others that have come before, but by presenting the connection so archly and so comically, the envoy asserts that the importance of the *Clerk's Tale* looms larger than that of such a debate or theme: to read in such a way is to reduce it. Even in his farewell and envoy, the Clerk himself comically takes the responsibility for misinterpreting Griselde, as if parodying a process of misunderstanding he is sure will begin.

The next stanza (IV.1170–76) has perhaps elicited more comment than any other in the ending of *Clerk's Tale*, because of its startling mention of the Wife of Bath and "al hire secte." I am inclined to think of the problematic "secte" as a pun, including the legal, gender, and religious definitions all in one, at least partly because a pun would be appropriate to the sort of voice the Clerk is now assuming. Aside from its startling break in decorum and its relation to the Court of Love quality of the "marriage debate," the address has other implications. As I suggested, it ties the ending of the tale to some of Chaucer's short poems and their epistolary style. But the "secte" of the Wife conjures the image of a regiment of women following her antirule like the regiment of poets following Golias (those poets being fond of

titular names such as "Primas" or the "Archpoet"). The voice of the demure
Clerk becomes indistinguishable from that of goliard poetry:[5]

> I wol with lusty herte, fressh and grene,
> Seyn yow a song to glade yow, I wene;
> And lat us stynte of ernestful matere.
> Herkneth my song that seith in this manere.

(IV.1172–76)

The Clerk shows that he can compete with the Squire in song and enjoy-
ment of life. It may well be considered a dangerous revelation, given the
portraits of clerks and of singing, in, say, the *Miller's Tale*, but it shows the
Clerk's ability to join in with, indeed, to match, a certain quality of celebra-
tion from which he seems to have kept some distance before. The Clerk we
saw in the General Prologue is the Clerk in his study. The Clerk we see now
is the Clerk as a student in town, the student as participant in such celebra-
tions as the Feast of Fools.[6]

The lines that introduce the Wife of Bath, "whos lyf and al hire secte
God mayntene / in heigh maistrie," also suggest the festive quality of the
Clerk's humor. The comic reversal of sexual roles, as of most normative
roles, is a constant of carnival imagery. There is probably also a literary pun
here: the "lyf" of the Wife of Bath is not only her existence, it is also her
autobiography (as if her biography were akin to the *vita* of a saint), which
is to say the performance of her prologue, and Chaucer's own text. The
Wife of Bath becomes the very sort of authority against which she argues,
something the Clerk shrewdly seems to understand. Not only does the
Clerk answer her here, but she is quoted within the *Merchant's Tale* and
referred to Bukton by Chaucer himself in another "Lenvoy"—*Lenvoy de
Chaucer a Bukton*—on marriage (29). The Clerk's line freely admits the
literary power of the Wife's discourse and even blesses it in a spirit of plen-
itude that recalls *The Romance of the Rose*.

What marks the envoy most strikingly is its verse form, though we may
forget that in astonishment at its other qualities. However loosely, it uses
only three rhymes throughout six six-line stanzas in an ABABCB pattern. Like
Chaucer himself, the Clerk lavishes the most elaborate care on what he pre-
sents as an ephemeral and secondary performance.[7] The verse form also dic-
tates, in an extremely playful way, what is often a bizarre and comic diction.
Rhymes not only match in a stanza, but each stanzas rhymes with the next,
so it is impossible for a word of a certain level of elevation to sustain its dig-
nity. The stateliness of "assaille" and "faille" in the first stanza of the envoy
would not be out of place in the tale itself, but the second stanza subverts
that level of diction with a slightly less dignified "mervaille," a much less
dignified "tonge naille" and an almost physically lowered "entraille."

This lowering of the diction inevitably results in the animal images that mark the envoy. The "archewyves" are as strong as "a greet camaille" or "egre as is a tygre." However grotesque and exuberant, these phrases recall learned and biblical images, at the same time that they suggest the upside-down world of travel fantasies such as that of Mandeville, who describes places and peoples whose behavior and appearance is as grotesque as the Clerk finds that of the "archewyves." There is a more popular note to the bizarre devouring beast, "Chichevache," who seems to step right out of popular folklore, and whom we find in other writings of a more or less popular nature on marriage.[8] Similarly, the defeated and bound husband is akin to a "quaille," a word which here nicely combines the implications of prey, food and a hint of pity and terror. The noble world of the hunt and the lower—but related—world of the kitchen are combined.

So from one point of view the Clerk seems, like his creator, to have it both ways. He is able to tell the sort of moral tale that many of the other pilgrims have not been able to realize. At the same time, he enters into Harry's spirit of play, if only as an afterthought, and "quites" the Wife of Bath. But the parodic note in the envoy, meant to playfully answer the Wife, in a way reveals a certain triumph of her point, for it reveals a side of the Clerk that he has suppressed in his tale and that has a tradition insofar as his class and his profession are concerned. For such songs, like the songs of the Goliard poets and the pranks of the Feast of Fools, display the carnival anarchy of university celebrations—certainly more pointedly witty and calculated than those of village festival, but nonetheless related in spirit. Yet the very fact that the Clerk must offer this playfulness as a coda to his main presentation is an implicit critique of the limits of his perspective. In the *Nun's Priest's Tale*, for instance, the profoundly comic quality derives from the indistinguishability of unofficial and apparently official cultures. Like his heroine, the Clerk has some problems that derive from the purity of his intentions.

There was a time when critics agreed that the problem of the *Clerk's Tale* was the monstrous Walter, but there is now some disagreement as to who the real monster of the tale might be. There are ways in which Griselde herself seems monstrously passive, or, to be more accurate, passive-aggressive. But behind these "monsters" lurks another perverse sensibility, that of the Clerk. It is hard to think of the Clerk in negative terms. The General Prologue presents him as without doubt among the most admirable of the pilgrims. Yet the Clerk is not without his flaws, more serious than a venal love of well-made books. For that, intellectuals may be admired. But for a greater fault, the tendency to sacrifice human desire and personal happiness to theoretical constructs, the Clerk betrays the human sense of meaning that inhabits so much of Chaucer, particularly the General Prologue. This is the treason of the Clerk, and it is evident in his tale, which in a small way betrays him.

For he embodies one of the characteristic intellectual vices, the impulse to impose abstract order on experience. Moreover, even his humor is suspect. He virtually requires an *ad hominem* argument to make his case. The comedy is drier and less motivated than the similar flyting between, say, the Miller and the Reeve or the Friar and the Summoner. The one obvious motivation, that as an intellectual he is called upon to defend the tradition that the Wife questions, is itself ironic, for he does so in a manner that reflects not the older authority of the Church, but the new style of humanism, acerbic, superior, ironic. The problem is compounded by the fact that as readers we find a natural point of contact in the most silent and literate of Chaucer's pilgrims.

The Clerk condescends in some fashion to the pilgrims. Even in Petrarch's version, the tale of Griselde owes much to fairy tale, much to myth. Petrarch, the Clerk tells us, "with high style . . . enditeth," but the Clerk has presumably "lowered" the tale for us, even if the result is in keeping with the spare elegance of early humanist style. In what follows, he lowers it even further, to the point of parody. In the fashion of parable, the tale seeks to make the complex simple, but the problem with the tale is its complexity, not its simplicity. In its appropriation of mythic device, it embodies the central problem of Christian intellectual life in the Middle Ages: to embody in narrative and image what would seem to be recalcitrant, even opposed to such representation, to protect from misunderstanding that which by its very nature remains a mystery. In so doing, the Clerk, like many patristic authorities, must resort to creating another myth and falls subject to his own critique.

The Clerk's weak point, however, is located precisely in his greatest triumph of wit, the envoy itself. For the envoy reveals a certain playfulness in the Clerk, one missing from his tale, where the only version of play is Walter's sadistic cat-and-mouse game. The envoy explicitly answers and implicitly echoes the Wife of Bath, but its ironic intent is more general, to parody the extremely personalized, even sexualized, form of interpretation that the Wife offers of authoritative texts—indeed, of any story. The Clerk lampoons the tendency of lay readers to search texts for practical advice, to center all speculation on their own experience. He may be thinking of interpreters like Harry Bailly, who only understands the *Melibee* in relation to his own marriage. The Clerk first points out the official interpretation of his own tale and then offers a lampoon of what he regards as the way in which his tale may be misunderstood. The Clerk pretends to be converted, as the knight in the Wife's own tale is converted. But the Clerk's revenge, while only pretending to defer to the Wife, literally defers to her: she controls his words and images as the books she seeks to controvert control her discourse. The allusion to "Ekko that holdeth no silence" (IV.1189) is perhaps a fleeting reference to the Wife's own travesty of the tale of Midas. The Clerk possibly echoes the leonine imagery of the Wife, "Who peyntede the leon?" (III.692) in his sarcastic urging that wives be as fierce as "a tygre yond in Ynde" (IV.1199). However consciously he seeks to parody her method, his own images change from the spare diction of the tale of Griselde to the animal world of carnivalized texts: "Chichevache," the proverbial camel, the fierce tiger.

For some poets, this would indeed be a defense of poetry—or at least of correct interpretation—and we could imagine the poet, not his character speaking. But Chaucer has already displayed his willingness to let interpretation take its own course and to allow meaning to be generated by response. The Clerk knows that this will happen, but he is not happy about it. He seeks to control but knows the limits of his control and has recourse to that sentimentality of the intellectuals, sarcastic irony.

The Clerk's discourse, however, must take responsibility for this process of misinterpretation, and it is that responsibility which is avoided through irony. It is avoided by being forced upon the reader. As a result, the difficulty of the passage becomes paradigmatic, not only of problems of Chaucer criticism, but of Chaucerian poetics, for the Clerk in a sense localizes Chaucer's own most characteristic move, which is to constantly shift the problem of perception and right understanding to the reader. This shift results in those effects we regard as most "Chaucerian," most ironic and most comic, but there is some evidence, perhaps most clearly in the retraction and in the place of the *Parson's Tale* at the end of the *Canterbury Tales*, that Chaucer regarded this central aspect of his aesthetic as problematic. If there is a serious dimension to the envoy and the two stanzas preceeding, it is as a meditation, and perhaps as a defense against the implications of this problem, for the Clerk has made clear what the story should be about. By continuing, he merely resigns himself comically to its inevitable misinterpretation. Yet the question of responsibility cannot be so easily avoided, for if the contribution of Chaucer criticism over the past two decades can be itself misinterpreted to suggest a consensus, it is that the Clerk himself is culpable, taking part in this misinterpretation by highlighting certain dramatic and narrative aspects of the tale itself. In so doing, he "plays" with the reader much as Walter "plays" with Griselde. Chaucer himself, however, is aware in some fashion of the kinship as the Clerk is not. What the Pardoner's performance, for instance, demonstrates is that effect is not always allied with purity of intention and that perhaps the obsession with creatural reality that the Pardoner exploits might well have its own truth.

At least one strain of the commentary on the *Clerk's Tale* has been the argument that the voice in the envoy is that of the poet rather than his character. As Muriel Bowden (1964, 129) succinctly puts it, "to the present writer the satire (surely foreign to the Clerk) and change of meter would indicate that those six stanzas are meant to be the poet's interruption." What I have tried to point out in suggesting an analogy between certain festive forms and the *Clerk's Envoy* is that if we take the Clerk as a type, the satire is by no means beyond him. Still, Bowden and others have a point that is borne out by my constant reference to Chaucer's short poems. The Clerk speaks in a voice that we can call, with some caution, Chaucer's own informal poetic voice, one we find in the more comic moments of the short poems. The extravagant diction, the odd rhymes, the reference to the Wife of Bath as an adviser and adversary at once can all be found in Chaucer's own short "envoys."

We can be sidetracked here, I think, by further arguments about persona, performance, and who is speaking where and when. But what I do want to claim is that the kinship between the two voices accords the envoy some importance as more than a mere appendage to the *Clerk's Tale*. For in his ambivalent and ironic attitude towards popular misunderstanding and interpretation, the Clerk exhibits a secret ambivalence and dependence that Chaucer also manifests. Robert A. Pratt (1966) once wrote an important article on Chaucer's difficult relation to his learned sources wittily titled "Chaucer and the Hand that Fed Him." But Chaucer feeds out of another hand, which he also bites. His attitude towards the nature of popular reception, a reception that has ironically kept the tradition of his poetry alive even during periods of learned neglect, is much more difficult and ambivalent than it might seem on the surface. The Clerk's irony reveals that ambivalence.

It is usually argued that a great deal of satirical poetry, particularly that aimed at the higher reaches of the church hierarchy, has its origins in the Feast of Fools. Taken in its largest sense, the poems thereby reflect the radical urge of comedy: all those who agree to abandon the pretense of authority and imposed order are welcome to the feast; those who do not join in (or pay the celebrants) are excluded or indeed ridiculed. What we find in the envoy is a remarkable twist. The language of satirical Latin poetry is aimed squarely at wives who would impose their own order upon the state of things. But the Wife of Bath's program has already turned things upside down. The Clerk seeks to use the language of unofficial culture to critique that culture.

The problem is that the parodies and travesties of the Wife are already a critique, and the extreme posture of the envoy suggests that perhaps she does not go far enough and does not take her proposals to their logical or illogical extremes. The Clerk is in a sense correct. What is striking about the Wife of Bath is as much her acceptance as her rebellion against the way things are. That is very much her problem: her imagination and her discontents work in opposite ways. But the Clerk has another problem, not unrelated to his own story, an obsession concerning order and control, an obsession from which even the Knight distances himself. The language on which the Clerk calls to answer the Wife of Bath has a life of its own, and looked at carefully it calls into question his own understanding of the very point he raises in appending the song: how we understand stories, how we test fiction against the realities of life.

Chapter Six

POETICS IN THE PROLOGUES

I HAVE ARGUED that the apparently unconscious jocularity at the end of the *Clerk's Tale* disguises what is in fact a considerable problem of poetics for Chaucer. It reveals some of the difficulties in negotiating the distance between popular discourse and high literary purpose. This chapter investigates a similar dilemma in some of Chaucer's most apparently admirable characters, not only the Clerk, but also the Franklin and the Squire. Uncontrollable and recalcitrant forms, the fabulous and the folkloric escape these narrators' attempts to deduce, and sometimes invent, a stable set of literary and social values. This conflict between the anarchically improvisational demands of literary performance and the obsession with values that mark Chaucer's most socially prominent speakers is also dramatized in the discussions preceding the *Nun's Priest's Tale*. In pursuing the implicit aesthetic arguments of these interchanges, I am less interested in character or dramatic consistency than I am in the ways in which Chaucer, consciously or not, externalizes some of the conflicts in his own poetic.

. . .

Some of Chaucer's tale-tellers reveal considerable anxiety about the status of their art, which is to say, about their own status. These are the pilgrims who are most explicit about the self-consciously literary nature of their enterprises: such characters as the Squire (who resembles as much a Renaissance courtier as a medieval knight), the Franklin (who, as has been remarked, has about him all the values of an eighteenth-century country squire), and the Clerk (whose proto-humanism is revealed in his reverence for Petrarch). The tales that they tell also share an interesting problem: an uncertainty, verging on embarrassment, as to the status of the magical, the fairy tale, the wonder that inhabit their plots and link their stories to a world they would seek to leave behind. For all his love of "medieval" paraphernalia, for instance, the Squire ends up constructing the atmosphere of precisely those romances that would prove increasingly fashionable and popular as literacy became widespread (Goodman 1983). In its very exclusion of ethical and philosophical issues it predicts the schizoid nature of what Arthur Ferguson (1960) called "the Indian Summer of English Chivalry." The Franklin also tells a romance, but again the class basis of chivalric romance is turned against itself. The Clerk, in his search to pare down his narrative to essential form, without, however, reverting to allegory, ends up writing something very much like a fairy tale.

Elements of fantasy and fairy tale had always been part and parcel of romance. Auerbach (1953, 123–42) argues that this fantastic element reveals the obsolete position of the aristocracy, who must now define their role in sheerly idealistic plots. It may be argued with equal historical authority, however, that the integration of such simple folk forms as fairy tales illustrates the hegemonic power of aristocratic culture, so that even potentially unruly forms are subsumed to the general thesis of romance. Even Freud referred to the fantasy of many of his patients that they were in fact the offspring of some mysterious royal or aristocratic figure as "the family romance."

In the most theatrically realized performances, such as the Wife of Bath's or the Pardoner's, we find precisely the ironic awareness of fiction and interpretation that marks the popular theater. These characters quite literally use tradition in heterodox and highly personalized ways, playing upon often primitive prejudices and fears, while at the same time forging a certain individual dynamism. The self-satirical and apparently cautionary discourse they engage in can also express forms of discontent and protest that must be avoided by exemplary and virtuous figures. The relative force of Dante's infernal characters is at least partly attributable to this sense of self-definition, but Chaucer includes such discourse in a framework neither apocalyptic nor allegorical.

In contrast, the Franklin, for instance, is concerned much more with the creation of a finished work that explains itself in terms of obvious, included values, even when those values become difficult for his own position. He seeks to be rhetorically and stylistically coherent and self-conscious and to articulate a certain version of modernity. He is concerned, that is, with certain ethical, even proto-humanist, implications of his narrative voice. The Clerk is similarly impelled to stress a particular style and rhetoric and a set of serious values over the efficacy of performance and self-delineation and self-realization. This is not to say that the Clerk and the Franklin tell tales that are less appropriate to them, or that the Wife or the Pardoner do not tell effective stories. But the latter appropriate many more aspects of popular theatricality, while the former seek more to create articulate public and ethical voices—predicting a direction that would become more prominent in fifteenth- and sixteenth-century humanist literature.[1] And this difference, although certainly an aspect of character, is accentuated by their self-presentations and their relative concerns with consistency and the value of their fictions. This is why the Clerk's parody of the Wife's performance at the end of his own tale is such an interesting and important moment, for it demonstrates Chaucer's awareness of his appropriation of one kind of literature and his role in creating quite another, a tradition more civic and rhetorical than most modern versions of Chaucer allow.

The difference in self-consciousness between these different sort of tale-tellers—those who justify themselves dramatically such as the Wife and the Pardoner and those who justify themselves by their ethical consistency—suggests also a radically different orientation to popular mentality. It is perhaps no accident that the Wife and the Pardoner deal head on or play with theological controversies and in so doing express a good deal of ir-reverence. Indeed, even the contempt the Pardoner expresses toward the "lewed folk" is itself part of the self-mockery implicit in such popular irreverence.

What marks the performances of this other group of pilgrims, the Fran-klin, the Squire, and the Clerk, is the lack of integration of fantastic and folk themes in their narratives. Rather, the opposite happens: it is precisely these elements that frustrate the development of either narrative or ideas in their tales. We have the paradox of figures who represent the very social forces that will soon transform the balance of power in aristocratic society struggling not against the values of the present ruling order, but against some older and more amorphous stratum, as if in conflict with their own cultural pasts. If any of the pilgrims represent the creation of a new voice, it is these pilgrims, yet that voice must articulate itself against not so much the styles of aristocratic culture, with which it may politely debate, but also and more inchoately the forms of popular and folk life.

The generic claim of being a "Breton lai" in the Franklin's introduction has obscured the largely performative and self-defining quality of his speech. Recently, however, Anne Middleton's analysis of his tale (1980a) has alerted us to the "self-fashioning" aspects of this introduction. The speech is not a perfectly consistent unity but ties together a number of different literary contexts and traditions:

> Thise olde gentil Britouns in hir dayes
> Of diverse aventures maden layes,
> Rymeyed in hir firste Briton tonge,
> Whiche layes hir instrumentz they songe
> Or elles redden hem for hir pleasaunce;
> And oon of hem have I in remembraunce,
> Which I shal seyn with good wyl as I kan.
> But, sires, by cause I am a burel man,
> At my bigynnyng first I yow biseche,
> Have me excused of my rude speche.
> I lerned nevere rethorik, certeyn;
> Thyng that I speke, it moot be bare and pleyn.
> I sleep nevere on the Mount of Pernaso,
> Ne lerned Marcus Tullius Scithero.

> (V.709–22)

The *Franklin's Prologue* divides into three parts. The first part is concerned, as is Chaucer, with the traditional genesis of tales. In the Franklin's literary history, however, oral transmission and presentation are evidence not of folk origin, but of the noble origins of stories. Like the eighteenth-century readers whom he so resembles, the Franklin promulgates an Ossian-like origin for literary performance. We may take the Franklin's stress on the misty noble origins of story as an example of what is sometimes thought to be his social climbing. Or we may take it as a correction to a modern populist conception of oral performance, that it is somehow always evidence of the creativity of ordinary people. For the Franklin, evidently, oral culture is not necessarily popular culture. In any case, he admits of reading as one of the ways in which noble folk entertained each other.

The Franklin's preface may tell us that a medieval audience did not make distinctions between popular and elite modes quite in the same way we do. As Charles Muscatine (1986) argues in his book on the fabliaux, a "popular" culture may well have been everyone's primary culture, and elite culture, such as that of the court, may have been a secondary, restricted, coterie culture, to which some may have had access in addition to their participation in "popular," which is to say, primary, culture. Chaucer, however, presents this to us as a matter of distinctions being made. Clearly the Franklin feels a certain pride in being able to tell a story whose origins are "noble," and this pride is clearly related to his admiration for the Squire's performance and his disgust with his downwardly mobile son. Perhaps fabliaux were by no means "popular" forms, but Chaucer goes out of his way to have them voiced by appropriately scurrilous characters. So too, perhaps, noble and commoner shared in a common spring of story. But the Franklin highlights the purely noble run of that spring, and he is deeply concerned in his story and his presentation with access to noble values. As a result, the values of his story, themselves ironically dependent on folk-tale for their transmission, are presented as borrowed from a higher and finer social world.

Of course, what the Franklin imagines in his description of the Breton lay is something very much like Arthurian court culture, not our modern, romanticized version of Celtic folkloric improvisation. In the next part of his three-part prologue (ll. 721–28) he moves us from courtly to learned performance. Rhetoric here becomes a matter as much of oral as of written presentation. In the same way as he suggests that he knows about and understands the niceties of aristocratic performance despite his class position, so too does he suggest that in his inability to apply the colors of rhetoric he fully understands the options.

All of this is comically deflated in the last few lines, where, like the Wife of Bath, the Franklin tries to state that his real authority is experience itself, and that the colors of the physical world are his real materials: "Colours ne knowe I none, withouten drede, / But swiche colours as growen in the mede" (V.723–24). He speaks now in the language of a Franklin, or perhaps the language that a scholar or a lord might expect a Franklin to speak in. This is a crucial distinction, because the modesty of these last few lines is as calculated as that of the first two parts of this passage. Of course, one of the ironies of the story he tells is that the colors and shapes of fields and seas may not be exactly what they seem.

The irony of this last point may be taken as a sly witticism on the part of the Franklin, or it may be read as a deconstructive moment. But there is another aspect to the Franklin's obsession with the sources of story, for he shares that obsession with his creator. Readers at the moment may find themselves still in reaction to Kittredge's famous ascription of Chaucer's own voice to the Franklin and his confident assertion that the *Franklin's Tale* is none other than Chaucer's solution to the Marriage Debate and its real conclusion (Kittredge 1911–12, 467). But there is indeed a tone of the poet's own voice here, especially so since the passage is describing the origins of literature itself. This authorial voice is, however, not a solution to anything, for it represents again Chaucer's struggle with the multifarious forces of literary culture.

The Squire, on the other hand, does not describe the literary context of his performance in much detail. He merely accedes to Harry's request to tell something of love. This very modesty, itself a symptom of courtly behavior, parodied in other speakers such as the teller of *Sir Thopas*, is thus a significant act. For Harry, the Squire looks like a lover and so ought to be able to make some literary capital out of his experience. But the Squire elegantly denies this, despite the trappings of the outfit we marvel at in the General Prologue. Rather, he suggests in his denial that his knowledge of love is in fact part of a larger education, one still in process.

This may seem to be a complex way of explaining an embarrassed silence typical of a certain stage of youth. Indeed, as recently as a decade ago, the Squire was seen as a nostalgically satiric figure. He was regarded as an embodiment of what Huizinga (1954) calls "the waning of the Middle Ages"—the gradual exhaustion of aristocratic culture as it flowered in its last blooming (Kahrl 1973). For others, his tale was an example of the absurd turn that romance had taken, and Chaucer's lack of completion a symptom of the poet's own weariness with the joke. But interpretation of the tale has taken a different turn over the past decade. For Anne Middleton (1980a), the Squire is one of Chaucer's "new men," articulating a new and significant concern with the public status of fiction, one shared by Chaucer himself. For Jennifer Goodman (1983), the *Squire's Tale* represents not a parody of decadent romance, but an example of an extremely fashionable new current in fourteenth-century literary culture. Like his clothes, then, these interpretations of the Squire argue for an aura of modernity rather than of obsolescence.

But what is the significance of the Squire's relatively taciturn preamble to a long tale? The answer, I think, is found in the fact that it is the Franklin who provides the afterword, rather than the introduction, to the Squire's poetic. Aside from its actual content, the very reflection of this articulation to the Franklin is significant. For the Squire represents both the best and the most limited in courtly consciousness. Like the courtier who will follow him in the literature of courtesy books, he has a problem with language in relation to the self. Except for highly stylized denials of exceptionality and some self-deprecating laments, praise of self must always be voiced by someone other than himself. Moreover, it is very often action, not language, by the lady, his fellows, or followers, that defines his virtue. To voice it himself, even to explain the process of assumptions, would be to make the entire enterprise vanish. This paradox is also the paradox of the courtesy books. How does one actually explain courtesy? To do so is to render grace graceless and clumsy. The courtesy books themselves, as important as they are for the development of certain strands of thought, are in fact extremely awkward guides to the elegance and grace that they seek to encourage. One born to their highest aspirations hardly needs them. One who seeks to use them too assiduously may render their advice futile, perverting or appropriating their uses to very different ends.

It is this Shakespearian turn to the uses of courtly style that motivates the articulation of the Squire's poetic, spoken not by the Squire himself but by the Franklin:

> "In feith, Squier, thow hast thee wel yquit
> And gentilly. I preise wel they wit,"
> Quod the Frankeleyn, "considerynge thy yowthe,
> So feelyngly thou spekest sire, I allow the! . . .
> I have a sone, and by the Trinitee,
> I hadde levere than twenty pound worth lond,
> Though it right now were fallen in myn hond,
> He were a man of swich discrecioun
> As that ye been!

(V.673–86)

In so doing, Chaucer enacts the social and literary paradox at once. By defining the Squire's self, the Franklin allows us to judge, presumably admirably, his character, but the terms he uses inevitably are ones that the Squire could not use for himself, which also change somewhat the context of his performance.

The Squire becomes, for the Franklin, a model for behavior (defined by the negative model of his own son), in the same way that the virtues the Squire embodies are themselves embodied in the courtesy books. In so doing, a life becomes a text. In the extreme dichotomy of the Squire's performance, on the one hand his modest demeanor and self-deprecating rhetoric, on the other the extravagant and excessive gestures of his narrative, there is evident an effort to avoid precisely the kind of "model" the Franklin sees in him. Chaucer is aware of the comedy and adolescent self-consciousness of the Squire's performance, but he is also aware of its serious and important sides. The Franklin is not stupid (nor is he excessively diplomatic, as some critics have argued, diplomatically praising the Squire in order to save the young man's literary face) but he does willfully rewrite the relation of the Squire's performance to normative behavior.

Equally important, the Franklin historicizes the Squire's values and performance. This procedure, to historicize and to textualize a pilgrim's performance, is one that Chaucer indulges in occasionally: the Wife of Bath is perhaps the best example, as she recurs in the *Clerk's Envoy* and the *Merchant's Tale*, as well as Chaucer's own advice to Vache. In the Franklin's case, it is combined with another Chaucerian response, which is to personalize impersonal forces, to take things not only literally but biographically. But it is this historicization which is the chief unique contribution of the Franklin here, for the values that in the *Squire's Tale* are evidently free of the determining factors of history and geography (as is his tale in its present form) are now phrased by the Franklin as dynamic, historical, and changing. They become subject to redefinition, while in the *Squire's Tale* they were presented as in the process of discovery. One of the ironies of the Franklin's response, and his deep admiration of the Squire's eloquence, is itself the historicization of his images. His son is acting out the negative image of the courtier, one against which recently arrived established figures like the Franklin tend to rail. In this parallel between Knight as father to his Squire and the Franklin as father to his son, there may be some reference to actual social mobility. The Franklin and his son may have a good deal more "propertie" than the Knight and his. The parallel may be a matter of pattern, for this is one of the very few images of fathers and sons in the *Canterbury Tales*, except for the frightening pathos of Hugelino in the *Monk's Tale*. Such a parallel develops another theme entirely, the historical continuity of values and of order, a theme at the center of the *Knight's Tale*. It matters, then, that the universe of the *Franklin's Tale* not only rationalizes that of the Squire and his use of magic and of setting, but utopianizes that of the Knight. In this case, it is the representative of the older knightly class who is presented as "realistic." In his endeavor to yoke utopia with reason, the Franklin predicts the history of his own discourse in following centuries.

.   .   .

If any tale throws itself into the obsessive human dialectic of certainty and uncertainty, it is that of the Nun's Priest. Yet even this tale exists in a position of considerable uncertainty, partly in terms of its place in the *Canter-*

bury Tales and partly in the details of its prologue. Neither problem is unimportant, though the first has been extensively discussed and the second hardly at all.

The first problem is the question of the place of this tale in the order of the tales as a whole.[2] If the *Tales* are regarded as a sequence, this becomes a crucial question, for it matters whether the *Nun's Priest's Tale* comes in the middle or closer to the end. For its remarkable perspective regards all of the concerns of Chaucer and his characters and the literary and philosophical traditions he has called upon. If this anti-summa comes in the middle of the tales it is one thing, if towards the end, quite another. Are we to read the ending of the *Canterbury Tales* as we do Book 3 of the *Troilus*, as a celebration and exultation, comic and generous at once, of human possibility and sensibility? Or are we to read the last section of the *Canterbury Tales* as if it were akin to the end of the *Troilus*, with its somewhat darker and more problematic vision of human existence in time? These quandaries are only abated somewhat if we agree, as seems to be the consensus, that the tale represents relatively late Chaucer, and that its perspective is one of a poet looking back upon the range of his art, with both skepticism about its uses and fondness towards its possibilities. But only somewhat, for if the tale is read earlier, the range of possibilities for the rest of the *Canterbury Tales* are somewhat more limited, as if Chaucer had begun to limit himself. If the tale is read later, it provides a summing up and a critique from a profoundly comic point of view, but its skepticism about human nature and awareness is picked up and amplified unmercifully in some of the tales that follow. The one tale in which Chaucer seems to summarize and include all he has mastered turns out to be a highly unstable center.

The lesser problem of the speakers in the prologue affects the potency and seriousness of the ideas in the tale as opposed to the idea of the tale:

> "Hoo!" quod the Knyght, "good sire, namoore of this!
> That ye han seyd is right ynough, ywis,
> And muchel moore; for litel hevynesse
> Is right ynough to muche folk, I gesse.
> I seye for me, it is a greet disese,
> Whereas men han been in greet welthe and ese,
> To heeren of hire sodeyn fal, allas!"
>
> (VII.2767–73)

In some manuscripts, the interruption of the Monk is instigated not by the Knight but by the Host. Scholars have plausibly suggested that Chaucer might have briefly considered giving these lines to Harry and then reconsidered the matter from the point of view of social niceties or the repetition of Harry's interruption of *Sir Thopas*.

At the same time, this dramatic and formal appropriateness obscures other questions raised by the canceled assignment of the lines to the Host. For in fact they sound different assigned to the Host or to the Knight. From Harry, with some slight revision, we could have argued for an increasingly flat-footed and rude progress in his speech. But from the Knight, the speech requires interpretation as it stands. We can understand why Harry would want the tale to stop, but why should the Knight interrupt at this point?

The answers to this question have been at the center not only of readings of this passage, but of interpretations of the Knight and his tale over the past few decades, and the question raises issues that range widely over the *Canterbury Tales* (Gaylord 1967, Kaske 1957). For in the voice of the Knight, these lines address issues of authority, tradition, and the status of normative ideals in the *Canterbury Tales*. If one major and important revision of these questions has been an explanation of the seriousness and power of tales like that of the Knight, against an earlier condescension towards "medieval convention," another revision has suggested that perhaps the situation is not that clear-cut, and that for all its majesty and for all his virtue, the world of the Knight and the world of his tale are not without limits.

But in fact this discussion of poetics is part of a prolonged discussion that inhabits the prologues and afterwords of many of the surrounding tales. The earlier attempt by Harry to lighten the mood after the *Melibee* generates some of the most interesting comments about the nature of poetry in the *Canterbury Tales*, but it also suggests some equally interesting observations about the nature of the audience of that poetry. Harry's naturalism, for instance, leads him into those peculiar comic speeches, revealing in one case the fabliau-like nature of his own marriage to a wife who seems to combine the worst of the Wife of Bath's verbal threats with the worst social pretensions of the wives of the five guildsmen:

> "For she nys no thyng of swich pacience
> As was this Melibeus wyf Prudence.
> By Goddes bones, whan I bete my knaves,
> She bringeth me forth the grete clobbed staves,
> And crieth, 'Slee the dogges everichoon,
> And brek hem, bothe bak and every boon!'
> "And if that any neighebor of myne
> Wol nat in chirche to my wyf enclyne,
> Or be so hardy to hire to trespace,
> Whan she comth hoom she rampeth in my face,
> And crieth, 'False coward, wrek they wyf!
> By corpus bones, I wol have thy knyf,
> And thou shalt have my distaf and go spynne!' "
>
> (VII.1895–1907)

This explicitly sexual interpretation leads obsessively to his inappropriate flattery of the two prelates, the Monk and the Nun's Priest. To the Monk he says,

> "Thou woldest han been a tredefowel aright.
> Haddestow as greet a leeve as thou hast myght
> To parfourne al thy lust in engendrure,
> Thou haddest bigeten many a creature."

(VII.1944–48)

Harry Bailly strikes us as one of those characters who, through their vivacity and autobiographical indiscretion, burst from the frame of literary convention. There is, however, a ghostly quality to the host in that he mirrors the function of the creator of the poem. He literally takes over from the narrator at the end of the General Prologue. As Gaylord (1967, 235) puts it, "Harry is the Apostle of the Obvious, Chaucer is the Master of Indirection." But in so doing, he displays two tendencies that the narrator also exhibits. One is to draw a portrait of the character addressed, partly for our benefit as readers, but with an ironic result, for Harry's observations are too often off the mark, or, rather, too accurate. It is likely that any of the pilgrims hearing their description in the General Prologue might find something to be pleased at. Indeed, though it is all done from memory after the fact, it is all done with the greatest of tact, as if to avoid libel. But where Chaucer lets us make our own mind up, Harry tells us what to think. (Of course, in the same way that the narrator's nondirective quality is a form of coercion, Harry's bullying has a reverse effect on our value in his judgment.) The other peculiar quality that Harry shares is a tendency to assume some qualities of whomever he is addressing. He imitates in some fashion what he takes to be their habit of speech or mind. Again, there is something of this in the General Prologue (Nolan 1986, Mandel 1977). It is perhaps a habit that Chaucer learned from Dante, who ever so slightly mirrors the quality of whomever he addresses. But for Harry, it tends to lessen empathy, in that he underlines qualities that the character might not want to see, and we are forced to wince at his parody of tact.

Harry is perceptive enough about human character but not particularly helpful in the matter of the uses of fiction and the relation of fiction to social life. What the *Monk's Tale* does is not only defend the Monk's character against infamy, by reasserting his monkishness, but also reinforce the relation of genre to audience. This, for the Monk, is art, in which history and fable are one. It is in this effort to reinstate the estates of literature, as of men, that the Knight's reply to the Monk must be read. The moment has usually been explained in terms of the Knight's tact—that Harry, confused as to the profusion of sententious fiction that he presumes to approve of, fails to stop it, and that the Knight, symbol of order on the pilgrimage, steps in to balance the scales, "for litel hevynesse is right ynough to muche folk." On another level, the Knight means to suggest that the Monk's strained seriousness is also ultimately philosophically flawed, in that it leaves out the Boethian distance from Fortune that makes the difference between philosophy and pessimism. Harry, now converted by the greater authority of the Knight, belatedly adds his criticism, which is an attempt to rephrase the Knight's tactful speech, but which seems mistakenly to criticize the Monk for not showing that Fortune has a good side. "Swich talkyng," says Harry in a tone-deaf metaphor, "is nat worth a boterflye" (VII.2790). He says that if it were not for the jingling bells on the Monk's bridle, he would have fallen asleep. Harry's naivete gets right to the point, for the jingling bells show up the pretensions of the Monk's philosophy. What both damns and redeems the pilgrims is not philosophy but personality. Their ideas are never displayed independent of their embodiment in this or that person, which perhaps accounts for why debates as to who is right or wrong still go on.

In the abstract, the Knight's objection is expressed in philosophical terms, but it can be seen to be representative of the perspective of his class. The Knight tends to see the values appropriate to his position as appropriate to society as a whole. A member of the armed nobility would indeed object to the fatalism of monastic history—their very definitions of history contrast. In answering the Monk, the Knight defends a chivalric conception of human action, which would seek to emphasize a degree of mastery and control of human action and affairs. Notably, his protest is not selfishly justified, and he raises the discussion to a level far above that of social class and position.

Of course, the Knight's interruption bears with it some serious thinking and reservation. His own tale was painfully aware of the limits of human action. To act with prudence is one thing, good for rulers or any people with responsibilities. But the Monk's "tragedies" are the tragedy of any action. The debate, as always in Chaucer, is ironically qualified in the struggle between ideology and character. However conventional the content of the debate, the frame and the personality of the speakers complicate matters. The *Melibee*, the *Monk's Tale*, and the Knight's speech all say what we would expect to be said, but not always from a speaker we might expect.

These different conceptions of human action and their literary representation are part of the subject of the *Nun's Priest's Tale*, which takes them up by sending them up. It has been pointed out how it satirizes all our pretensions about human order by parodying rhetoric, which is the linguistic counterpart to that order. But the tale also concerns itself with rhetoric as a series of conventions about communication, how we address and thus affect our audience. The Nun's Priest, as if bemused by Harry's flattery, constructs a fiction that ravages those who do not pay attention to the jingling of bells or would disparage the butterfly of language. The tale is the last defense of poetry in the work, unlike the Manciple's and the Canon Yeoman's, which question and even attack the uses of fiction.

Like the *Nun's Priest's Tale*, which parodies this concern, the *Monk's Tale* attempts to order the world on a historical pattern. Its failure engenders the Knight's concern, since he seeks to do much the same, but with a more profound awareness of the difficulties involved. For the Monk, the world is sad, but simple. For Harry, the world is equally simple, if only comically sad. Indeed, we see in Harry's response to the *Melibee* and his overture to the Monk a suggestion of the theme to follow. Again, Chaucer works his way into and out of his tales with an associational and parodic series of borrowings and suggestions among his characters.

Harry has responded to the *Melibee* in a wonderfully inappropriate way, autobiographizing its political and moral message, lowering it to the commedia dell'arte level of his own marriage. Here we find the image of marriage in the *Wife of Bath's Tale* and in the envoy to the *Clerk's Tale* presented as an actual experience rather than as a prescription. The Monk, both virile and unencumbered by women, represents for Harry a certain kind of ideal. But he is aware of the difficulty of this ideal, and he addresses this difficulty by a historical paradigm, that in this decadent age, all the real men are in the cloister. Laymen, exhausted by the perverse demands of modern society, can no longer assume their rightful place. Even humankind shrivels as a result: "Religioun hath take up al the corn / Of tredyng, and we borel men been shrympes" (VII.1954–55).

It is a remarkable diatribe, and shocking in its intimations. The Monk reacts with clerical decorum. He is offended by Harry's innuendo. Yet at the same time the tales he tells are not unrelated to Harry's speech, which images a pattern of decline. Like Harry, the Monk sees decline everywhere and seeks to trace its pattern. This effort is probably doomed from the start, for the Monk seeks to offer an interpretation of history that denies the possibilities of human history. Even his opening remarks suggest that the most obvious ordering of even monastic chronicles, simple chronology itself, will not be followed, for he cannot quite remember it straight. This excuse is echoed elsewhere; it is Harry's complaint after the tale is stopped that the presentation is such that he isn't sure of the message. But more oddly, the Monk's excuse about proper order recalls a much more striking moment in the General Prologue, when the narrator himself tries to put the pilgrims in proper order.

The Knight's interruption of the Monk, however welcome, is itself fraught with difficulty. One could take the Knight's speech as being more comical than this, to say that his wish for another turn of the wheel (VII.2775–79) and his stress on his own response ("I seye for me. . . . As it thynketh me") is a rationalization of his own social position and his discomfort at the thought of himself being subject to fortune, but this would be to discard the evidence both of his tale and of his prologue. Were the interruption by the Man of Law, for instance, perhaps the only other pilgrim with the social standing to interrupt at this point, we might so take it, but it matters that the Knight speaks. He asks for balance and for the possibility of human control, which, in however compromised a form, Theseus seeks in his own tale. If this speech reveals anything negative about the Knight, it is that he seems to have lost the perspective he has as narrator of his own tale and identified once again with its efforts and ideals rather than its disturbing distance on those efforts and ideals. The teller of the *Knight's Tale* can hardly stand on the laurels of having told a light tale, or one that shows both sides of fortune's influence: it does in one way but in another does not. Of course, the Knight is quite right in pointing out the lack of balance or relief in the Monk's tales. Oddly, he does not suggest the obvious question of length—that it would be equally jejune to tell the sort of tale he asks for in the form of the Monk's monastic exercises.

The Knight's apparent aesthetic of scholastic integrity is reinterpreted by Harry Bailly in a much more unidirectional affective aesthetic. As Harry says, there isn't much point in making a point if there isn't anyone around to listen. Harry here articulates his own dislocated aesthetic: first, that the only use of literature is for its immediate audience's delectation, and, secondly, that it should provide an immediate moral or point or use. In a more sophisticated form, this is an old and honorable poetic position, but it does not leave very much room for other modes of existence of literature. He makes his point by saying that he did not quite catch the Monk's point—"I noot nevere what." Harry is not that stupid, and no one could have failed to catch the Monk's point, but Harry is reduced to that level of skeptical articulation by his own bullheaded poetics.

In contrast to the Knight's criticism that a serious moral requires also a serious breadth of vision, Harry returns to his consistent see-saw version of poetics, that we must have both seriousness and frivolity, both entertainment and edification. He is most pleased when both occur as a result of the same performance, but his strategic aim is balance. This sometimes results in odd contradictions, for instance, his tendency to take the most abstract lessons, such as that of the *Melibee*, and apply them very practically to his own life, while skirting around the scandalous personal attacks between the pilgrims, which motivate the most entertaining of the tales. The Nun's Priest responds to this most fully, because he in fact indulges in a literary scandal, pulling the metaphysical rug from beneath most of the narratives we have listened to so far, yet he presents this as a moral lesson. The *Nun's Priest Tale* also negatively fills Harry's prescription without Harry quite realizing it. For the tale entertains profoundly under the guise of a moral, but that moral could be replicated or separated or read in a thousand different ways. On this metaliterary level, then, the tale suggests the signature of the poet, for the Nun's Priest, in his acceptance of his charge, rewrites Chaucer's most concise defense—"Blameth nat me"—as "But I be myrie, ywis I wol be blamed" (2817).

Harry's largely separable, rather than integrated, view of art results also in the series of "judgments" he makes in this link. He suggests to the Monk that he draw upon his experience—tell us something about hunting, he says—the first and last resort of the creative writing teacher. The Monk has a right to be insulted, of course, for not only his hunting but his monastic learning is part of his experience. In reaction to this assertion of a lack of consonance among exterior and interior states, a question not without application to the uses of language and rhetoric, Harry empirically changes his strategy and turns to the Nun's Priest in the hope that a lack of consonance may in fact be the very key he seeks. The Nun's Priest is not dressed particularly well, and his horse is unkempt and, unlike the Prioress' dogs, apparently underfed. The old classical connection between the control of the rhetor and the horses of rhetoric may not apply after all. Despite this, of course, Harry's physical categories remain the same, for he is as impressed with the Nun's Priest's masculine appearance as with the Monk's. He may not mind the Clerk appearing "maidenly" and reticent and telling a serious and perhaps even depressing (despite its ending) story, but for the Monk to do so amounts to a betrayal of the relation of appearance and reality, or language and its referent, if we are to take Harry's references to clothes and horses as metaphorically descended from medieval metaphors for aspects of language.

The Prologue to the *Nun's Priest's Tale* is more than a contribution to the roadside drama—the Knight's place as a principle of order within the frame—or of roadside comedy—Harry's inflated jousting with the Monk. Insufficient attention is paid to the most glaring fact here, which is that this is the introduction to the *Nun's Priest's Tale*. And the Nun's Priest, we know, says very little. Why is such an articulate poetic fashioner not given a place to explain his own poetic principles? One answer is characterological. It may well be in the nature of this sly and intelligent man, surrounded by and subject to the Prioress and her nuns, to simply listen in wry amusement at what is said around him. (In the fabliau world he will have a sexual rather than linguistic analogue: the apparently mute farmhand who is taken in by one nun after the other in the convent at which he works, a tale found in its archest form in *Decameron*, Day 3, Story 1).

But the question may be regarded from another point or points of view. The Nun's Priest's poetics are revealed here, but indirectly, as with the Squire, who must have his poetic program articulated by the Franklin, just as the values he represents are to be codified in the literature of the gentleman, courtly behavior adapted to wider, and utterly changed, circumstances. In the case of the Nun's Priest, however, his poetic context is revealed not by the statement but by the form of this prologue. For the Nun's Priest works by means of parodying and contrasting dissonant voices, inverting levels and register, toying with the desperate human needs for communication and understanding. Like the narration of his tale then, his prologue reveals a series of voices, cacophonous and hopelessly at odds with each other's meanings, while he stands aside and admires the sound and light—or heat. It hardly needs to be said that this is in a sense the mode of Chaucer himself, both in an actual creative sense and in the role he casts for himself, early on in the dream visions and as the narrator of the *Canterbury Tales*.

The ultimate irony of the Knight's remarks is that the Nun's Priest tells exactly the sort of tale the Knight asks for, but in such a way as to call into question the bases not of the *Monk's Tale*, but of the Knight's own tale. The *Nun's Priest's Tale* is the true Monk's last tale, and his secret revenge against the Knight. A consummate tale-teller himself, the Nun's Priest may be taken as avenging any sort of censoring, or even of editing, within the work. In his tale, two conflicting tendencies within the *Canterbury Tales*, towards infinite Scheherezade-like replication and towards silence of various sorts, are unified. He himself is relatively silent and self-effacing, and his tale, for all its glorious language and twists and turns, is a parody of our efforts at naming things and seeking to control them through language.

The central place of parody in the *Nun's Priest's Tale* is itself a sign of the tale's special status in the workings, if not the order, of the *Canterbury Tales*. It stands at once as the most perfect example of their art, or the baldest revelation of the scandal, of the *Canterbury Tales*. The *Tales* have been often described as an anthology of medieval literary forms, but it would not be amiss to describe them as a parody of medieval literary forms. Either in their structure or their style, or in the context in which they are set, traditional literary attitudes are caricatured, if not subverted. Nor does such a description reduce them. Literary languages all over Europe engage in a parody, and sometimes a travesty, of the very languages they seek to replace. At the same time, these languages also parody the register and ranges of sublanguages and dialects that grow all around and beneath them. In a formal sense, this is also true of some of the great works of early modernism. Joyce's *Ulysses* consists almost entirely of parody, and Eliot's *Waste Land* includes the languages and dialects of modern life as forms of a new Babel.

This sense of playfulness and parody must certainly have inhabited some sectors of the court and the circles in which Chaucer moved—not, perhaps, the official and ceremonial center of court life, but the culture at the fringes of the court. Chaucer's short poems give us a glimpse of this little world. Although one suspects it was imbued with more self-importance, the *pui*, if it had much importance in London literary life, would also have had the air of contest and competition that we see in the *Canterbury Tales*. One imagines that if Chaucer played a role in the operations of such a guild, he would have done so with mock modesty, by a gentle comic outdoing, excelling his competitors by pretending not to.

Parody and playfulness of various sorts are shared by early humanism, but to a different end. If Petrarch is an example, they represent in a sense a new conception of the literary monument as precisely that, a monument. In inventing literary history as we know it, Petrarch introduces a secular canon of authorities. The humanist conception of literary history, far from celebrating heteroglossia and plurality, makes a claim to hegemony. Oddly enough, most preabsolutist and prehumanist court culture had more in common with popular culture in displaying an awareness of its provisional and consciously structured nature.

Even the most differing interpretations of Chaucer in the past decades have sought to place him as one of the last representative poets of the Middle Ages. But that status implies a certain central and magisterial place against which I suspect the parodic art of the *Canterbury Tales* works. From a sheerly literary point of view, Chaucer's art seems a devilishly inspired program to "outdo" the available variety of genres, themes, and types. He not only does it all as well as or better than anyone else, but also does so in a fashion that makes anyone who comes after necessarily be implicated in parody. The painful avoidance of irony in fifteenth-century poets is in a sense a way of going on anyway, for to admit to the implications of Chaucer's irony would be not to write at all. In a sense, "the father of English poetry" shares with some of the other "strong" poets that Harold Bloom (1973) describes a potential for inducing a crushing anxiety among his poetic descendants. Interestingly, Chaucer's attraction to parodic and ironic contexts derives at least partly from a lack of security about vernacular and secular poetic possibilities. The parody of the *Canterbury Tales* extends to the forms and genres themselves, for by having certain tales parody others, the work as a whole calls into question the prerogative of any forms to represent reality. By collocating subversive popular cultural voices with more learned parodic literary traditions, Chaucer engages in a difficult maneuver, for either end of his spectrum of voices, festive abandonment or metaphysical distance, constantly invades and calls into question the balance and moderation for which he has always been praised.

Chapter Seven

THE NOISE OF THE PEOPLE

THIS CHAPTER seeks to contribute to an ongoing revision in our under-
standing of what may be called Chaucer's politics. In place of a detached,
perhaps self-protective, skeptical, moderate, and reasonable Chaucer, cur-
rent studies, some conservative and some methodologically radical in their
approach, have given us a Chaucer much more deeply implicated in four-
teenth-century controversy, particularly the crises of schism, rebellion, and
authority that plagued England then.[1] Chaucer studies had avoided this
position for a long time, partly because of the assumption of a certain
Chaucer behind the text, partly because of a critical enterprise concerned
with making a case for either Chaucer's literary coherence or his theological
and philosophical significance—an enterprise that depends upon an as-
sumption of stability and stasis. The presumption of a Chaucer, or a Chauc-
erian text, serenely removed from crisis and disruption is one rarely held
now, despite the construction of such a presumption as a straw man by
myself as well as others.

Instead of pointing to issues of explicit policy, however, I seek to locate
what I would have liked to call Chaucer's political unconscious, had the
phrase not already become part of our critical lexicon in other ways. This
chapter centers on some apparently minor moments in Chaucer, moments
when an analogy is made between social disruption and what might be
stylistically identified as popular voices, moments that result in narrative
crises of one sort or another. This chapter returns to some of the issues
touched upon in Chapters 2 and 3, which now appear in a more powerfully
disturbing context. I want to point towards certain moments in Chaucer
that represent a pattern of containment and release, a formal analogy to
Chaucer's ambivalent and difficult relation to the power of popular dis-
course, most intense when it seems most parodic and scornful, and fre-
quently distant when it seems most respectful. My argument begin on the
level of imagery and moves towards larger and larger formal structures, in
an effort to suggest the uses of one of the most fertile critical endeavors of
the past few years, the close interaction of historiography, critical theory,
and literary analysis.

I shall concentrate on four problematic passages, though I shall allude to
other works as well. The first is a peculiar description of the Trojan parlia-
ment in *Troilus and Criseyde* (IV.183–96), "The noyse of peple up stirte

thanne at ones," variously glossed as a punning reference to the revolt of 1381 or to Chaucer's own experiences with Parliament. Here the forms of discourse taken in most *Troilus* studies to be synthesized break out in open conflict. The apparent and perhaps conscious identification with the political and linguistic restraint of aristocratic authority is called into question by the power of disruptive imagery. In this passage, public language, frequently allied with alliterative poetry, is criticized as profoundly limited. However tragically the resolution is imagined in *Troilus*, however stoically in the *Knight's Tale*, the result is not easily explained by recourse to traditional Boethian paradigms. Whereas courtly restraint is represented almost as an attempt to resist or deny history, popular voicing is represented as one of history's several agents.

My second example is an equally puzzling reference to the revolt of 1381, this time in a comic context, at the end of the *Nun's Priest's Tale* (VII.3375–3400). Here the apparent neutralization of the highly charged political reference is in fact only apparent. Chaucer conflates this peculiar allusion with a description that most resembles, of all his analogues, the *Roman de Fauvel*, arguably and controversially one of the earliest literary records of the charivari. The "noise of the people" is represented in animal form in the tale. However articulated through the rather different subversiveness of clerical play, the passage accords considerable power to this noise. My third example is Saturn's speech in the *Knight's Tale* (I.2458–69), which also refers to the rebellion and popular complaint, but this time in a sardonic and frightening context.

My fourth example will be the ending of the *Miller's Tale*, which, although it has no direct reference to the revolt, has, as several critics have noted, some at least poetic analogy to it (David 1976, 90–107; Patterson 1987a; P. Olson 1986). The image of community we find at the end, however, has the ambiguity of Bakhtin's "carnivalesque." The potentially revolutionary force of the "voice of the people" breaks through in some of the less direct images I have discussed, but here, in its most direct representation, it is muted by its articulation as festive release.

This last point relates to what might be called a methodological rather than Chaucerian conclusion, for it addresses the problematics of using precisely the "new historical" (as distinct from "new historicist") materials I have called upon here, particularly those that have appropriated anthropological and poststructuralist methodologies. The explicit move of this enterprise, open among anthropologists, sometimes disguised among historians, is the attention to context, setting, and motive that once fueled the New Criticism. Yet the stasis and idealism that lay at the end of the exercise of literary reading is now no longer possible. Specifically, the model of festivity as release and refreshment, a controversial position in the interpretation of such festive materials, which I have admitted may well be the

case at the end of the *Miller's Tale*, is revealed as a Chaucerian position and
not necessarily historical reality. In other contexts and other apparently less
threatening voices than those of the Miller, in contexts, that is, that seem
less subversive, Chaucer accords to popular voices considerable power.

As for my Chaucerian conclusion, what I seek to locate on a microscopic
level is something I have tried to describe on a larger scale in the previous
chapters: Chaucer's difficult and ambivalent relation to the power of popu-
lar discourse, a discourse on which he depends for much of his own poetic
power, but whose implications he is compelled to constrain. The result of
this strategy of containment is a poetic and political stance that we might
take to be more benign and distant than it is.

·   ·   ·

My first example is a strange possible pun that occurs in Book 4 of *Troilus
and Criseyde*:

> The noyse of peple up stirte thanne at ones,
> As breme as blase of straw iset on-fire;
> For infortune it wolde, for the nones,
> They sholden hire confusioun desire.
> "Ector," quod they, "what goost may yow enspyre
> This womman thus to shilde and don us leese
> Daun Antenor—a wrong wey now ye chese—
>
> That is so wys and ek so bold baroun?"

(IV.183–90)

The paradisiacal bliss of Book 3 has ended. Calchas, Criseyde's father,
makes overtures to have her join him among the Greeks. The point under
discussion is an exchange between Criseyde and the Trojan Antenor (who
will eventually become a traitor). Hector has just made a resonant aristo-
cratic defense of Criseyde, "we usen no wimmen here to selle," an allusion
in its own way to the origins of the war. But the "peple"—who here be-
come metonymically one with the Trojan Parliament—dismiss his defenses
almost by dismissing an entire courtly code. Their bald, cold, military rea-
soning is not itself wildly irrational (the image of possession is probably not
superstition, but a way of asking Hector if he has lost his reason), but the
shouts and murmurs that precede it and that are no doubt the tenor of the
famous image—"as breme as blase of straw iset on-fire"—are described
with such contemptuous force that they overpower the entire exchange.

The possibility of this allusion is a possibility of a pun, and it is arguable
to what extent Chaucer uses puns. The pendulum seems to be swinging in

favor of Chaucer's wordplay, but to what extent is still an open question. "As blase of straw iset on-fire" may refer to Jack Straw, whose name appears as a leader of the Peasants' Revolt, and who may well have been symbolic rather than historical. Gower makes a similar pun in Latin, which we are meant to catch, in the *Vox Clamantis*. But the identitification of this parliament with the rebels of 1381 is by no means an open-and-shut case, even if, as Chaucer might have known, their deliberative procedures are more reasonable than that of Parliament itself. The other possible reference here, generally regarded as even more doubtful, is to the Parliament of 1386, which may have put Chaucer in some jeopardy, as it indeed put some of his friends in more than jeopardy (Brown 1911, McCall and Rudisill 1959, Fisher 1964). The identification of either allusion, to the Merciless Parliament or to the Peasants' Revolt, rests on less-than-solid evidence. But if the possibility of allusion exists, I see no reason why Chaucer may not have conflated into this image two expressions of group action, politically very different, but both hostile to his political position, indeed, to his position in general.

The power of this image suggests something about the strange alternation of decisive action, usually military and legal, on the part of Chaucer's most admirable aristocratic or royal figures, and their curious passivity or fitfulness, usually in the face of confrontation or consultation with popular deliberative or appellant bodies. The list is long and various: Theseus takes pity upon the train of weeping women; Walter agrees to give up his bachelor existence and marry; Hector's stern speech has no consequence. We do need to consider the possibility that Chaucer is engaging with current political controversies surrounding the questions of advice and the prerogatives of rule (P. Olson 1986; Patch 1930), perhaps even criticizing the impulsive tendencies of some of his superiors, but we also need to keep in mind that narrative is not the same as legal record, and that Chaucer is under no obligation to provide a complete account of the administrative and consultative deliberations of his characters. In general, these actions, or inactions, are presented as positive virtues in the context of the narrative. Under the circumstances, Hector and Troilus act as best they can, for to take what we would regard as decisive action would be to continue the cycle of sacrifice, abduction, and imprisonment that generates the violence and chaos of the Trojan War itself. Nevertheless, the understatement of these nobler characters is continually drowned out by what Chaucer calls in an ironic but loaded phrase the "noise of peple."

This is, moreover, one of the few places in Chaucer where the verbal associations of alliteration, not as we find them in common speech, but as we find them in alliterative poetry, are given full weight. The Parson dismisses the possibility of alliterative poetry ("I kan nat geeste 'rum, ram, ruf' by lettre" [X.43]) but he is after all dismissing the possibility of speaking in any sort of verse. The politics of alliterative poetry are still a matter of question to my mind, even if we accept Elizabeth Salter's (1966a and 1966b) correction of the old Hulbert thesis, which proposed that alliterative poetry was consciously fostered by a largely northern baronial elite as a nationalist antidote to what they perceived as the soft dangers of a southern cosmopolitan and internationalist Ricardian court. Salter established that the audiences were interchangeable. It has never seemed to me impossible that these audiences may have imagined themselves in different roles, even politically, in different venues, but all that is beside the point. What is to the point is that if I hear correctly an alliterative echo in the image describing Chaucer's Trojan Parliament, Chaucer is associating a dangerous popular blindness with a certain Langlandian tone. In the *Parliament of Foules*, the birds speak almost by nature in alliteration as they dismiss the discourse of their betters. Moreover, these echoes, even if I am hallucinating them, may underline the twist that the very conception of the *Troilus* offers to its own tradition, for many of the other great late medieval versions of Troy either are in or call upon alliterative verse and at the same time more prominently highlight the aspects of public experience that the *Troilus* renders only rarely.

One way of regarding this complex is to stop at that point, to say that Chaucer regards mass, popular, or even democratic action as bad and self-serving, out of kilter with the harmonious and hierarchical way things ought to be. And if there were some way of having Chaucer reappear and articulate his politics editorially he would probably come close to saying something like that. But set against the experience of the poem, popular response acquires a different significance. For this disturbance parallels other disruptive forces within the world of this fiction, not least of all the processes of history itself, partly expressed through the vicissitudes of the plot, partly expressed through the background of war and violence. Even erotic experience, benign in Book 3, is attended by images of disorder in Books 1, 4 and 5. These various disruptive forces, social, historical, and sexual, are only temporarily contained by the heroic action of princely figures such as Troilus and Hector. The *Troilus*, whatever the class origins of its stylistic traits or the class valence of the narrator's distance from the action, subsumes its values to that of its aristocratic, even royal, central figures. These figures stand almost as individual, rather than class, heroes, against the vicissitudes of history and the unreliability of the social order. History itself is perceived through the filter of our and the narrator's reconstruction of the perspective of the noble characters. Chaucer allies himself with this focus of values, even as the work itself reveals the limitations of those values against the disorienting forces of time, society, and nature, which no longer seem to align themselves with the ideology of the protagonists. The passage we are looking at, as a stylistic and narrative moment, encapsulates the larger pattern that the poem as a whole projects.

But the political implications of these stylistic tensions are ambiguous, as they are in Chaucer's *Knight's Tale*. The official and expressed approval of heroic aristocratic action is set against much more powerfully disruptive chthonic forces, and, as in the *Knight's Tale*, the power of poetic imagery tends to stress the gaps, fissures, and limitations of hegemonic culture. I will turn to an example of that imagery momentarily, but in the context of discussing another example of the "noise of the people" and its attendant historical allusions, at the end of the *Nun's Priest's Tale*.

· · ·

The profoundly serious, even tragic, representation of popular disruptive-ness is not the only Chaucerian response. Another famous topical allusion to the Peasants' Revolt is contained in a peculiarly unfunny joke in the *Nun's Priest's Tale*:

> So hydous was the noyse—a, benedicitee!—
> Certes, he Jakke Straw and his meynee
> Ne made nevere shoutes half so shrille
> Whan that they wolden any Flemyng kille,
> As thilke day was maad upon the fox.
> Of bras they broghten bemes, and of box,
> Of horn, of boon, in whiche they blewe and powped,
> And therwithal they skriked and they howped.
> It semed as that hevene sholde fall.
>
> (VII.3393–3401)

This is the scene at the end of the tale, in which the widow, the animals of the barnyard, even the bees buzzing out of their hive, form an Edenic alli-ance to rescue Chaunticleer, who relies also on his own newly discovered wit. Here again we find the association of revolt—Jack Straw and his co-horts—with pure noise.[2] But the tone of the reference is ironic, even fes-tive. Although it is sometimes mentioned in a catalogue of analogues, no one to my knowledge has suggested the association of this scene with the bizarre Dionysian parade of the *Roman de Fauvel* (1914), or with the ritual of charivari to which that parade may be the earliest literary allusion—here set in a political rather than erotic context (Ginzburg 1981).

To point to festive, even carnivalesque moments in the *Nun's Priest's Tale* seems almost redundant. But the association of this moment with Jack Straw and 1381 and one of the most ferocious episodes of the revolt is something else again and repays close attention. "Turneth agayn, ye proude cherles alle!" This is what Chaunticleer, acting as a speechwriter, tells the fox, who holds him by the neck, to say. He continues with his prompting: "A verray pestilence upon yow falle!" "Pestilence" may in fact denote a number of ills and diseases, but it is impossible that it does not bear the freight of black humor, referring to the Black Plague. Nor can the aristocratic disdain of line 3408 not remind us of Richard II's contemptuous dismissal of the rebels: "Rustics you were and rustics you are still."

Chaunticleer's script for the fox conflates the two great cataclysms of late fourteenth-century English society, the revolt and the plague, yet it does so by placing them in this ironic context, so that their horror is rendered comic. Moreover, the arrogance of the speech is a parody of an aspect of aristocratic discourse, the other side of courtliness. But like some plays within plays, it is only rehearsed and coached. The fox cannot both act and speak, and as he voices those words, which proclaim his power, he becomes powerless, and Chaunticleer escapes.

Earlier scholars who were fascinated with the roman à clef and topical possibilities of this tale may have been barking up the wrong tree, but at least they were barking. The story is not politically topical, but it does address questions of language and power, even if through a parodic inversion that makes it difficult to say what its politics are. The playfulness and wit of clerical misrule allow a comic improvisation on the most serious questions, and it is in the tradition of clerical misrule to make language play an instrument of power.

The words are not magical. The fox does not recite them and thus free Chaunticleer, he merely verbally agrees to say them: "in feith, it shal be don" (VII.3414), "don" because part of the speech would announce the fox's actual eating of Chaunticleer. No doubt some wicked sacramental parody is behind this particular joke, but for our purposes it is more important to point out the paradoxical humor of Chaunticleer's speech, freeing himself from powerlessness by voicing for someone who holds him within his power a defiant and arrogant expression of contempt for "cherles." As in the *Miller's Tale*, the discourse of courtliness and its parodic inversion becomes the means by which peasant cunning, the almost palpable weapon of the powerless, becomes manifest. Chaunticleer is both courtly and a parody of courtliness, both powerful and powerless.

His speaking, a deferred and quoted discourse never voiced in its apparently intended context, speaks as if in the voice of authority, while its parodic quality actually establishes it as part of the noise we hear in the lines following, the noise of the people, however disguised as animals the revelers as rescuers might be. Expressed in the archly sympathetic tone of the Nun's Priest, the description of the animal pageant of this chase, and particularly its "rough music," ends in one of the images typical of apocalyptic rhetoric: "It semed as that the hevene sholde falle." It only "semed swich," of course, since this is the Nun's Priest's voice, and one of the constants of clerical parody is a parody of apocalypse itself, from the eschatological jokes of the *Apocalypsis Goliae* to the utopian caricatures of the *Land of Cockaigne*.

But even so it links this barnyard revolt with the terrifying apocalyptic appeals of the anarchic peasant rebellions chronicled in Norman Cohn's classic study, *The Pursuit of the Millennium* (1963; see also Bloomfield 1964). Apocalyptic thinking was of course by no means limited to the dispossessed. Apocalyptic themes inform most of the other great fourteenth-century works: *Piers Plowman*, *Pearl*, *Vox Clamatis*. In all these works, apocalyptic transformation is deferred or qualified, but it is nevertheless important to note that Chaucer alludes to this obviously central chord in his culture only indirectly, and only in comic moments such as this, when it may serve as a metaphor for something else.

Nevertheless, metaphoric vehicles can have a life of their own, and whether intentionally or not, the festive chase collates an allusion to the rebellion and its "noise" with the eschatological and millenial hopes that provided its primary ideological framework. Chaucer and the Nun's Priest refer to this matrix ironically: the tone of "they yelleden as fendes doon in helle" is hardly laudatory. It may allude to the chronicles of the uprising itself, which of course refer to the horrors of the mob in such conventionally extravagant images, but it also may be read as a theatrical allusion to the devils in the mystery plays, for in those plays noise, and rebellion and gossip and rant, are automatically associated with those who frustrate or deny a divinely designed plan.

.   .   .

Within the world of such works as the *Miller's Tale* and the *Nun's Priest's Tale*, however differently they handle "the noise of the people," this matrix of apocalyptic imagery, rebellion, and festivity are merged in relatively liberating or at least renewing ways. But some of the same ingredients are included in a much more problematic way in the *Knight's Tale*, particularly in Saturn's great speech to Venus, in which he promises to assist her in guaranteeing victory to Palomon:

> Myn is the stranglyng and hangyng by the throte,
> The murmere and the cherles rebellyng,
> The groynynge and the pryvee empoysonyng;
> I do vengeance and pleyn correccioun,
> Whil I dwelle in the signe of the leoun.
> Myn is the ruyne of the hye halles,
> The fallynge of the toures and of the walles
> Upon the mynour or the carpenter.
> I slow Sampsoun, shakynge the piler;

> And myne be the maladyes colde,
> The derke tresons, and the castes olde;
> Myn lookyng is the fader of pestilence.

(I.2458–469)

And in the next line he says to Venus, in what may be read as Chaucerian humor, "Now weep namoore." A peculiar and savage movement takes us from Saturn's opening line, "my deere doghter Venus," to "myn lookyng is the fader of pestilence," so that Venus herself is implicated in the forces of anarchy and disease. More to my point here is that we find the disruptive and festive imagery of the *Nun's Priest's Tale* and the *Miller's Tale* presented in a frightening and sinister, which is to say its original, context. Indeed, in some smaller way, the same tone as Saturn's speech can be located in the description of the Trojan parliament, which in a sense is a harbinger of ruined towers and treacherous plots to come in the Trojan legend. Antenor will prove a traitor. The metaphor of fire that describes the murmuring of the people there will become literal in the destruction of Troy. As in the association of images in the *Nun's Priest's Tale*, Saturn's speech associates noise and rebellion, "the murmere and the cherles rebellyng." Rebellion is associated syntactically with the pestilence with which the catalogue ends, and with the imagery of ruins and toppled towers that resounds through the passage.

Saturn's speech, in its frightening grandeur, is often paralleled with the terrifying imagery depicted in the Temple of Mars: the sow eating the child in the cradle, the cook scalded by his own food, the hunter killed by the wild bears who are his prey, the carter run over by his cartwheel. And it true that the chaos of these images derives from a similar inversion of the normal order, a world turned upside down. But the difference between Saturn's speech and the Temple of Mars is even more important, for what the Temple of Mars portrays (however symbolically) is the acknowledged reality rather than the repressed fantasy of the knightly world: this is the reality that their activity, war itself, creates. It is not controllable in any real sense, and it represents part of what Theseus seeks to avoid by mandating the tournament. But it is an extension of the aristocratic ethic, and one it is prepared to acknowledge.[3]

This is not the case with Saturn's speech. The disorder it projects is not one continuous with the imposition of authoritarian order: it is that which escapes and confounds that order. Saturn voices those forces that, although we may see them partly as humanly motivated, the world of the Knight can only entertain as disruptive natural eruptions, a sort of unnatural nature.[4] So the plague and the rebellion and apocalyptic images are equated. That is, the *Knight's Tale* and these other festive moments such as the end of the *Nun's Priest's Tale* agree on all the signs but disagree as to their value. The *Nun's Priest's Tale* represents as comic and liberating farce what the Troilus and the *Knight's Tale* associate with historical tragedy. The *Canterbury Tales* repeats itself, the first time as tragedy, the second time as farce.

.   .   .

But there is a complex mediation between those poles, one that we might take as innocent, even the very ceremony of innocence. It is the *Miller's Tale*, particularly its ending. For here the festive and communal imagery profoundly politicized elsewhere is represented as a safety-valve for danger-ous social forces. In the world of the *Miller's Tale*, the noise of the people is laughter at their own foibles, which while renewing and celebratory, and even in its own way democratic, is so profoundly taken with the comedy of all possible human actions that it renders action itself comic rather than transformative, or even, as it is in the world of the Nun's Priest, associated with power. In typical Chaucerian complexity, the festive release itself is ineffective, for the Reeve's response, and even the Cook's, suggest divisions within the ranks that finally dilute the sense of threat that this inventive and improvisational popular discourse might contain.

Indeed, the *Miller's Tale* announces itself as revel, as festival. It stresses the gap between public rather than private enactment of revels, and in so doing suggests an observation of the physical source of such revels:

> Ther was the revel and the melodye;
> And thus lith Alison and Nicholas,
> In bisynesse of myrthe and of solas,
> Til that the belle of laudes gan to rynge,
> And freres in the chauncel gonne singe.
>
> (I.3652–56)

In the largest sense, the *Miller's Tale* is itself a revel, and the specifically sexual use to which the word is put here reveals a witty determinism as to what our revels are all about. The embodiment of the *Miller's Tale* as festival, not only as including images of festival, is here made clear. Even its language manifests an expressive as well as a descriptive dimension. Its most significant statements are anarchically preverbal or paraverbal: "Teehee"; "I wol crie out 'out, harow' and 'alas' "; the laughter of the neighbors at the end. In its combination of verbal mockery and physical abuse, the tale embodies the rough music of popular festive forms.

The *Miller's Tale* hides behind its comically proper language the brutal directness of popular wisdom.

He knew nat Catoun, for his wit was rude,
That bad men sholde wedde his simylitude.
Men sholde wedden after her estaat
For youth and elde is often at debaat.

(I.3227–30)

It presents as polite and literary "debate" the festival spirit of charivari pro-
testing mismatched marriages. The language of the *Miller's Tale* has a
starkly bodily and sexual quality even when it seems not to. This is also
revealed in the veiled wit of Nicholas's revelation to John, but occurs
throughout:

"And after wol I speke in pryvetee
Of certeyn thyng that toucheth me and thee.
I wol telle it noon other men, certeyn."

(I.3493–95)

There are enough puns on "pryvetee" in this work to alert us to another
level entirely here, but the "certeyn thyng that toucheth me and thee" is not
only the situation, but Alisoun's body itself, her "pryvetee." Not only does
the language of the poem describe intellectual activity through sexual or
bodily analogues, language itself seems equivalent to sexual activity. The
nearly parodic rhyme scheme only barely rhymes in its most explicit cou-
plet: "As clerkes ben ful subtile and ful queynte; / And prively he caughte
hire by the queynte" (I.3275–76). The *Miller's Tale* is replete with self-
quotation and references to other moments in the *Canterbury Tales*,
though it is perhaps not nearly as full as that of the Nun's Priest. It echoes
other tales and characters with a subtle verbal quotation that is as sophisti-
cated as its humor is rough. Nicholas's pretensions are not unique, though
his books "grete and smale" certainly recall the Clerk's volumes of Aristotle,
also alluded to ever so lightly in the devilish wit of Absolon's portrait, "In
twenty manere koude he trippe and daunce / After the scole of Oxenforde
tho" (3328–29). In the fashion of great farce, the transposed qualities of
the Clerk and the Squire, who represent socially authorized versions of
everything the Miller is not, are mirrored in Absolon and Nicholas.

The references to the play of Noah that run through the *Miller's Tale* are
not only parodic. At the end, as at the end of the *Nun's Priest's Tale*, there
is an effect not very different from the end of the biblical Flood narrative,
in which the unity of the entire community, animals and all, is affirmed. It
is a moment similar to the images of festive community, and sometimes the
dances, at the end of the late romances of Shakespeare. Such archetypal
endings stress the sense of festive renewal and of purification—from false
morality as well as from corruption—that breaks down the boundaries that
divide us from nature and from each other. Whereas the apocalyptic images

of the other passages I have discussed are either satirically or seriously threatening, the *Miller's Tale*, like the Flood, has only been a test.

At the end of the *Miller's Tale*, Chaucer's most direct ascription of popular discourse (for even if the literary origins of fabliaux are aristocratic, Chaucer presents the tale as if it were popular performance), the potentially subversive festive action is presented as the laughter of the community at its own members. On the one hand this laughter represents a sense of freedom and breadth of vision that is its own way subversive, but on the other, it seems to suggest that the renewing power of the *Miller's Tale*'s festive discourse is a matter of release rather than revolt. In the other images of popular disruption I have pointed to in Chaucer, we find a serious, even threatening, political dimension missing here.[5]

There is of course no reason why Chaucer should be held responsible for a Zola-like representation of historical reality or a Brechtian explicitness about the political implications of his narrative. Yet the contrast is problematic for two reasons. One is that Chaucer himself allows even a dangerous power to the voice of the people elsewhere, when it speaks indirectly. The other is that we may be tempted to read the action of the *Miller's Tale* mimetically anyway, to argue that its sense of innocent release is precisely the function of medieval festival.

The place of such subversive currents in Chaucer has a curious analogue in debates among historians and anthropologists. The charivari is perhaps an example of such a debate. Lévi-Strauss (1969, 285–342) puzzles over the peculiar reaction of Brazilian Indians to an eclipse of the sun. They sought to dispel the aberration by banging on pans and chanting in a way that struck Lévi-Strauss as remarkably similar to charivari festivals in his own France, which bemoaned ill-matched marriages in their communities. The underlying analogy, he decided, was a protest against the reversal of the natural order of things. It was this comparative and structural conclusion that motivated the response by E. P. Thompson (1972), in which he argued that such popular festive forms have functions that change historically, that they can be appropriated to specific political and cultural crises, and that their meaning derives from their function within the life of their community. It is not, I think, terribly off the mark to see this debate as the beginning of the interesting synthesis of anthropology and history, with its stress on context and political purpose, that one sees in the work of Geertz (1973), Davis (1976) and Ginzburg (1980).

This is what I have tried to do, to pay attention to the context of Chaucer's festive imagery. The result is that instead of the mythicizing and dehistoricizing tendency of such studies—and even Bakhtin, on whom I have depended so much, is a problem here—I find that Chaucer frequently speaks against himself, at times obscuring, and at other times revealing, the power of the "noise of the people."

But this is more than a matter of Chaucer's opinions. I said in opening this chapter that I wanted to help define Chaucer's politics, but I have ended up writing as much about his poetics. That is because my argument has been that his poetics are his politics, his politics are his poetics. Chaucer's ambivalent and problematic relation to the power of popular discourse is in fact a reflection of, even an allegory of, his own making of poetry, which appropriates the power of popular performance and response as it distances itself from it, at least partly by the process of the fictionalization of its own apparent origin as hearsay, gossip, just talk. Indeed, at times, Chaucer seems to be aware of, even celebrating, the anarchic power of his own poetry. The next chapter, by way of conclusion, turns to these moments.

Chapter Eight

FORMS OF TALK

FROM VAUCLUSE, Petrarch writes to complain of the vogue of poetry writing among the inhabitants of Avignon and its surroundings. He complains that he can barely leave his home:

> Carpenters, cloth fullers, farmers have deserted their plows and their other tools to talk about the Muses and about Apollo; I am not able to tell you how far this plague has spread, which a short time ago affected few men. . . . I seethe in my home and hardly dare to go out in public; indeed frenetic men run to me from all directions, arguing, asking questions, grabbing. . . . If it spreads further, it is all over: shepherds, fishermen, hunters, plowmen, even the cattle themselves will moo in verse and will chew only poems for cud.[1]

Petrarch's parody of the Avignon literary scene could be a fair description of Chaucer's *Canterbury Tales*, though Chaucer seems to appreciate rather than scorn the resulting melange. Of course, none of the Canterbury pilgrims crowd around Chaucer the poet. Either he is much less famous or much more modest than Petrarch. He apparently celebrates the possibility that ordinary people have the capacity to engage in poetic discourse, that even, under certain conditions, the "cattle themselves will moo in verse." Chaucer inverts the articulate disdain that Italian writers level against popular understanding and interpretation. Although it is unlikely that Chaucer could have come across any of Petrarch's famous letters, there is a good deal of circumstantial and some direct evidence to suggest that he was familiar with his conception of poetry. I want to consider, that is, the *Canterbury Tales* as an answer to Petrarch's nightmare. In their literary performances, the Canterbury pilgrims themselves externalize the "noise of the people" inscribed in the imagery described in the last chapter.

Perhaps as a function of what it imitates as much as a reflection of the conflict between oral and written forms of memory and entertainment, the *Canterbury Tales* always negotiates playfully and carefully its status somewhere between talk and writing. Indeed, it presents talk as high art. The reason for this is more than a simple transition from a public, oral mode of presentation to a private, individual, written mode.[2] At least for the late Middle Ages, it would seem that such an assumption is fraught with complexities (Eisenstein 1979, Stock 1983). Given the way books were read in early modern and late medieval Europe, they encouraged rather than silenced conversation. They literally gave people something to talk about. Hence, the bookishness and source-oriented quality of the *Canterbury Tales* by no means contradicts its status as an imitation of verbal gesture, talk, and gossip. If one chooses to savor books silently, as Petrarch and as Chaucer the narrator of the dream visions seem to, it is in isolation from the local community and in communion with a similar body of readers from antiquity to posterity. Of course, reading aloud often has its private uses. The Wife of Bath's learned husband reads to her from his book. In fact, the respect for books that we find in Petrarch and in Richard de Bury—and in Chaucer—ought not mislead us. From the point of view of some of the pilgrims, the silent and individual study of a character like the Clerk might be regarded as the slightest bit peculiar.

Chaucer's poetry obscures any easy distinction between orality and literacy, subsuming both to a more generalized category of performance. This theme of performance and the performances themselves negotiate dialectically between talk and text, so that we are never entirely sure where one begins and the other leaves off. The blurred distinction may be observed in Chaucer's own self-presentation of the *Canterbury Tales*: it is a book, but it is also a record of what the narrator has heard. This dichotomy suggests yet again the uneasy relations between official and popular cultural forms in the *Canterbury Tales,* for we conventionally associate literacy with official culture and orality with popular expression. But Chaucer's work suggests that this dichotomy may not be so easily drawn.

There has traditionally been an assumption that the skeptical, realistic, and empirical strain in Chaucer derives from bourgeois values. In the rationalist and humane balance of his vision, we see embodied the values of early capitalism and the access to knowledge on a broad scale implicit in the age of print. But in fact the experiential, empiricist strain in Chaucer is nearly always in contrast with books and authorities, and represents, as often as not, a residue of oral and popular culture, a suspicion of, at the same time as it rewrites, official and institutional culture. It is not the literate and stylistically consistent Clerk who is the most radical member of the pilgrimage, and certainly not the Merchant. Rather, it is the Wife, whom the Clerk seeks to refute, and who refers to books and learning in them with the particular tendency towards bizarre and concrete reinterpretation that marks oral and popular sentiment.

The contrast between books and lived experience is not just an idea addressed in the work: it is embodied in the very experience of Chaucer's poetry. In the same way that the fiction of oral address is built into texts that stylistically and formally are written and meant to be read, so too is the theme of knowledge gleaned from books, also something of a fiction.[3] Chaucer has the habit of presenting what is often nearly journalistic observation as if it were something he had read somewhere. At other points, as we know from many studies of the General Prologue, he presents hoary commonplaces as his own inventions. For all the explanations of the conflict between innocence and authority in sociological or literary historical terms, it is a conflict that finds its expression most radically at the level of our experience of reading the text, which thereby itself becomes an authority.

Whether or not the *Canterbury Tales* are read as drama, it is clear that their immediate fiction is as forms of speech. The tales presume to be the record of the pilgrims' talk. Such talk takes a number of forms. In a world before print communication of much scale, talk assumes an importance and variety of functions: gossip, news, instruction, encouragement, argument, the expression of intimacy. Obviously talk has been superseded by other media for the more public of these purposes. The *Canterbury Tales* is on one level a written document attesting to the importance of talk. But there are many forms of talk, and the *Canterbury Tales* embodies various official and popular forms: the talk of the court, the talk of the marketplace, the talk of women, apprentices, students, the poor, the rich. There are other medieval texts that imitate this variety of speech. What is unique about Chaucer's text is the manner in which it embodies as well as imitates such talk. Even the most rudimentary forms of conversation, the language of traders, the language of children, make comments about their own volume, tone, or intelligibility. Chaucer's forms of "talk" comment on the act of speech itself. As courtier, politician, Londoner, diplomat, let alone poet, he must always have been alert to the varieties of register, the unspoken behind the spoken. Even in the most touching moments of the *Book of the Duchess*, the cacophony of the *Parliament of Fowls*, and the very subject of the *House of Fame*, there is much talk about talk.

As the *House of Fame* demonstrates, however, the distinctions between popular and courtly forms of talk and between gossip and news form a thin line. This blurring of distinctions is no doubt part of the poem's meaning, but it is also part of Chaucer's style. English did seem to have had comparatively free intercourse between popular and aristocratic forms of speech; even before "bastard feudalism" the English aristocracy never required the elaborate class markings of French court life. But it is clear that what Chaucer saw as a subject for comic aside in the early poetry he gradually came to regard as substance for his later poetry. What marks these assumptions towards talk and gossip in the earlier and later poetry is as much the attitude of the included audience as it is the attitude of the poet. The frenetic, consuming obsessions with news and gossip in the *House of Fame*, which paradoxically sounds more like a marketplace than a court hall, contrast radically with the relatively genteel patience of the pilgrims, who admittedly, have less use for news and the status it confers in a place of power like the court.

Throughout the *Canterbury Tales* we must trust the world of the speaker. Spoken conversation, anecdote, and tale become a way of discovering and dealing with the world. The array of genres, types, characters, and even the world and historical perspective stretching from the classical past to the present day, from England to Tartary, seem unprecedented, auguring the mastery of the geographical and commercial world that the Renaissance would usher in (Zacher 1976). But in another sense it is a world communicated, even reduced, to conversation, hearsay, and anecdote. This reduction is evident in a local, detailed sense, in the nearly deliberate exclusion of the here and now of London, the slightly off-focus shift of the beginning of the *Tales* to the suburbs and the continuation away from the city. But even as the stories get under way, our attention focuses on the journey, not the place, and especially on the stories that are meant to pass the time. Even the places that the poet "knows" are slid over—a bit of London, a bit of Oxford. Even the Italy that Chaucer knows is notably represented in stories that give little sense of place. Hence, our perception of reality is always dependent on the details chosen by the speaker. Although this is so in all literature, there is a degree to which most narrative fictions pride themselves on providing data for readers so they may make up their minds themselves. Here the secondary and filtered nature of reality is stressed.

This speaking voice, as much as the world to which it refers, is the reality of the *Canterbury Tales*.[4] This is not to say that some tales are not excessively formal, or even impossible as "talk." Chaucer is aware that common speech can be as deadening as court discourse. Moreover, the nuances and rhetorical ploys in which many characters engage are those that Chaucer uses to great advantage in the early poems. That talk might be a form of entry into a poem, giving the illusion of intelligibility and accessibility, was something that he could have learned from texts as available as the *Romance of the Rose*, which is almost entirely talk. Indeed, what Chaucer learned from Jean de Meun and both learned from the languages of popular culture was that even the most abstract and forbidding categories could be given the illusion of immediacy by being represented as talk.

Chaucer even refers to his own presentation in oral terms. The pilgrimage will unroll before us "as I telle." The phrase has about it a pseudo-minstrel air, and carries on the fiction of popular presentation. In Chaucer's terms, "poetrie" is something Dante or Petrarch or Virgil does. Chaucer himself will only "telle," like the voice of apparently popular romances. At other times, he uses the term *endite*. The term has scribal and rhetorical connotations, although Ovid also apparently "endites." Chaucer will also ascend to call himself a "maker," a more honorific title, but hardly a vatic one. Of course, in the *House of Fame*, where the question of poetry and its sources is one of the points, Chaucer is by analogy learning about poetry.

But perhaps in circling around the term, he is suggesting that he seeks to accomplish something not normally regarded as "poetic" in either the prophetic or the courtly sense. It may well be that much of the "talk" in the *Canterbury Tales* is a form of anti-poetry, or poetry in spite of itself. Chaucer manages an explicit emblem of such a transformation in *Sir Thopas*, where his voice is in the register of the popular minstrel. Like some modern writers and artists, Chaucer seems to play with the limits of what is or what is not suitable for artistic representation. The text of the General Prologue, however artfully constructed, exposes raw conflicts in the appeals it makes to us: as book, as high rhetoric, as journalistic observation, as pilgrimage, as procession, as just talk.

Conversation, in common or elevated speech, is one of the remarkable strengths of much medieval narrative, as Chretien or the *Gawain*-poet illustrates. Indeed, it is partly this conversational ventriloquism that is behind the obsession with "drama" as a metaphor, as I explain above. What medieval narrative poets do well is also what some eighteenth- and nineteenth-century dramatists also do well. Partly this conversational mimicry is a result of finely tuned ear for society and social level in medieval narrative, but even in relatively abstract narrative ordinary talk is managed surprisingly well.

The characters to whom the modern reader is liable to react as the most "realistic" in Chaucer—and this includes characters in other works than the *Canterbury Tales*—are precisely those in whom the rhythms and diction of popular speech are most clearly featured. What we perceive as realism is the style of speech appropriate to the interchanges of everyday life. In this sense, "realism" is not only found in the speech of lower-class characters; Pandarus and Criseyde and the Eagle in the *House of Fame* all speak in the style of everyday speech. Indeed, Chaucer suggests the perspectives, objects, sounds, and sights of everyday existence less by extensive description than by the inclusion of certain images and frames of reference in the speech of his characters. Food imagery, domestic imagery, animal imagery, all are found not as fixtures in the Chaucerian landscape, but as "sayings" in the mouths of his characters, usually as proverbs, oaths, or homespun metaphors. Thus, instead of fixing our perspective on the action through naturalistic description, the language of his most "realistic" characters involve us in an unreal, or perhaps surreal, relationship to phenomenal reality: quotidian existence is embodied in forms of talk that keep us shifting from one plane of social life to another, that suggest relationships between speakers (or between the speaker and us) rather than draw portraits or genre scenes that we may disinterestedly observe.

The meeting point of popular and learned wisdom is the proverb. Indeed, proverbs often consist of wisdom that official knowledge has repressed or rejected. Although not the only or the most prevalent aspect of

everyday speech imitated in Chaucer's "real talk," proverbs seem to be es-
pecially noticeable, perhaps because they are self-contained and quotable
units—critics and readers end up using those proverbs in the same way as
Chaucer's characters. Again, perhaps because proverbs are part of "natural
speech," a wide range of Chaucer's characters use them, and it is the ques-
tion of how they are used and misused that seems to be at issue. Proverbial
knowledge may be parodied, but at other times Chaucer's speakers can use
proverbs in speeches of some dignity and elevated importance. For
Chaucer the poet, proverbs are less gems of wisdom than texts he can set
within various contexts and contrast with other forms of discourse and
knowledge.[5]

Proverbs themselves are implicated in the difficult circle of popular and
elite cultures. For by their very form—the fact that they are quotable and
separable from an extended learned context—proverbs lend themselves to
transmission to a popular audience, by mottoes, songs, and sermons. At
the same time, the expression of proverbs in elite literature is often as a
commonplace, generally acknowledged by all, and hence claiming to be
general, if not folk, knowledge. Proverbs are probably one of those forms
circulated from one stratum of culture to another and back again. As with
fabliaux, however, Chaucer makes it seem as if a genre not entirely popular
in origin or reception were "naturally" popular. It is not only the love of
proverbial wisdom by the middle classes that in following centuries that
makes his proverbial statements seem "popular": it is rather the way in
which his speakers use these phrases.

Popular sermons, which feature on the one end an elevated single speak-
ing voice, and on the other end a silent multitude, are subject to a similar
conversion in Chaucer. The condition of the *Parson's Tale* approaches such
a final authority, but in fact it is not based on sermons, but on specific
written manuals. Elsewhere in the *Canterbury Tales*, particularly in the re-
markable performances of the Pardoner and the Wife of Bath, we find the
influence of sermon language more directly evidenced. As in sermons
themselves, little dramas and dramatic dialogues are set within the larger
discourse, and the level of language at one moment soars to that of theolog-
ical speculation, and the next sinks to street language and gossip. This is
also true of tales themselves, like that of the Nun's Priest (Gallick 1975 and
1978). The style of the speaker constantly imagines and responds to the
response of the listeners, even when it has, now wittingly, now unwit-
tingly, created that response. The language of these latter performances
more nearly approaches dialogue, even when the characters seem to be
engaging in what we now call "dramatic monologues." Their speeches are
filled with the language and utterances of others, and everywhere they
seem to be answering questions and responding to comments so that one
could reconstruct a whole set of questions asked by imaginary interlocu-

tors. All of these performances are imbued with a sense of the provisional status of language, and they are prepared to abandon one level of diction for another as the moment demands. All speak as if, indeed, on condition that they do not always and consistently mean what they say.

This stress on talk may help us to think of the settings of the *Canterbury Tales*—and by this I mean not just the General Prologue, headlinks, and endlinks, but also the ways tales are led into and out of by their tellers—in ways less dependent on a pictorial metaphor, the notion of "framing," and more responsive to an explicitly linguistic metaphor, the idea of quotation. Indeed, the tales, even the roadside drama, are forms of retelling, forms of direct discourse, and as such are a complex layering of direct and indirect discourse. They are, as a sociologist (Goffman 1981) has recently said about so many of our responses, "forms of talk." Like talk, and unlike fine writing, there are shifts of position, internal contradictions, ironic self-observations. The sense of quotation implies the sense of dialogue rather than the sense of absolute statement that could be claimed by some of Chaucer's stories. We need to be attuned to the ways in which meanings are created or qualified by the same means talk is, by interruptions, pauses, qualifications, or meanderings. The notion of quotation, rather than framing, may help us notice that texture. Such an enterprise both borrows from and contradicts the basic impulse of much practical criticism, which seeks unity and coherence in formal literary statements, whereas I am suggesting that we look for the ways in which a poetry like Chaucer's seeks to create and complicate meanings by the disruption of coherent statements.

Much of the talk in the *Canterbury Tales* is "traditional" in the sense that speakers are repeating information they have gotten elsewhere. Of course, this is the definition of communication, but it is more than a redundant observation. That is, jokes, gossip, news, or "tydings" are first heard by the speaker and then repeated to another group or member of a group. Their importance is in creating a sense of kinship among the speakers as much as in communicating information. When the speakers of the *Canterbury Tales* quote from books, they footnote carefully. When they tell their stories, they are inventing and performing, but the assumption, spoken or unspoken, is that the story was first heard elsewhere. It is the originality—the "modernity"—of Chaucer that he places traditional story and its art in the mouths of concrete and historically defined characters, so that their impulses and individual quirks and personalities "make it new." What he alerts us to is that the meaning of a discourse may be as much its context as its text. But the implications of this are revolutionary: tradition itself may be then regarded as a series of contexts rewritten for special and momentary purposes. Perhaps the received meaning of any of these stories may themselves have been a historically limited interpretation. In the *Canterbury Tales*, in its form and way of addressing us, rather than in its content and doctrine, the disturbing political implications of the conflict between literate and traditional society can be located.

This is not the place to do yet another close reading of the General Prologue to establish what it is "really about," but I would like to point to a set of details that might be regarded as suggesting that it is at least partly concerned with degrees of literacy and literary taste and versions of literary transmission. The General Prologue underlines the capacity of the pilgrims to articulate their literary and sometimes subliterary efforts through speaking, singing, reading, and writing. For some of Chaucer's tale-tellers, how they talk is important as a way of defining who they are. Indeed, even their portraits in the General Prologue stress their performative and interpretative abilities, their literary competence as it were.

The General Prologue, particularly as Harry Bailly announces the rules of the game, is filled with overt and covert references to the art of poetry. The pilgrimage will be a metaphor for as well as premise for the writing of fiction. Such images include the narrator's famous disclaimer (720–46), the Host's description of the contest (790–800), which not only induces a legal consent to his laws (784–87) in a manner that resembles Chaucer's own previous allegiance to the laws of the God of Love but also begins the pilgrimage as if it were a race or hunt: its images combine elite and popular games. The end of the General Prologue thus reflects on the material of its making and the making of the stories that follow. In each portrait, along with a number of other obsessive themes that critics have noted, is a careful notation of the speech and language and sound of each pilgrim. This concern with speech and language embodies the dialectic that informs many of Chaucer's mimetic details, between a self-reflexiveness that threatens to ironize each moment and gesture and a vision that allows each individual character human faults and a history.

The portraits assemble details that communicate the type and character of the pilgrims but also imply their fitness for literary exercise. The Knight's portrait is filled with the language of values that permeates his tale. The Squire and the Prioress, with varying degrees of success, practice artful language and song. The Monk is described in terms of his questionable interpretation of monastic rules. The Friar is skilled in ambiguously "fair language." The Clerk's literacy as well as his speech is stressed, as in counterpoint is the writing and more calculatedly restrained speech of the Man of Law. This reticence is also evident in the portrait of the Physician, who is described as much in terms of what he does not read as in terms of what he reads.[6] Despite, or perhaps because of, its materialism and its chthonic imagery, the Physician's portrait calls itself up against the Parson's. The Parson's portrait, for all its rough-and-ready earthiness, is also filled with references to reading and texts. He is "lerned." The very preaching in which he presumably engages is itself a form of literature in the late Middle

Ages. He teaches the Gospel. He quotes a "figure." Indeed, his unity of theory and practice represents an ideal "poetics" that is beyond poetry.

Another subset of characters, however, beginning as early as the Yeoman, have a more strained relation to official literature. Like the Yeoman, the Cook and the Shipman hardly form part of what we might regard as a participatory literary public. Instead, they represent "subcultures," groups within medieval society that might be assumed to have their own popular forms. This is obviously true of the Shipman, for sea ballads and ditties form a considerable part of popular literature in later ages. The guildsmen and their wives, for instance, are described as if they were in a civic procession, one of their contributions to medieval theatricality. With the introduction of the Cook and Shipman, complicated by the addition of other pilgrims, the images of literacy and literature become even more disorienting. The Miller, for instance, is described as a "janglere" and a "goliardeys," an expounder of low forms of literature, but literary nevertheless. The Summoner seems to have a frighteningly parrot-like relation to language: for him it is pure imitation, parody. The startling proverb that a jay can say "Watte" as well as the Pope suggests a nihilistic relation to language that, although not much in evidence in his tale, does have a place in the last sequence of Canterbury tales. The Pardoner, too, sings a popular song, but in a bizzare context. It predicts the stress on deceptively excessive performance, on pure display, that he features in his own prologue later. We find ourselves in the "literary" world of Hoccleve's autobiographical passages and, later, of Villon's. It is an association that poets will cultivate on and off for centuries up to the present day.

Thus, the "literary" theme in the General Prologue reflects the social and ethical patterns that also operate in it. We begin with an assumption of a cohesive literary tradition and a description of members of groups who might differ in purpose but share values. As the portraits move on, however, we become aware of startlingly different versions of the uses of language, speech, and literature. Indeed, this difference begins almost immediately and becomes increasingly stark. Moreover, we become aware that the "official" consensus is only the tip of the iceberg, and that beneath the surface, worlds of simultaneously thriving subcultures have their own languages and their own definitions of performance.

It is precisely that pluralism which the Host's plan attempts to control and which, quite against his intention, he encourages. He sets the game in motion and thereby immediately compromises his goal of a harmonious social group and controllable literary standards. Harry thus epitomizes the dilemma, not of "medieval" culture, but of bourgeois and "modern" culture. The means by which he attempts to establish order are in fact the forces of constant change and relative perspectives, which thereby undermine absolute values.

We are part of that subversion, for we must constantly test our interpretations against the responses of the pilgrims. We are made aware, as perhaps Chaucer's own audience was, of the differences between certain social and historical values, and of the stark differences that individual personality can make in the perception of meaning. Moreover, the pilgrims and their voices mean that no tale can be read in isolation. They create new contexts, which change the authority of tradition itself.

This "modernity" is obscured, willfully, by Harry's plan, for he seeks to impose an ancient sense of community on the pilgrims. The tale-telling contest is itself an old form of folk celebration, and the fact that "eating" rather than money or fame is the reward celebrates that older sense of community. It is perhaps a limitation of nostalgia to think that that communal world will be any more unified and stable than the world we have made, if only because that older image is equally constructed and subject to human failings. As a form of communal celebration, nearly always festive, the ideal of a tale-telling contest verges on my expanded version of theatricality. But in its allusion to the highly literary sense of the *Canterbury Tales* as poetry, the theme of the poetic contest touches upon the generating dialectic of the *Canterbury Tales*, its existence as event, record, and poetic text simultaneously, a condition that qualifies its apparent celebration of the popular.

No doubt for even a sophisticated audience such as that of the Ricardian court, tale-telling and impersonation had a purpose beyond mere entertainment. I have tried to suggest some of the more public and less conscious purposes earlier. But the court, like many little communities, must have shared in the appreciation of such tale-telling on a much less sophisticated basis. Storytelling, not unlike ghost stories on a child's camping trip, has also a ritual quality, in cementing a shared experience among the listeners.[7] This is precisely the quality highlighted in the General Prologue in the sense of camaraderie that Harry seeks to instill among the pilgrims. At the same time, throughout the tales, we are made aware first of the limitations of that possibility, as all sorts of external and internal conflicts divide the pilgrims. More importantly, the qualities that Chaucer displays in common with popular performances and theater are those that call into question the ritual and communal nature of the storytelling. We are made aware, as Chaucer is most certainly aware, of a larger literate public above and beyond both pilgrims and listeners and even a circle like the court. Indeed, we are that public, and the difference is as marked as the difference between a ritual in which the entire community participates and a performance at a commercial theater. The *Canterbury Tales* constantly accentuates the limits of traditional story and its ritual function. By exploiting rather than lamenting these limits, Chaucer has access to a richness and flexibility in narrative presentation that predicts Shakespeare's depth in manipulating popular dramatic conventions.

But talk and performance are matched by a curious counter-theme. Among the rhythms and tensions of the *Canterbury Tales*, the most contradictory is the generation of tale-telling itself, a result only partially of the confusions surrounding manuscript order. For from its inception, the *Canterbury Tales* alternates between a sense of rest, closure, and completion on the one hand and an obsession with continuation. Even the pilgrims are torn between telling the next story and having the last word.

The first tale, the Knight's version of Palamon and Arcite, ends with an apparently unanswerable vision of existence, one that calls into question the potential of language to interpret, or, at least to console. It is partly the genius of the *Miller's Tale* to define new terms with which to answer the *Knight's Tale*, and it does so, it hardly needs to be said, by inverting the categories of the Knight's version of existence. The *Miller's Tale* insists on the poetic possibility of the material, of precisely that which the *Knight's Tale* insists is ephemeral and illusory.

Of the many contrasts between the *Knight's Tale* and the *Miller's Tale* not the least is the difference between the stress on memory surrounding the *Knight's Tale* ("it was a noble storie / and worthy for to drawen to memorie" [I.3111–12]) and the stress on spontaneous performance and momentary invention that inhabits the *Miller's Tale*. Rhymes and paired words, not always significant in other parts of Chaucer, here become important aspects of meaning, sometimes with an air of seriousness, as indeed, the pairing of "memorie" and "storie" illustrates. Even when a few lines later the narrator offers his famous defense, "turne over the leef and chese another tale," he only pretends to take the part of official culture as it is expressed in the *Knight's Tale*, partly by stressing the bookishness of his own discourse, which is therefore offered as official, partly by reminding us of the pastness of the action. But we are reading in the present and have little choice but to be therefore identified with the celebration of the moment that is the point of the *Miller's Tale*.

The *Canterbury Tales* is torn between a generative, even redemptive, view of language on the one hand and a view of language as illusory or misleading on the other. It continues and develops its own grounds for continuation partly by questioning the absolute contrast between these two views. In the most avowedly confessional performances—the Wife of Bath's and the Pardoner's—this difficult doubleness of language is most evident, for these characters come close to self-redemption through verbal performances that quite often depend upon outright fabrication and wild misstatement.

This alternation between generation and cessation is exemplified at least partly by the frequent imprecation to silence, to stop speaking, which functions as an opposing impulse to Harry's concern with keeping the tales going. Sometimes this impulse is apparently verbalized by Harry himself, as when he tries to stop the Reeve, the Miller, or the Summoner from telling their stories, but usually the reason is that the telling might stop if a tale were told, for the social concord would be upset. Harry is downright uncomfortable with silence and seeks another sort of discourse rather than none at all. Even the Knight's appeal to the Monk—"Ho namoore of this"—identifies a particular kind of discourse, not language itself.

In general, the real imprecations to silence are highly personal rather than philosophical in nature. The Reeve seeks to stop the Miller, the Friar the Summoner, the Canon his Yeoman. Moreover, but for the problematic example of the Clerk (and perhaps the Plowman), characters associated with silent demeanors such as Geoffrey the pilgrim, the Reeve, and the Manciple, range from foolishness to knavery in their behavior. The professional reserve of the Man of Law, exemplified by a certain silence, is countered by his verbosity, particularly in the introduction to his tale.

It is within the tales themselves that language receives its harshest criticism. In the world of the *Manciple's Tale*, as in the *Shipman's Tale*, a cynicism about the relation between language and reality is evident, as recent scholarship has argued (Harwood 1972); the *Manciple's Tale* begins not with a statement but an enactment that verges on a ritual entry. On one level it is pure, even literal, horseplay. But on another level, its jokes and slightly sinister action—pouring more wine down the throat of the nauseatingly drunken Cook, apparently to silence him—has about it certain symbolic resonances. The most obvious of these resonances might seem to be sacramental parody. But beyond whatever eucharistic allusion may be here lies also another sacrament that is parody, a Dionysian indulgence in the netherworld that precedes, significantly, a tale of an Apollo who acts more Dionysian than Apollonian.[8] Chaucer may not have been familiar with either Nietzschean dichotomies or anthropological theories of the origin of Greek drama and myth. But the satyr-play rhythms of the Manciple's prologue and its obsession with the grotesque, which resemble the actions we find in Langland's description of Gluttony in *Piers Plowman* and the actions of mystery-play devils, imitate that function.

The poetic status of the *Canon's Yeoman's Tale* is established not so much by the Canon's Yeoman himself as by collaboration with Harry Bailly, who takes a prominent role as dramatic interlocutor in this prologue. Indeed, he induces something akin to a confessional mode by appropriating the voice of a character in a morality play. Whatever the "dramatic" basis of the "frame," this moment at least has about it the air of a true dramatic prologue. But the uneasy combination of confessional and demonic notes in the conversation and the tale that follows recalls an earlier Chaucerian rather than analogous dramatic moment. It is in fact the horseback conversation in the *Friar's Tale*, when the summoner meets and interrogates his true "brother," the "feend" who "dwelle in helle." The *Canon's Yeoman's*

Prologue and *Tale* inverts, or perhaps merely extends, the hidden statement of the earlier tale, that finally men make their own images of hell. Like the *Friar's Tale*, the *Canon's Yeoman's Tale* makes this point by a stress on fraud and self-deception. Like the tale also (at least in terms of its answering statement in the *Summoner's Tale)*, it suggests that to some extent the narrator is not entirely free of the delusion he describes—the Canon's Yeoman seems to state this at times. One's guess is that the tales of the Friar, Summoner, and Canon's Yeoman are all very late Chaucer. They share in the freedom and breadth and spontaneity of a master's late sketch. But by rewriting the playful slander of the earlier diptych of Friar and Summoner (even including its substantial intellectual and technical content), Chaucer raises these questions in a more serious context.

Related to the theme of silence is the way in which some of Chaucer's speakers tell us what kind of tale they will or will not tell:

> "Thou gettest fable noon ytoold for me;
> For Paul, that writeth unto Thymothee,
> Reepreveth hem that weyven soothfastnesse,
> And tellen fables and swich wrecchednesse.
> What sholde I sowen draf out of my fest,
> Whan I may sowen whete, if that me lest?
> For which I seye, if that yow list to heere
> Moralitee and vertuous mateere,
> And thanne that ye wol yeve me audience,
> I wol ful fayn, at Cristes reverence,
> Do yow pleasaunce leefful, as I kan.
> But trusteth wel, I am a Southren man,
> I kan nat geeste 'rum, ram, ruf,' by lettre,
> Ne, God woot, rym holde I but litel bettre;
> And therfore, if yow list—I wol nat glose—
> I wol yow telle a myrie tale in prose
> To knytte up al this feeste and make an ende."

(X.31–47)

We are so used to thinking of the Parson's words as an explanation of what follows in his tale and as a rejection of all that came before that we are likely to overlook the fact that this rejection is itself expressed in comic and parodic terms. In his own way, the Parson for a moment enters the spirit of the game, if only to say that the game is over. In order to reject "rym" he must resort to verse. At the same time, it is with a certain relish that he describes his position, a relish that energizes his stern message as a sermon well done might. His first sentence is a stern rejoinder to Harry's rather loosely worded imprecation to tell his tale, one in which Harry's oath seems to slip out as if beyond his control. The second is almost addressed to himself, as if he is explaining to himself both the opportunity for a redeemed discourse and talking himself out of the apparent problem of engaging in entertainment during what should be a very different sort of experience. The third ironically engages that experience by parodying a call to attention of a courtly, or even popular, versifier: "Do yow pleasaunce leefful, as I kan." This last clause, usually a filler in Chaucer, sometimes also occurs, perhaps by accident, in poetic apologies, as in the beginning of the *House of Fame*, where the first few lines of the Aeneid are inscribed on a tablet of brass. These lines of formal and humble presentation open into a broader, comic self-definition by way of mock self-criticism ("I kan nat geeste 'rum, ram, ruf' "). Beneath the broad humor we find the voice of the Parson virtually undoing the screens and the ironic portraiture that the Chaucerian narrator has built between self and representation since the early poems. In the Parson's description of how he wishes to frame his following words, we find a reversal of the procedure that Chaucer the poet has developed to allow his own words to be framed from the earliest poetic efforts. The Parson does not so much reject poetry or fiction as parody its most ingenious efforts to represent either phenomenal truth or the self, and he does so in a method that can only be regarded as itself poetic. Moreover, he envisions, and asks the assent of the group in also envisioning, his tale not as a rejection but the final expression of the "feeste." The Parson and his tale function much like the "doctor" at the end of certain mystery plays, elucidating a moral that should have been obvious, as if the playwright were protecting himself against the anarchy of art's signification. The image of Carnival here begins to give way to the image of Lent, but it still does so theatrically. This is not the case when the *Parson's Tale* is itself ended, and the poet speaks, or writes, not to us, in his own rather than a borrowed voice.

. . .

Here we have a work which, by the wildest conceit, purports to be recorded speech. At the same time, if we look at how talk works among the participants in the telling, we find a peculiar dialectic. Rather than a celebration of popular speech on the one hand or an obeisance to the written text on the other, we find both media as contested ground, each capable of disruption and confusion. While the presumption of the tale-telling fiction is that language and shared narration help us communicate and understand each other, the actual workings of the *Canterbury Tales* suggest a darker and less optimistic alternative, which is that the uses of fiction and talk are more important than their innate nature. In the guise of a communal and traditional social setting, Chaucer actually articulates the sense of potentially divisive modernity that haunts any age, no matter how holistic its world view.

The dark view of language and human communication that inhabits the end of the *Cantebury Tales* is admittedly thematic. The poet is clearly closing his book, as James Dean (1979; 1985) has argued. I agree that this theme is part of a closing phase in the Tales, but I would also point out that this sardonic attack is not separable from the uneasy and perhaps ironic relation of the *Canterbury Tales* throughout to its fictional medium of the spoken voice. In this respect, as in others, the *Canterbury Tales* reveals a difficult relation, nostalgic and cooptive at once, to both its official and its unofficial literary and cultural traditions. As with his contemporaries Petrarch and Boccaccio, Chaucer pursues a new ideal of poetic autonomy. He pursues this ideal less programatically, with an apparent sympathy for the values inevitably transformed by his literary exploitation of their traditional cultural forms. It is as if the humanist reading so much a part of modern Chaucer criticism from Kittredge to Donaldson is dependent upon Chaucer's wary distance from the rigors of a newly emerging conception of the poet inextricably related to Renaissance humanism.

I call Chaucer's sympathy apparent only to avoid reintroducing the modern humanist conception rendered problematic by my argument. Nevertheless, however much it calls into question the formal coherence and confined intention necessary to the humanist Chaucer, Chaucerian theatricality performs an existential paradigm of poetic freedom and autonomy, always in temporary and intermittent resistance to the forces of necessity and authority. In so doing, the *Canterbury Tales* not only enacts the divided loyalties of its poet and its age, but engages us in that struggle.

1. The question of Chaucer's relation to court and political expression has been revived in important studies by Anne Middleton (1978). Middleton identifies a "public" voice in Ricardian poetry, one that speaks "as if" to the commonwealth as a whole rather than to the court or coterie. She in a sense both fictionalizes and pushes Ferguson's (1965) historical notion of the "articulate citizen." Middleton bases her analysis largely on Gower and Langland and suggests that when Chaucer appropriates this voice it is only, as it were, in quotations.

2. Tout (1929) and others have documented concern with establishing a uniform administrative system. Chaucer's own career is a testament to the increase in diplomatic activity. The growth in the royal bureaucracy required the enlistment of talented commoners and the cultivation of similar talents in the members of the aristocracy. It is to this larger circle, rather than to the small circle of the household itself, that we should look to in deducing Chaucer's immediate reception, as has been stressed by Strohm (1977).

3. Literary performance has reemerged as an important category of Chaucer criticism. For an assessment of this trend, see my review-essay, "Chaucerian Performance" (1989), which discusses Leonard Koff's *Chaucer and the Art of Storytelling* (1988), Laura Kendrick's *Chaucerian Play* (1988), Betsy Bowden's *Chaucer Aloud* (1988), and Carl Lindahl's *Earnest Games* (1987).

4. These later arguments seem to me to grow out of, and perhaps beyond, Bakhtin's chiefly literary interest, but not against them. See Ginzburg 1980, Davis 1975, and Abelove et al. 1983, 99–121. In *The Old French Fabliaux* (1986, 164), Charles Muscatine levels a pluralist critique against Bakhtin, arguing that Bakhtin lumps together too broad a variety of comic forms as "popular" or "grotesque." Far from expressing "popular" unrest in opposition to official authority, fabliaux, for instance, underline a "stratum" in medieval culture, as in human culture in general, of the "skeptical," "materialist," "sensual," that only in hindsight and by contrast with the development of later gentility appears as obscene. The "unofficial" is not marginal or repressed, but is an expressed part of the culture taken as a whole. Interestingly, Muscatine, like Bakhtin, has to negotiate between a historical and cultural foundation for his readings. On Chaucer and Bakhtin see Andreas (1979; 1984).

5. Brewer (1968), although not discussing questions of audience, remains helpful in suggesting interlocking rather than distinct class separations.

6. Compare Kellogg (1977, 659):

If Chaucer needed more narrators than his own learned, courtly genteel persona, he also needed a more varied audience if he were to explore the full range of narrative possibilities. His pilgrim narrators do more than suggest the kind of people we might expect to hear such stories from; they suggest the kind of audience to which such stories are most appropriately directed. When Chaucer refers to a "cherles tale" he means not only one told by a churl but one especially enjoyed by a churl. Unless we are going to turn the page and choose another tale we must prepare ourselves to listen as a churl would listen. Both the narrators and the implied audiences have been generated by the various generic characteristics of the stories in the *Canterbury Tales*.

`CHAPTER TWO
BAKHTIN, CHAUCER, CARNIVAL, LENT

1. Derek Brewer (1974, 223) is one of the few critics to remind us continually of Chaucer's debt to popular sources. He argues against an excessively restricted notion of Chaucer's sources: "It must be questioned because it places Chaucer in the learned, exegetical Latin tradition of the official culture; whereas it seems that the bulk of Chaucer's work must be placed in a different, secular and unofficial tradition, which was in some respects opposed to the official." See also Elizabeth Kirk's intelligent survey, "Chaucer and His English Contemporaries" (1975) and the essays collected in Heffernan (1985).

2. Compare Howard (1980, 102):

Tidings are where events and language meet, where the world becomes preserved in words. They are the end of action; they are the beginnings of legends and fictions, the raw stuff of literature. Chaucer came to be interested in the uniqueness and delimitedness, the puzzling authenticity of each personage and each tiding, and the randomness with which tidings are heard and reiterated. From this point of view, each of the Canterbury tales is a tiding. . . . We have to seek out and decide upon the truth and authenticity of tidings. . . . This idea of a literary idea was risky and theatrical, distanced, highly disciplined. It calls upon a frame of mind in us, anticipates that frame of mind and in part inculcates it. It is not a strategy. . . . It is rather a stance, that invites and permits.

On some possible varieties of Chaucerian fiction, see Burlin (1977).

3. See Kristeva (1973, 111):

The author is not the ultimate example who might guarantee the truth of this meeting of discourses. His conception of the character, according to Bakhtin, is the conception of a discourse (of a word), or, better still, of the discourse of the other. The author's discourse is a discourse arising from another discourse, a word within the word, and not a word about the word (that is, not a true metadiscourse). There is no third person to bring unity to the confrontation of the two: the opposing of discourses are brought together but do not share identity, they do not culminate in a stable "I" which would be the "I" of the monologic author. The "dialogic" of the coexistence of opposites [is] quite different from the "monologic."

4. Polyglossia is literally the condition of England two centuries before Chaucer. For a different but important statement about Chaucer's position on the related matter of translation, see R. A. Shoaf (1979).

5. I have silently modernized archaic letters in quotations from *Handlyng Synne*.

6. All citations from Chaucer in my text are to *The Riverside Chaucer*, ed. Larry D. Benson et al. (1987).

7. On Chaucer and the hermeneutic circle, see Ferster (1985).

8. The classic study of Chaucer's place in relation to other fourteenth-century writers is Burrow (1971).

9. From an orthodox Boethian perspective, the distance between a controlling order and the multiplicity of phenomena is not a problem. See Lawler (1980).

CHAPTER THREE
THE POETICS OF THEATRICALITY

1. This chapter was written before I read Lindahl, *Earnest Games* (1987), an important study of Chaucer and certain folkloric forms. I had already consulted many of the sources Lindahl cites, but I have also abbreviated some of my descriptions in this chapter, since Lindahl's thorough analysis and description is so directly relevant. Lindahl analyzes the structure of a number of medieval festivals—the *Cour Amoureuse*, the love debates, the London Pui, the courtly Mayings, the Feast of Fools, the Boy Bishop ceremonies, the Riding of St. George, mystery plays, Christmas guisings, and Lord of Misrule ceremonies—and compares them to the *Canterbury Tales*, seeking to demonstrate that the entire enterprise is "socially appropriate" to the performers. Lindahl delineates a number of traits shared by all these ceremonies and the *Canterbury Tales*. A list of these traits alone suggests what Lindahl has to say about them: autocratic rulers, strict measures to ensure participation, amateur performers, rigid formality, processional form, mingling of sacred and profane elements, a surrounding festive context, strong competitive elements, and a hierarchical structure. The "churls'" games, however, differ in regard to these last two elements, since in non-gentil celebrations competition was by faction, rather than by individual participant, and whereas gentil festivals duplicate the order of society, "churls'" festivals seek to subvert that order. Lindahl's description of how Harry Bailly moves between behavior appropriate to one or the other social level is especially successful.

2. See Fifield (1967), who describes some of the masque-like qualities of the *Squire's Tale*, the *Franklin's Tale*, and the *Merchant's Tale*. For another allusion to popular theater, see Haskell (1975).

3. See Burke (1978, 198):

A charivari was, to follow a famous seventeenth-century definition, a "public defamation," more especially "an infamous (or infaming) ballad, sung by an armed troop, under the window of a young dotard, married, the day before, unto a young wanton, in mockery of them both." It was normally accompanied by "rough music.". . . It was not only the old man married to a young woman (or vice versa) who might be the object of a charivari, but anyone marrying for the second time, or a girl marrying outside the village, or a husband who was beaten or made a cuckold by his wife.

On the charivari, see also Davis (1975), and on its expression in Chaucer, Kern (1980).

4. If the scene in which Absalon visits the blacksmith reminds us of a peculiar inversion on the theme of Venus and Mars, it is perhaps because the structure of the story of Venus and Mars is itself like a fabliau. Moreover, the folk image of the blacksmith has sexual overtones. In Venice, hammers and anvils were carried about in processions as explicitly sexual symbols (Muir 1981, 158, 173).

5. For a critique of current assumptions about the literary history of the mystery plays, see Nelson (1974). On the evidence for the continuity of theatrical perform-ance, see R. Loomis (1945). On the concept of "theatrica," see the important article by G. Olson (1986).

6. Some of these points are raised by Prior (1986). As her title, "Parodying Typo-logy in the Miller's Tale," indicates, she is concerned largely with Chaucer's parody of typological interpretation, and therefore clerical interpretation in general, but she also suggests that Chaucer "calls into question the legitimacy of other artistic and clerical endeavors: in the Canon's Yeoman's tale the alchemist's art . . . in the Franklin's Tale the French clerk's magic and illusions and in the Knight's Tale Theseus' spectacle" (72). On other dramatic allusions in Chaucer, see Peterson (1976) and Lancashire (1975).

7. On Chaucer's gestures, the most detailed study is Windeatt (1979).

8. The most articulate case for Chaucer's awareness and defense of the morally limited nature of poetry is made by David (1976). Some members of Chaucer's immediate circle may have understood and appreciated the bold experiments of the *Canterbury Tales*, but "one may sympathize with other members of Chaucer's audi-ence, . . . of limited and established literary tastes, who would regard the lower characters in the General Prologue, not to mention their tales, with dismay" (122). David contrasts the critique of Gower's and Chaucer's work by the Man of Law with the rejection of poetry offered by the Parson. "Worldly poetry can defend itself against worldly men and specious critics like the Man of Law. The Parson's Prologue, however, contains an attack on poetry for which the . . . medieval poet . . . does not have a good answer" (131). See also Hanning (1984).

9. Throughout P. Olson (1986) runs the argument that Chaucer agrees with Wyclif's critique of the clerical hierarchy and to some degree with his analysis of the decline of the estates order, but proposes a much less radical, non-Wycliffite solu-tion. Olson does stress, however, Chaucer's general orthodoxy.

10. The relation of the *Shipman's Tale* to the Wife of Bath is perhaps most succinctly put by Donaldson (1958), who observes that "the theme illustrates one of the basic motifs in the Wife's character, her preoccupation with the possibility of exploiting physical charms for financial gain" (1094). But Chaucer reassigns the tale to allow her "enthusiastic partiality," "fully developed humanity," and "rich personal interpretation," at the same time allowing what is then the "carefully worked out equations" of the *Shipman's Tale* to "perform their own cold demon-stration" (1096), resulting in a work not unlike the *Merchant's Tale* in atmo-sphere.

11. A case for revision of the Wife herself is made by Pratt (1969), who assumes that the Wife had originally been assigned the *Shipman's Tale* and that aspects of the tale, particularly the wife's attitudes towards husbands in it, and the love of dancing and clothing, reflect the Wife of Bath. As Chaucer worked more on the character,

however, he worked in images from traditional antifeminist literature. For our purposes, Pratt's most interesting suggestions are not about her development, but about the use of those "static" antifeminist images.

12. One of the few cases made for the Shipman as the teller of the tale (Chapman 1956) imagines the Shipman himself as a consummate storyteller, miming various parts of the tale using different voices and pitches.

13. As Cooper (1984, 127) observes, "In changing tales, Chaucer also changes the Wife's character. In her Prologue she is colloquial, has a short way with moral abstraction. . . . Her tale introduces an unexpected note of idealism. With the fabliau, she would have been portrayed as a cynic; given her present tale, she is presented as an incurable romantic."

14. In her remarkable explanation of the Wife's use of romance, Fradenburg argues that "had the Wife told the Shipman's tale, it would have paradoxically dated her" (1986, 35). The Wife's "modernity," asserts Fradenburg, is partly created by her ambivalent handling of romance itself.

15. Perhaps because of its minimal suitability to dramatic theory, the most fertile ground for criticism of the *Shipman's Tale* has been its imagery and language. Silverman (1953) points out the rich associations and puns surrounding "tailye," "dettor," "chaffere," and so forth, suggesting the identity in the tale between sex and money. Levy (1967) extends these observations more pervasively and not always convincingly, but makes the astute observation that the monk and the merchant assume each other's role. See also Hermann (1985). Abraham (1977) convincingly suggests that this pun, conflating relationships and deception, is in fact central to the tale itself. Keiser (1978) demonstrates how characters in the tale use language to camoflauge their petty motivation and suggests also that the narrator can be shown to be implicated in this debased use of language. He argues further that the (sometimes) unnamed pilgrim who objects to the Parson at the end of Fragment B1, according to the Bradshaw Shift, reveals attitudes towards language and the ethical status of literature entirely consistent with the *Shipman's Tale*. The tale seems to implicate critics in its own workings, since evidence from close verbal analysis and dramatic consistency seems to conflict with evidence from manuscript authority.

16. On the "idealism" of the Wife, see Carruthers (1979).

CHAPTER FOUR
CHAUCER, BOCCACCIO, LONDON, FLORENCE

1. Translation in the text is mine. Sacchetti (1938, 119–20):
Andandosi un di il detto Dante per suo diporto . . . , e partando la gorgiera e la bracciaiuola, come allora si facea per usanza, scontro uno asinaio, il quale avea certe some di spazzatura innanzi; il quale asinaio andava drieto agli asini, cantando il libro di Dante; e quando avea cantato un pezzo, toccava l'asino, e diceva:—arri.—Scontrandosi Dante in costui, con la bracciaiuola gli diede una grande batacchiata su le spalle, dicendo:—Cotesto *arri* non vi mis'io.—Colui non sapea ne chi si fosse Dante, ne per quello che gli desse; se non che tocca gli asini forte, e pur:—arri, arri.

2. Translation in the text is mine. Petrarca (1926, [I, 12] 10:52): "Ergo sutrina et pistrina et vilissime mechanicarum artium, si necessitas nobilitare illas potest, nobilissime omnium fient."

3. Petrarca (1926, [XXI, 15] 13:99): "Fullonem et cauponem et lanistarum ceterorum."

4. My assumption is that Chaucer had some access to the *Decameron* as a collection, but even Petrarch claims not to have seen the entire work until very late. The case is still open. The standard recent discussions are summarized in McGrady (1977).

5. P. Taylor (1982) and Kirkpatrick (1983) also notice the analogy between Ciappelletto and the Pardoner. For my discussion of Boccaccio, I am obviously indebted to Almansi (1975).

6. See Kirkpatrick (1983, 222–30):

Indeed, in the *Decameron*, hypocrisy has almost invariably a creative aspect; the shifts and convolutions of the conscience serve to stimulate the tongue to new audacity. There is no such creativity in the Pardoner, nor any such complaisance in Chaucer's representation of him. . . . In the Pardoner, Chaucer has created a thoroughly Dantean figure. . . . the Pardoner cannot conjure this reality in the manner of Cipolla. . . . an elemental decency rebels against the viciousness of his tone, as it does later in the Host's response.

7. Translation of the *Decameron* in my text is by Musa and Bondenella (1983). Boccaccio (1955, 756):

Noi, come voi sapete, domane saranno quindici dì, per dovere alcun diporto pigliare e sostentamento della nostra sanità e della vita, cessando le malinconie e' dolori e l'angoscie, le quali per la nostra città continuamente, poi che questo pestilenzioso tempo incominciò, si veggono, uscimmo di Firenze; il che secondo il mio giudicio noi onestamente abbiam fatto; per ciò che, se io ho saputo ben riguardare, quantunque liete novelle e forse attrattive e concupiscenzia dette ci sieno, e del continuo mangiato e bevuto bene, e sonato e contato, cose tutte da incitare le deboli menti a cose meno oneste, niuno atto, niuna parola, niuna cosa né dalla vostra parte né dalla nostra ci ho conosciuta da biasimare; continua onestà, continua concordia, continua fraternal dimestichezza mi ci è paruta vedere e sentire. Il che senza dubbio in onore e servigio di voi e di me m'è carissimo. E per ciò, acciò che per troppa lunga consuetudine alcuna cosa che in fastidio si convertisse nascer non ne potesse, e perché alcuno la nostra troppo lunga dimoranza gavillar non potesse, e avendo ciascun di noi, la sua giornata, avuta la sua parte dell'onore che ancora in me dimora, giudicherei, quando piacer fosse di voi, che convenevole cosa fosse omai il tornarci là onde ci partimmo.

8. Boccaccio (1955, 761): "Chi non sa ch'è il vino ottima cosa a' viventi . . . e a colui che ha la febbre è nocivo? . . . Niuna corrotta mente intese mai sanamente parola; e così come le oneste a quella non giovano, così quelle che tanto oneste non sono la ben disposta non posson contaminare, se non come il loto i solari raggi o le terrene brutture le bellezze del cielo."

9. Boccaccio (1955, 4):

E chi negherà, questo, quantunque egli si sia, non molto più alle vaghe donne che agli uomini convenirsi donare? Esse dentro a' dilicati petti, temendo e vergognando, tengono l'amorose faimme nascose, le quali quanto più di forza abbian che le palesi coloro il sanno che l'hanno provato e provano; e oltro a ciò, ristrette da' voleri, da' piaceri, da' comandementi de' padri, delle madri, de' fratelli e de' mariti, il più del tempo nel piccolo circuito delle loro camere racchiuse dimorano, e quasi oziose sedendosi, volendo e non volendo in una medesima ora, seco rivolgono diversi pensieri, li quali non è possibile che sempre sieno allegri.

10. Auerbach (1965, 239) offers the classic definition of a literary public, which in fact includes the problematics of popular connections: "a social group corresponding to what in modern times is termed the literary public in contrast on the one hand to the great mass of the uneducated and on the other hand to those who made literature and learning their profession." Auerbach cautions against too strict a line between this public and "the people." "The transitions were fluid, and without constant contact with the lower levels no literary public can maintain its function and character" (240).

11. The art of the nobility, complains Lovato de Lovati in the early fourteenth century, has been deserted for the songs of the people. He describes a singer on a platform in the piazza "reciting the story of Charlemagne and the *gestes* of the French. The rabble hang around, listening intently, charmed by their Orpheus" (Larner, 1971, 176–77). On Boccaccio's debt to popular romance, see Wallace (1985).

12. Compare Wilkinson (1969, 226): "Geoffrey could come to the common man; but he still reflected the outlook of the poet of the court. He did not, like Langland, give a new significance to the poor. He talked of villages, but usually of the village aristocracy. Similarly, the lower citizenry of London had a scant place in his grand panorama, though he saw them daily in the streets."

13. Boccaccio (1955, 24):

Qui è bello e fresco stare, e hacci, come voi vedete, e tavolieri e scacchieri, e può ciascuno, secondo che all'animo gli è più di piacere, diletto pigliare. Ma se in questo il mio parer si seguitasse, non giucando, nel quale l'animo dell'una delle parti convien che si turbi senza troppo piacere dell'altra o di chi sta a vedere, ma novellando (il che può porgere, dicendo uno, a tutta la compagnia che ascolta diletto) questa calda parte del giorno trapasseremo.

CHAPTER FIVE
CARNIVAL VOICES IN THE *CLERK'S ENVOY*

1. The most sober and thoughtful of these is McCall (1966). An interesting demonstration of the seriously ironic "purgatorial" note in the envoy is Cherniss (1972). Morse (1958) associates the Clerk with Ockhamism, Wycliffism, and other contemporary forms of skepticism or critical reform. "At heart he was on the side of the Wife of Bath, and in mocking her he was also examining, once more and yet once more, his own restless intelligence" (4). The Clerk "breathed an atmosphere

charged with individualism and incipient revolt" (14–15). As convenient as Morse's argument would be for my position, it still seems to me that if the Clerk is of the Wife's "secte" it is without knowing it, and that it is his own language, which he is obviously so proud of controlling, that subverts him. For a compelling argument that the envoy does represent a successful recovery on the part of the Clerk from the dangers of his Tale, see Frese (1973). In a sentence that perhaps predicts my entire argument, Donaldson (1975, 1083) observes that "in his Envoy, an uproarious *tour-de-force*, the Clerk—and Chaucer—restore the balance by reasserting those everyday values that the tale has held in subordination." The "popular" quality of the envoy is touched on by Winny (1966), who also reads it as an example of Chaucer's "late style," contrasting with the hard-won elegance of the tale itself, which he sees as typical of an earlier phase of Chaucer. The envoy "offers a direct contrast of style . . . the sardonic advice to the Wife of Bath and her tribe which rounds out the story, are as remote from the lyrical mood of the tale as street-cries from madrigals" (14–15).

2. The lines following 1112 in Robinson, containing Harry's autobiographical reaction to the tale, occur in only some manuscripts. It is possible that these lines originally ended the entire tale at 1162, before the Clerk asks for "o word." My reading does not require these last lines to be finally intended by Chaucer after 1212, but they fit in comfortably. I suspect that a poet like Chaucer, while attracted to the manuscript linkage of the last lines of the Envoy with the "wepyng and waylyng" that opens the *Merchant's Tale*, would also have sought to soften a too blatantly paralleled transition. But see Dempster (1952) and Severs (1954).

3. Although the most flamboyant evidence of clerical misrule exists elsewhere, there is some testimony and certainly enough cross-fertilization in the strongly international university culture to suggest a healthy English tradition of student parody. One typical example is the parody of the Kyrie eleison twisted to allow a "Jankyn" to serenade an "Aleyson" (Robbins 1952, 27). The combination of learning and irreverence is not unique. During the unsettled early years of Richard II's rule, a royal officer on a visit to Oxford was greeted by students singing a song that cast aspersions on the king's honor, and arrows were shot into his quarters, the result of which was that the Chancellor of the University was removed when the culprits went unpunished (R. Wilson 1952, 201–2). In 1381, although overshadowed by other events, there was a violent attack by Oxford townsmen upon some university students. A century before, an attack by students had resulted in a number of deaths among the townsmen.

4. In the *Squire's Tale*, the treachery of the falcon's lover is described as "the sophymes of his art" (V.554). The OED cites a damning definition included in a Wycliffe sermon: "This is a foule soffyme, a foul and sotil disceit." In some other Chaucerian uses, "study" and "studien" imply a state of abstracted reverie, sometimes bordering on vexation, akin to the Old French "studie." This latter sense is the one called upon by the Knight, who speaks with gentle irony about the sudden change in Arcite's mood: "Into a studie he fil sodeynly, / As doon thise loveres in hir queyntes geres" (I.1530–31). A "studye" is a state verging dangerously close to melancholy. Indeed, in the *House of Fame* melancholy and study itself are associated syntactically, for "som man is to curious / In studye, or melancolyous" (29–30). In

Sir Gawain and the Green Knight, Sir Gawain is described as being "in a study" when he learns the identity of Lord Bercilak and is told of the trick played upon him; Gawain "in a study stod a gret whyle" (2369) before an understandable but immoderate outburst. In *Troilus and Criseyde*, Pandarus seems distracted when Criseyde suggests that they go in to dine, "But Pandarus, that in a studye stood, /Er he was war, she took hym by the hood, / And seyde, 'Ye were caught er that ye wiste!' " (II:1180–82) a statement truer of her own situation. As with most of Pandarus's moods, it is difficult to tell whether this moment of being "in a study" is calculated to allow the import of Troilus's letter to sink in. Pandarus is not the kind of character one would expect to be "in a study," though, unlike Harry, he might well respect such introspection.

5. By Chaucer's time, "goliard" no longer had, or never did have, the specific meaning it has in romantic literary history. The Miller is described as a goliard in the General Prologue (560), and the terms seems intertwined with general minstrelsy, although in Langland "goliard" is associated with Latin. (*Piers Plowman*, B, Prol. 139). See the MED for further references. But I appropriate the term here to indicate an underground and unofficial tradition of student life, which by its very nature seems to demand a subculture close to that which we call "bohemian," even if we discount the excesses of writers like Villon as self-dramatization. I do not mean that the Clerk is a "wandering scholar," but that he appropriates this unofficial voice for his own witty (and orthodox) purposes. Perhaps one of the most widespread goliardic satires, at least partly because its attack upon the abuses of the clergy was consistent with traditional Christian moral values, was the *Apocalypsis Goliae* (Wright 1841), which McPeek (1951) suggests Chaucer may have known. This poem is a mock dream vision, in which the narrator comes across the great authorities of classical tradition in absurd postures and positions, followed by a parody of the opening of the Seven Seals, in which the emblems of the four evangelists somehow become corrupt bishops, popes, and other high church officials. The language of the poem itself lampoons learned exegesis and etymology: "hinc nomen ducitur officialium / qui, ut officiant, habent officium" (ll. 251–52). Even clerks are subject to criticism, for one seal is dense with interlinear gloss, delineating the vices of clerks. Indeed, in a satire written for clerks by clerks, it is not surprising to find such harsh but knowing treatment. The clerks are kept up all night by their so-called studies. Throughout the *Apocalypsis Goliae*, the satire is informed by the earthy images of a comic point of view, images of food, sensuality, animal behavior, money, hunting, gambling—activities and qualities rather celebrated in other goliardic verse. Such images occur in more indignant railing against corruption (compare the *Pardoner's Tale*, for instance), but here they are presented with a nearly worldly humor. It is the Angels opening the seals in this poem (like Piers the Plowman in the pardon scene) who are horrified and outraged. An important summary of Chaucer's access to "goliardic" materials is Jill Mann (1974).

6. Perhaps the most notorious expression of student revelry in the Middle Ages was "festum stultorum," the Feast of Fools. The examples we have records of are largely French. Typically it involved an inversion of the usual order of things, with the lower clergy in university and cathedral towns assuming the powers of their superiors. Clerks dressed as women dancing in the choir, playing dice in church,

censing the church with the smoke of burning shoes, riding through the town singing ribald songs—the evidence for all these activities comes typically from the observation of outraged opponents. Chambers (1903, 274–371) has a convenient description. One can argue whether these carnivalesque activities were condemned or shrewdly encouraged by the powers that be, but at least one consistent theme in the records is the singing of parodic and satiric, sometimes obscene, songs and poems. For a brilliant examination of the imagery associated with festive life, see Davis (1975, 97–123).

7. Middleton (1980b, 149) observes that part of the comedy of the envoy comes from a discrepancy between the comically practical quality of the Clerk's advice as understood by the Host and its form as "an extended *envoi*, a form associated with the conclusion, delivery and application of a lyrical fable to its princely audience, the handing over of an enigma as both game and counsel."

8. "Chichevache" is a horned beast who feeds on patient wives. In some transformations, "chichevache" seems oddly enough to be a cow, which is how Robinson glosses the reference. For a full discussion, see the introduction to Lydgate's "Bycorne and Chichevache" in Hammond (1927, 113–18). For the intriguing presentational context of Lydgate's poem, see the headings printed in Lydgate (1934).

CHAPTER SIX
POETICS IN THE PROLOGUES

1. I have in mind the tradition suggested by Ferguson (1965), but my terms here have been influenced by Middleton (1980a). This important article states the issue in some of the same terms, but sees the Clerk, Franklin, and Man of Law as articulating a similar sense of literary values, equivalent to social values. But Middleton sees this position as relatively consistent, and, indeed, mirroring Chaucer's own poetic concerns. My argument here is that these characters are concerned with literary and social values, and that Chaucer is concerned with some of the same issues, but that these characters voice these issues in profoundly discontinuous ways. Chaucer seems aware, as his characters are not, of the paradox of their efforts.

2. It is almost impossible to summarize the various arguments concerning the order of the *Tales* here, if only because the issues recently have become closely tied to some recent editions of Chaucer. A cogent summary concerning the place of the *Nun's Priest's Tale* is available in Pearsall (1985a). A sensible discussion and critique of alternatives to the Ellesmere order is in Cooper (1984, 56–71). For futher alternatives to traditional orderings, see Owen (1977).

CHAPTER SEVEN
THE NOISE OF THE PEOPLE

1. See P. Olson (1986) and Patterson (1987a). For an extended critique of the political implications of Olson and the theoretical implications of Patterson, see Fradenburg (1989).

2. The association of this scene, its language, and the revolt have been recently reexamined by Scanlon (1989, esp. 61–65), and Travis (n.d.). I am grateful to

Professor Travis for sharing an early draft of his article with me after I read this chapter as a paper. He convincingly explains the association of noise, animals, and revolt that I take here as a problem.

3. Even in its form the *Knight's Tale* suggests that the center cannot hold. Indeed, its center is the powerful ceremonial images that have consistently drawn the attention of critics, and that some, from Root to Kolve, have argued are the virtual meaning of the work. If so, however, that meaning is radically conditioned by various actions and gestures that nearly always disturb and sometimes subvert the ordering efforts of those ceremonial images. Kolve (1984, 85–157) takes full account of the disordering themes of such imagery. See also Hanning (1980).

4. Charles Muscatine (1950) argues that its form was its meaning, and that the pageantry and formal order of the work itself was integral to its theme, which was the "noble life," rather than love or philosophy (see also Muscatine 1957, 173–90). In arguing for a destabilizing and self-critical work, I share an interpretation with Westlund, who suggests "that the *Knight's Tale* presents the continual subversion of noble efforts to bring order out of disorder" (1964, 526). A pattern emerges in which "an ordered, formal situation is presented only to be immediately interrupted by forces which overthrow it. . . . At several points in the *Knight's Tale* a formal situation, rule, or pattern of conduct is set forth and given value only to be subverted later in the poem" (527). "The poem raises problems," argues Westlund, "which noble conduct cannot fully resolve" (532). My intention here is not to repeat a developed, if heterodox, position in commentary on the *Knight's Tale*, but to suggest that these issues acquire a different and crucial value within the *Canterbury Tales* as a whole. Westlund, for instance, after making his interesting case, suggests that the poem is as it is in order to establish the "pilgrimage theme" and sense of "spiritual quest" in the *Canterbury Tales*. He finally sees the themes of the poem as a "balance" (536–37).

5. P. Olson (1986) reads the *Miller's Tale* as an explicitly political statement, criticizing the failure of civil government to assure domestic order. Patterson (1987a) sees the tale and its narration as implicitly ideological, particularly in its suppression of the language of protest in the mouth of John the Carpenter.

CHAPTER EIGHT
FORMS OF TALK

1. Translation in the text is mine. Petrarca (1926, [13, 7] 12:82–84):
Carpentarii fullones agricole, desertis aratris et ceterarum artium instrumentis, de Musis et de Apolline fabulantur; dici non potest quam late iam vagetur hec pestis, que paucorum nuper hominem fuit. . . . Nam et domi estuo et vix iam in publicum exire audeo; occurrunt enim omni ex parte frenetici, percontantur arripiunt docent disputant altercantur. . . . Quod si serpere ceperit, actum est: pastores piscatores venatores aratores ipsique boves mera mugient poemata, mera poemata ruminabunt.

2. The question of whether Chaucer read his work aloud does not mean that he imagined it only to be presented in such a form. Nevertheless, studies of Chaucer's connection to oral culture are now only just being revived. See Lindahl

(1987), B. Bowden (1987), and Koff (1988). Crosby (1938) and Bronson (1940) remain important.

3. See the *Parliament of Foules*, 15–25.

4. I ought to add that it is the fiction of a speaking voice. The question of Chaucerian presence is presently under debate. See, for instance, Jordan (1987), Leicester (1980), and Gellrich (1985).

5. If the appearance of popular wisdom in Chaucer's characters is created at least partly by the frequent use of proverbs, we are reminded by Whiting's classic study (1934) that proverbs cannot be automatically associated with folk or popular wisdom (18). Some of Chaucer's most sophisticated characters, according to Whiting, use proverbs freely, and Chaucer's ability to encapsulate wisdom in proverbial form was admired by Renaissance commentators. But it cannot be denied that Chaucer makes his most down-to-earth characters—"strongest," in Whiting's terms—rely especially on proverbs. But if that is true, then the use of proverbial wisdom, even while it espouses Boethian stoicism, insists on the investment of these characters in material reality. Whiting (48–75) himself points out that in the *Troilus*, for instance, Pandarus and Criseyde use many more proverbs than Troilus himself. But that does not necessarily mark their sophistication in contrast to Troilus. Rather, it underlines their "realistic" perspective on things. See also K. Taylor (1980).

6. G. Olson (1982) argues that literature itself in the later Middle Ages was regarded as a kind of medicine. In addition, it was apparently a pleasant custom for the medical fraternities in Florence to take poets in as their brothers. Boccaccio apparently had such a connection.

7. Lindahl (1987) makes the important point that this effect is by no means unsophisticated; from his point of view, the court itself is a "folk community" (159–72).

8. Some of these points in one form or another have been made by previous scholars. Harwood (1972, 279) suggests that the tale is a "curtain-raiser—a kind of satyr play—before the Parson leads the pilgrims from 'ernest' into a 'game.' " Harwood also calls the Manciple's story a kind of "verbal Misrule" after the Host's "Misrule of the usual kind" in his praise of Bacchus. John Norton-Smith (1974, 150) points to an Ovidian scene in which Silenus falls off his ass in a procession. For an Ovidian reference, or a firmer location in Statius, see Baker (1984), who suggests some Bacchic-Apollonian tensions, if not in a highly codified form. Pearcy (1974) suggests the mystery-play staging as a source. See also Dean (1985).

WORKS CITED

Abelove, Henry, et al. 1983. *Visions of History*. New York: Pantheon.

Abraham, David. 1977. "Cosyn and Cosynage: Pun and Structure in the Shipman's Tale." *Chaucer Review* 11: 319–27.

Almansi, Guido. 1975. *The Writer as Liar: Narrative Technique in The Decameron*. London: Routledge and Kegan Paul.

Andreas, James. 1979. "Festive Liminality in Chaucerian Comedy." *Chaucer Newsletter* 1: 3–6.

———. 1984. "The Rhetoric of Chaucerian Comedy: The Aristotelian Legacy." *Comparatist* 8: 56–66.

Aston, Margaret. 1979. "England and the Waning of the Middle Ages." *Medievalia et Humanistica*, n.s., 9: 1–24.

Auerbach, Erich. 1953. *Mimesis: The Representation of Reality in Western Literature*. Princeton: Princeton University Press, 1953.

———. 1965. *Literary Language and Its Public in Late Latin Antiquity and in the Middle Ages*. Translated by Ralph Manheim. Bollingen Series, no. 74. New York: Pantheon.

Baker, Donald, ed. 1984. *The Manciple's Tale*. A Variorum Edition of the Works of Geoffrey Chaucer, The Canterbury Tales, vol. 2, pt. 10. Norman: University of Oklahoma Press.

Bakhtin, M. M. 1968. *Rabelais and His World*. Translated by Helene Iswolsky. Boston: Massachusetts Institute of Technology Press.

———. 1973. *Problems of Dostoevsky's Poetics*. Translated by R. W. Rostel. Ann Arbor: Ardis.

———. 1981. *The Dialogic Imagination: Four Essays*. Translated by Caryl Emerson and Michael Holquist. Austin: Univsersity of Texas Press.

Bakhtin, M. M., and P. N. Medvedev. 1985. *The Formal Method in Literary Scholarship: A Critical Introduction to Sociological Poetics*. Translated by Albert J. Wehrle. Cambridge: Harvard University Press.

Becker, Marvin B. 1967. *Florence in Transition*, vol. 1. Baltimore: Johns Hopkins University Press.

Benson, C. David. 1986. *Chaucer's Drama of Style: Poetic Variety and Contrast in the Canterbury Tales*. Chapel Hill: University of North Carolina Press.

Benson, Larry D. 1984. "The 'Queynte' Punnings of Chaucer's Critics." *Studies in the Age of Chaucer*, proceedings, no. 1, 23–47.

Bloch, R. Howard. 1986. *The Scandal of the Fabliaux*. Chicago: University of Chicago Press.

Bloomfield, Morton. 1964. *Piers Plowman as a Fourteenth-Century Apocalypse*. New Brunswick: Rutgers University Press.

Bloom, Harold. 1973. *The Anxiety of Influence: A Theory of Poetry*. New York: Oxford University Press.

Boccaccio, Giovanni. *Decameron*. 1955. Edited by Enrico Bianchi. La Letteratura Italiana, vol. 8. Milan: Ricciardi.

———. 1983. *The Decameron*. Translated by Mark Musa and Peter Bondanella. New York: Norton, 1983.

Boitani, Piero. 1982. *English Medieval Narrative in the Thirteenth and Fourteenth Centuries*. Cambridge: Cambridge University Press.

Bowden, Betsy. 1987. *Chaucer Aloud: The Varieties of Textual Interpretation*. Philadelphia: University of Pennsylvania Press.

Bowden, Muriel. 1964. *A Reader's Guide to Geoffrey Chaucer*. London: Thames and Hudson.

Branca, Vittore. 1956. *Boccaccio Medievale*. Florence: Sansoni.

Brandt, William J. 1966. *The Shape of Medieval History: Studies in Modes of Perception*. New Haven: Yale University Press.

Braswell, Mary Flowers. 1985. "The Magic of Machinery: A Context for Chaucer's Franklin's Tale." *Mosaic* 18: 101–10.

Brewer, Derek. 1968. "Class Distinction in Chaucer." *Speculum* 43: 290–305.

———. 1974. *Towards A Chaucerian Poetic*. London: Oxford University Press.

Bronson, Bertrand. 1940. "Chaucer's Art in Relation to His Audience." In *Five Studies in Literature*, 1–53. University of California Publications in English, no. 8. Berkeley: University of California Press.

Brown, Carleton. 1911. "Another Contemporary Allusion in Chaucer's *Troilus*." *Modern Language Notes*, 26: 208–11.

Bryan, W. F., and Germaine Dempster, eds. 1941. *Sources and Analogues of Chaucer's Canterbury Tales*. Reprint. New York: Humanities Press, 1958.

Burke, Peter. 1978. *Popular Culture in Early Modern Europe*. London: T. Smith.

Burlin, Robert. 1977. *Chaucerian Fiction*. Princeton: Princeton University Press.

Burrow, John. 1971. *Ricardian Poetry*. New Haven: Yale University Press.

Carruthers, Mary. 1979. "The Wife of Bath and the Painting of Lions." *PMLA* 94: 209–22.

Caspari, Fritz. 1954. *Humanism and the Social Order in Tudor England*. Chicago: University of Chicago Press.

Chambers, E. K. 1907. *The Mediaeval Stage*, vol. 1. London: Oxford University Press.

Chapman, Robert L. 1956. "The Shipman's Tale was Meant for the Shipman." *Modern Language Notes* 71: 4–5.

Chaucer, Geoffrey. 1987. *The Riverside Chaucer*. 3d ed., edited by Larry D. Benson et al. Boston: Houghton Mifflin.

Cherniss, Michael D. 1972. "The *Clerk's Tale* and Envoy, the Wife of Bath's Purgatory, and the *Merchant's Tale*." *Chaucer Review* 6: 235–54.

Chronicle of Lanercost, The. 1913. Translated by Sir Herbert Maxwell. Glasgow: Maclehose.

Clark, Katerina, and Michael Holquist. 1984. *Mikhael Bakhtin*. Cambridge: Belknap Press, Harvard University Press.

Cohn, Norman. 1963. *The Pursuit of the Millennium*. New York: Harper, 1963.

Cooper, Helen. 1984. *The Structure of the Canterbury Tales*. Athens: University of Georgia Press, 1984.

Covella, Sr. Francis Dolores. 1970. "The Speaker of the Wife of Bath Stanza and Envoy." *Chaucer Review* 4: 267–83.

Crosby, Ruth. 1938. "Chaucer and the Custom of Oral Delivery." *Speculum* 13: 413–32.

David, Alfred. 1976. *The Strumpet Muse: Art and Morals in Chaucer's Poetry.* Bloomington: Indiana University Press.

Davidson, Clifford, ed. 1981. *A Middle English Treatise on the Playing of Miracles.* Washington, D.C.: University Press of America.

Davis, Natalie Zemon. 1975. *Society and Culture in Early Modern France.* Stanford: Stanford University Press.

Dean, James. 1977. "Time Past and Time Present in Chaucer's Clerk's Tale and Gower's *Confessio Amantis.*" *ELH* 44: 401–18.

———. 1985. "Dismantling the Canterbury Book." *PMLA* 100: 746–62.

Dempster, Germaine. 1932. *Dramatic Irony in Chaucer.* Stanford: Stanford University Press.

———. 1952. "The Clerk's Endlink." *PMLA* 67: 1177–81.

Donaldson, E. T., ed. 1958. *Chaucer's Poetry: An Anthology for the Modern Reader.* 2d ed. New York: Ronald.

Doran, John. 1858. *The History of Court Fools.* Reprint. New York: Haskell House, 1966.

Eisenstein, Elizabeth. 1979. *The Printing Press as an Agent of Change.* Cambridge: Cambridge University Press.

Ferguson, Arthur B. 1960. *The Indian Summer of English Chivalry: Studies in the Decline and Transformation of Chivalric Idealism.* Durham, North Carolina: Duke University Press.

———. 1965. *The Articulate Citizen in the English Renaissance.* Durham, North Carolina: Duke University Press.

Ferster, Judith. 1985. *Chaucer on Interpretation.* New York: Cambridge University Press.

Fifield, Merle. 1967. "Chaucer the Theatre-Goer." *Papers on Language and Literature* 3, supplement: 63–70.

Fisher, John Hurt. 1964. *John Gower.* New York: New York University Press.

Fradenburg, Louise O. 1986. "The Wife of Bath's Passing Fancy." *Studies in the Age of Chaucer* 8: 31–58.

———. 1989. "Criticism, Anti-Semitism, and the *Prioress' Tale.*" *Exemplaria* 1: 69–116.

Frazer, Sir James. 1966. *The Golden Bough: A Study in Magic*, vol. 10. 3d ed. New York: St. Martin's.

Frese, Dolores Warwick. 1973. "Chaucer's *Clerk's Tale*: The Monsters and the Critics Reconsidered." *Chaucer Review* 8: 133–46.

Frye, Northrop. 1953. *Anatomy of Criticism.* Princeton: Princeton University Press.

Gallick, Susan. 1975. "A Look at Chaucer and His Preachers." *Speculum* 50: 456–76.

———. 1978. "Styles of Usage in the *Nun's Priest's Tale.*" *Chaucer Review* 11: 232–47.

Ganim, John M. 1983. *Style and Consciousness in Middle English Narrative*. Princeton: Princeton University Press.

———. 1989. "Chaucerian Performance." *Envoi* 1: 266–75.

Gaylord, Alan. 1967. "*Sentence* and *Solaas* in Fragment VII of the *Canterbury Tales*: Harry Bailey as Horseback Editor." *PMLA* 82: 226–37.

Geertz, Clifford. 1973. *The Interpretation of Cultures*. New York: Basic Books.

Gellrich, Jesse M. 1985. *The Idea of the Book in the Middle Ages*. Ithaca, New York: Cornell University Press.

Ginzburg, Carlo. 1980. *The Cheese and the Worms: The Cosmos of a Sixteenth-Century Miller*. Translated by John and Anne Tedeschi. Baltimore: Johns Hopkins University Press.

———. 1981. "Charivari, associations juvéniles, chasse sauvage." In *Le Charivari: Actes de la table ronde organisée à Paris (25–27 Avril 1977) par l'Ecole des Hautes Etudes en Sciences Sociales et le Centre National de la Recherche Scientifique*, ed. Jacques Le Goff and Jean Claude-Schmitt, 131–40. The Hague: Mouton.

Goffman, Erving. 1981. *Forms of Talk*. Philadelphia: University of Pennsylvania Press.

Goodman, Jennifer. 1983. "Chaucer's *Squire's Tale* and the Rise of Chivalry." *Studies in the Age of Chaucer* 5: 127–36.

Green, Richard F. 1980. *Poets and Princepleasers: Literature and the English Court in the Late Middle Ages*. Toronto: University of Toronto Press.

Greenblatt, Stephen. 1980. *Renaissance Self-Fashioning: From More to Shakespeare*. Chicago: University of Chicago Press.

Hammond, Eleanor, ed. 1927. *English Verse between Chaucer and Surrey*. Reprint. New York: Octagon, 1965.

Handlyng Synne. 1901, 1903. *Robert of Brunne's "Handlyng Synne" and Its French Original*. Edited by Frederick Furnival. Early English Text Society, Old Series, vols. 119, 123. Reprint. New York: Kraus.

Hanning, Robert W. 1980. " 'The Struggle between Noble Design and Chaos': The Literary Tradition of the Knight's Tale." *The Literary Review* 23: 519–41.

———. 1982. " 'You Have Begun a Parlous Pleye': The Nature and Limits of Dramatic Mimesis as a Theme in Four Middle English 'Fall of Lucifer' Cycle Plays." In *The Drama of the Middle Ages: Comparative and Critical Essays*, ed. Clifford Davidson, C. J. Gianakaris, and John H. Stroupe, 140–68. New York: AMS.

———. 1984. "Chaucer and the Dangers of Poetry." *CEA Critic* 46: 17–26.

———. 1985. "Roasting a Friar, Mis-Taking a Wife, and Other Acts of Textual Harrassment in Chaucer's *Canterbury Tales*." *Studies in the Age of Chaucer*, 7: 3–21.

Harder, Kelsie B. 1956. "Chaucer's Use of the Mystery Plays in the *Miller's Tale*." *Modern Language Quarterly* 17: 193–98.

Hardison, O. B. 1965. *Christian Rite and Christian Drama in the Middle Ages: Essays in the Origin and Early History of Modern Drama*. Baltimore: Johns Hopkins University Press.

Harwood, Britton J. 1972. "Language and the Real: Chaucer's Manciple." *Chaucer Review* 6: 268–79.

Haskell, Ann. 1975. "Sir Thopas: The Puppet's Puppet." *Chaucer Review* 9: 253–61.

Hauser, Arnold. 1951. *The Social History of Art*. 2 vols. New York: Vintage.

Heffernan, Thomas J., ed. 1985. *The Popular Literature of Medieval England*. Tennessee Studies in Literature, vol. 28. Knoxville: University of Tennessee Press.

Hermann, John P. 1985. "Dismemberment, Dissemination, Discourse: Sign and Symbol in the *Shipman's Tale*." *Chaucer Review* 19: 302–37.

Howard, Donald R. 1976. *The Idea of the Canterbury Tales*. Berkeley: University of California Press.

———. 1979. "Fiction and Religion in Boccaccio and Chaucer." *Journal of the American Academy of Religion* 47, no. 2, supplement: 307–28.

———. 1980. *Writers and Pilgrims: Medieval Pilgrimage Narratives and Their Posterity*. Berkeley: University of California Press.

Huizinga, Johan. 1954. *The Waning of the Middle Ages*. Garden City, New York: Anchor.

Jordan, Robert M. 1967. *Chaucer and the Shape of Creation: The Aesthetic Possibilities of Inorganic Structure*. Cambridge: Harvard University Press.

———. 1987. *Chaucer's Poetics and the Modern Reader*. Berkeley: University of California Press.

Kahrl, Stanley J. 1973. "Chaucer's *Squire's Tale* and the Decline of Chivalry." *Chaucer Review* 7: 194–209.

Kaske, R. E. 1957. "The Knight's Interruption of the Monk's Tale." *ELH* 24: 249–68.

Keiser, George. 1977. "Language and Meaning in Chaucer's *Shipman's Tale*." *Chaucer Review* 12: 147–59.

Kellogg, Robert. 1977. "Oral Narrative, Written Books." *Genre* 10: 655–65.

Kendrick, Laura. 1988. *Chaucerian Play: Comedy and Control in the Canterbury Tales*. Berkeley: University of California Press.

Kermode, Frank. 1967. *The Sense of An Ending*. New York: Oxford University Press.

Kern, Edith. 1980. *The Absolute Comic*. New York: Columbia University Press.

Kirk, Elizabeth. 1975. "Chaucer and His English Contemporaries." In *Geoffrey Chaucer: A Collection of Original Articles*, ed. George Economou, 111–27. New York: McGraw-Hill.

Kirkpatrick, Robin. 1983. "The Wake of the *Commedia*: Chaucer's *Canterbury Tales* and Boccaccio's *Decameron*." In *Chaucer and the Italian Trecento*, ed. Piero Boitani, 201–30. Cambridge: Cambridge University Press.

Kittredge, George Lyman. 1911–12. "Chaucer's Discussion of Marriage." *Modern Philology* 9: 435–67.

———. 1915. *Chaucer and His Poetry*. Cambridge: Harvard University Press.

Koff, Leonard. 1988. *Chaucer and the Art of Storytelling*. Berkeley: University of California Press.

Kolve, V. A. 1984. *Chaucer and the Imagery of Narrative*. Stanford: Stanford University Press.

Kristeva, Julia. 1973. "The Ruin of a Poetics." In *Russian Formalism*, ed. Stephen Bann and John E. Bowlt, 102–19. New York: Barnes and Noble.

———. 1980. *Desire in Language: A Semiotic Approach to Literature and Art*. Edited by Leon S. Roudiez, translated by Thomas Gora, Alice Jardine, and Leon S. Roudiez. New York: Columbia University Press.

Lancashire, Ann. 1975. "Chaucer and the Sacrifice of Isaac." *Chaucer Review* 9: 320–26.

Larner, John. 1971. *Culture and Society in Italy, 1290–1420.* London: Batsford.

Lawler, Traugott. 1980. *The One and the Many in the Canterbury Tales.* Hamden, Connecticut: Archon.

Lawton, David. 1985. *Chaucer's Narrators.* Chaucer Studies, no. 13. Cambridge: Boydell and Brewer.

Leicester, H. Marshall, Jr. 1980. "The Art of Impersonation: A General Prologue to the *Canterbury Tales.*" *PMLA* 95: 213–24.

Le Roy Ladurie, Emmanual. 1978. *Montaillou: The Promised Land of Error.* Translated by Barbara Bray. New York: Braziller.

Lévi-Strauss, Claude. 1969. *The Raw and the Cooked.* Translated by John Weightman and Doreen Weightman. New York: Harper.

Levy, Bernard. 1967. "The Quaint World of the Shipman's Tale." *Studies in Short Fiction* 4: 112–18.

Lewis, C. S. 1962. "The Anthropological Approach." In *English and Medieval Studies Presented to J. R. R. Tolkien,* ed. Norman Davis and C. L. Wrenn, 219–30. London: Allen.

Lindahl, Carl. 1987. *Earnest Games: Folkloric Patterns in the Canterbury Tales.* Bloomington: Indiana University Press.

Loomis, Laura Hibbard. 1958. "Secular Dramatics in the Royal Palace, Paris, 1378, 1379, and Chaucer's 'Tregetoures.' " *Speculum* 33: 242–55.

Loomis, Roger S. 1945. "Some Evidence from Secular Theatres in the Twelfth and Thirteenth Centuries." *Theatre Annual* 3: 33–43.

Lumiansky, R. M. 1955. *Of Sondry Folk: The Dramatic Principle in the Canterbury Tales.* Austin: University of Texas Press.

Lydgate, John. 1906. *Troy Book.* Edited by H. Bergen. Early English Text Society, old series, no. 97, vol. 1. London: Early English Text Society.

———. 1934. *The Minor Poems of John Lydgate,* pt. 2. Edited by Henry N. MacCracken. Early English Text Society, old series, no. 192. London: Oxford University Press.

McCall, John. 1966. "The *Clerk's Tale* and the Theme of Obedience." *Modern Language Quarterly* 27: 260–69.

McCall, John P., and George Rudisill. 1959. "The Parliament of 1386 and Chaucer's Trojan Parliament." *Journal of English and Germanic Philology* 58: 276–88.

McGrady, Donald. 1977. "Chaucer and the *Decameron* Reconsidered." *Chaucer Review* 12: 1–26.

McPeek, James A. S. 1951. "Chaucer and the Goliards." *Speculum* 26: 332–36.

Malone, Kemp. 1951. *Chapters on Chaucer.* Baltimore: Johns Hopkins University Press.

Mandel, Jerome. 1977. "Other Voices in the 'Canterbury Tales.' " *Criticism* 19: 338–49.

Mann, Jill. 1974. "Chaucer and the Medieval Latin Poets." In *Geoffrey Chaucer,* ed. Derek Brewer, 154–83. Writers and Their Background. Athens: Ohio University Press.

Mathew, Gervase. 1968. *The Court of Richard II.* London: Murray.

Middleton, Anne. 1978. "The Idea of Public Poetry in the Reign of Richard II." *Speculum* 53: 94–114.

———. 1980a. "Chaucer's 'New Men' and the Good of Literature in the *Canterbury Tales*." In *Literature and Society*, ed. Edward Said, 15–56. Essays from the English Institute, 1978. Baltimore: Johns Hopkins University Press.

———. 1980b. "The Clerk and His Tale: Some Literary Contexts." *Studies in the Age of Chaucer* 2: 121–50.

Morse, J. Mitchell. 1958. "The Philosophy of the Clerk of Oxenford." *Modern Language Quarterly* 19: 3–20.

Muir, Edward. 1981. *Civic Ritual in Renaissance Venice*. Princeton: Princeton University Press.

Muscatine, Charles. 1950. "Form, Texture, and Meaning in Chaucer's *Knight's Tale*." *PMLA* 65: 911–29.

———. 1957. *Chaucer and the French Tradition*. Berkeley: University of California Press.

———. 1986. *The Old French Fabliaux*. New Haven: Yale University Press.

Nelson, Alan H. 1974. *The Medieval English Stage: Corpus Christi Pageants and Plays*. Chicago: University of Chicago Press.

Nolan, Barbara. 1986. " 'A Poet Ther Was': Chaucer's Voices in the General Prologue to *The Canterbury Tales*." *PMLA* 101: 154–69.

Norton-Smith, John. 1974. *Geoffrey Chaucer*. London: Routledge and Kegan Paul.

Nykrog, Per. 1957. *Les Fabliaux: Étude d'histoire littéraire et de stylistique mediévale*. Copenhagen: Munksgaard.

Olson, Glending. 1982. *Literature as Recreation in the Later Middle Ages*. Ithaca, New York: Cornell University Press.

———. 1986. "The Medieval Fortunes of 'Theatrica.' " *Traditio* 42: 265–86.

Olson, Paul. 1986. *The Canterbury Tales and the Good Society*. Princeton: Princeton University Press.

Orgel, Stephen. 1975. *The Illusion of Power: Political Theater in the English Renaissance*. Berkeley: University of California Press.

Owen, Charles A. 1977. *Pilgrimage and Storytelling in the Canterbury Tales: The Dialectic of 'Ernest' and 'Game.'* Norman: University of Oklahorma Press.

Pace, George B., and Alfred David, ed. 1982. *The Minor Poems*, vol. 1. A Variorum Edition of the Works of Geoffrey Chaucer, vol. 5. Norman: University of Oklahoma Press.

Patch, H. R. 1930. "Chaucer and the Common People." *Journal of English and Germanic Philology* 29: 376–84.

Patterson, Lee. 1983. " 'For the Wyves Love of Bathe': Feminine Rhetoric and Poetic Resolution in the *Roman de la Rose* and the *Canterbury Tales*." *Speculum* 58: 656–95.

———. 1987a. " 'No Man His Reson Herde': Peasant Consciousness, Chaucer's Miller, and the Structure of the *Canterbury Tales*." *South Atlantic Quarterly* 86: 457–95.

———. 1987b. *Negotiating the Past*. Madison: University of Wisconsin Press.

Payne, Anne F. 1981. *Chaucer and Menippean Satire*. Madison: University of Wisconsin Press.

Pearcy, Roy J. 1974. "Does the Manciple's Prologue Contain a Reference to Hell's Mouth?" *English Language Notes* 11: 167–75.

Pearsall, Derek, ed. 1985a. *The Nun's Priest's Tale*. A Variorum Edition of the Works of Geoffrey Chaucer, The Canterbury Tales. Vol. 2, pt. 9. Norman: University of Oklahoma Press.

———. 1985b. *The Canterbury Tales*. London: George Allen and Unwin.

Peterson, Joyce E. 1976. "With Feigned Flattery: The Pardoner as Vice." *Chaucer Review* 10: 326–36.

Petrarca, Francesco. 1926. *Le Familiari*. Edited by Vittorio Rossi. Edizione Nazionale delle Opere di Francesco Petrarca. Florence: Sansoni.

Pratt, Robert A. 1966. "Chaucer and The Hand That Fed Him." *Speculum* 41: 619–42.

———. 1969. "The Development of the Wife of Bath." In *Studies in Medieval Literature in Honor of Albert Croll Baugh*, ed. MacEdward Leach, 45–79. Philadelphia: University of Pennsylvania Press.

Prior, Sandra Pierson. 1986. "Parodying Typology in the Miller's Tale." *Journal of Medieval and Renaissance Studies* 16: 57–73.

Robertson, D. W. 1962. *A Preface to Chaucer: Studies in Medieval Perspectives*. Princeton: Princeton University Press.

Robbins, R. H. 1952. *Secular Lyrics of the XIV and XV Centuries*. 2d ed. Oxford: Clarendon Press.

Roman de Fauvel, Le. 1914. Edited by Arthur Langfors. Paris: Didot.

Sacchetti, Franco. 1938. *Cento Novelle*. Edited by Raffaello Forniciari. Florence: Sansoni.

Salter, Elizabeth. 1966a. "The Alliterative Revival, I." *Modern Philology* 64: 146–50.

———. 1966b. "The Alliterative Revival, II." *Modern Philology* 64: 233–37.

———. 1973. "Courts and Courtly Love." In *The Mediaeval World*, ed. David Daiches and Anthony Thorlby, 407–44. London: Aldus.

Scanlon, Larry. 1989. "The Authority of Fable: Allegory and Irony in the *Nun's Priest's Tale*." *Exemplaria* 1: 43–68.

Severs, J. Burke. 1954. "Did Chaucer Rearrange the Clerk's Envoy?" *Modern Language Notes* 69: 472–78.

Shoaf, R. A. 1979. "Notes Toward Chaucer's Poetics of Translation," *Studies in the Age of Chaucer* 1: 55–66.

Silverman, Albert J. 1953. "Sex and Money in Chaucer's Shipman's Tale." *Philological Quarterly* 32: 329–31.

Singleton, Charles. 1944. "On Meaning in *The Decameron*." *Italica* 2: 117–24.

Sledd, James. 1953–54. "The *Clerk's Tale*: The Monsters and the Critics." *Modern Philology* 51: 73–82.

Speirs, John. 1957. *Medieval English Literature: The Non-Chaucerian Tradition*. London: Faber.

Stevens, John. 1961. *Music and Poetry in the Early Tudor Court*. London: Methuen.

Stillwell, Gardiner. 1944. "Chaucer's 'Sad' Merchant." *Review of English Studies* 20: 1–18.

Stock, Brian. 1983. *The Implications of Literacy*. Princeton: Princeton University Press.

Strohm, Paul. 1977. "Chaucer's Audience." *Literature and History* 5: 26–41.

Tatlock, J.S.P. 1907. *The Development and Chronology of Chaucer's Works.* Chaucer Society, 2d ser., no. 37. London: Chaucer Society.

Taylor, Karla. 1980. "Proverbs and the Authentication of Convention in *Troilus and Criseyde.*" In *Chaucer's Troilus: Essays in Criticism,* ed. Stephen Barney, 277–96. Hamden, Connecticut: Shoestring Press.

Taylor, Paul Beekman. 1982. "*Peynted Confessiouns*: Boccaccio and Chaucer." *Comparative Literature* 34: 116–29.

Thompson, E. P. 1972. " 'Rough Music': le charivari anglais." *Annales* 27: 285–312.

Tout, T. F. 1929. "Literature and Learning in the English Civil Service in the Fourteenth Century." *Speculum* 4: 365–89.

Travis, Peter. N.d. "Chaucer's Trivial Fox Chase and the Peasants' Revolt of 1381." Typescript.

Volosinov, V. N. 1976. *Freudianism: A Marxist Critique.* Translated by I. R. Titunik. New York: Academic Press.

Wallace, David. 1985. *Chaucer and the Early Writing of Boccaccio.* Cambridge: Brewer.

Weimann, Robert. 1978. *Shakespeare and the Popular Tradition in the Theater: Studies in the Social Dimension of Dramatic Form and Function.* Edited by Robert Schwartz. Baltimore: Johns Hopkins University Press.

Westlund, Joseph. 1964. "The *Knight's Tale* as an Impetus for Pilgrimage." *Philological Quarterly* 43: 526–37.

Whiting, B. J. 1934. *Chaucer's Use of Proverbs.* Cambridge, Massachusetts: Harvard University Press.

Wickham, Glynne. 1959. *Early English Stages,* vol. 1. London: Routledge.

Wilkinson, Bertie. 1969. *The Later Middle Ages in England, 1216–1485.* Harlow: Longmans.

Wilson, Enid. 1936. *The Fool: His Social and Literary History.* New York: Farrar and Rinehart.

Wilson, R. M. 1952. *The Lost Literature of Medieval England.* Reprint. New York: Cooper Square, 1969.

Windeatt, Barry. 1979. "Gesture in Chaucer." *Medievalia et Humanistica* 9: 143–61.

Winny, James. 1966. *The Clerk's Prologue and Tale.* Cambridge: Cambridge University Press.

Withington, Robert. 1918. *English Pageantry: An Historical Outline,* vol. 1. Reprint. New York: Blom, 1963.

Woolf, Virginia. 1925. "The Pastons and Chaucer." In *The Second Common Reader.* New York: Harcourt.

Wright, Thomas. 1841. *The Latin Poems Attributed to Walter Mapes.* London: Camden Society.

Zacher, Christian. 1976. *Curiosity and Pilgrimage.* Baltimore: Johns Hopkins University Press.

INDEX